Pre

Hull College
Libraries

This book must be returned on or before the
latest date stamped below

PRC

Pretty Pictures

PRODUCTION DESIGN AND THE HISTORY FILM

C. S. Tashiro

UNIVERSITY OF TEXAS PRESS, AUSTIN

First edition, 1998

Requests for permission to reproduce material from this work should be sent to Permissions, University of Texas Press, Box 7819, Austin, TX 78713-7819.

♾ The paper used in this publication meets the minimum requirements of American National Standard for Information Sciences—Permanence of Paper for Printed Library Materials, ANSI Z39.48-1984.

Library of Congress Cataloging-in-Publication Data

Tashiro, C. S. (Charles Shiro), 1957–
    Pretty pictures : production design and the history film / by C. S. Tashiro. — 1st ed.
        p.   cm.
    Revision of thesis (Ph.D.)—University of Southern California.
    Filmography: p.
    Includes bibliographical references and index.
    ISBN 978-0-292-78150-4

    1. Motion pictures—Art direction.   2. Motion pictures—Setting and scenery.   3. Historical films.   I. Title.
PN1995.9.A74T37   1998
791.43'0233—dc21   97-4762

To family and friends

Contents

Acknowledgments

Any author inevitably encounters the difficulty of deciding whose help to acknowledge, which in turn leads to the question of just what to consider part of the writing process. Since this book presents a significantly revised version of my Ph.D. dissertation from the University of Southern California School of Cinema-Television's Department of Critical Studies, it makes sense to mention the many people who helped me out during my doctoral work, but I must here restrict my specific thanks only to those directly related to the writing and research.

However, as will become clear to anyone who reads what follows, I believe strongly in a synthetic approach to criticism that as much as possible refuses to draw limits around experience in order to privilege one aspect of it over another. It is therefore difficult for me to think of "writing" isolated or different from a range of actions that influence each other. Anyone who has, like Proust's Marcel, allowed sensuous experience to overwhelm reason in a torrent of feeling will know what I mean. Under such circumstances, it is impossible to insist that only those books and the people who helped me retrieve them have contributed toward the final product.

With that reservation in mind, I must begin the list with my mother, Charlotte Tashiro. In addition to providing financial support during my days as a Ph.D. candidate, she more importantly started my thoughts about historical representation with the costumes she made for my first "historical" movie back in Falmouth, Massachusetts. It was also she who first made me aware of the sensual qualities of fabric and, by implication, its contribution to the enrichment of life and cinema. In this same regard, I would like to thank all those people, particularly my sister Stephanie, who in the past have served as actors in my film and video projects. Too numerous to list, they each contributed without knowing it to my thoughts about the importance of the human form in relation to visual design.

Jumping ahead, I would like to thank Petter Magnus Nordin, Neela Sastry, and Sarma Bala Kameshwara Vrudhula for "conspiring" to send me back to graduate school for a Ph.D. It is a safe bet I would never have done it were it not for their encouragement and goading. I would also like to thank Dorab Patel for much the same involvement, for reading an early revision of the book, and for providing many meals beyond the budget of a starving student. In the same spirit, I would like to thank Scott and Jill Kalter, whose enthusiastic support and weekend retreats in Malibu provided incalculable relief and refreshment from academic doldrums.

As for USC, it is difficult to single out fellow students for thanks, since part of the process of graduate education is to test your ideas against the opinions of others. If I mention specific colleagues, such as Donna Cunningham, Harry Benshoff, Tracy Biga, Vicky Johnson, Chris Lippard, Mark Wolf, Doug Troyan, and Susan Robinson, it is not to overlook others, but to recall those people with whom I most often discussed ideas. I would, in addition, like to thank my friends and chief "sparring partners" in the department, Tassilo Schneider and Jonathan Schwartz, who always could be relied upon for honest opinions. That is, of course, another way of saying that they could always be relied upon to tell me when I was full of it.

From the USC administration, I would like first to mention the helpful support of the staff of the Critical Studies Department. Chief among these would be Lee Stork, Owen Costello, Casandra Morgan, and Anne Bergman. I would also like to thank Dean Elizabeth Daley of the USC School of Cinema-Television for her support of several projects on which I worked as a student and her continued support of my work as an Annenberg Fellow. I am, of course, also thankful to the staff of the USC Cinema-Television library, particularly Ned Comstock and Steve Hanson. Thanks, too, to Gino Cheng and Max Nikias of the School of Engineering for allowing me access to play around with the computers in the basement of Electrical Engineering.

I would like to thank Professors Rick Jewell and David James for agreeing to sit on my exam committee and for reading an early draft of this work. I would also like to thank Professor Victor Regnier of the USC School of Architecture for gamely venturing into the unknown of Ph.D. work with an untried quantity such as myself. To Professor Lynn Spigel I offer special thanks for her always fresh and unique perspective.

I would also like to thank my advisor, Professor Marsha Kinder, for her always energetic, enthusiastic, honest, and complete support. If the mark of a great teacher is the ability to advance her ideas, while providing ample room for the student to develop his own, Professor Kinder has all the traits of greatness. It has been a privilege to work with her for the past four years. Without her encouragement, this project might well have withered on the vine of good intentions.

Finally, I would like to thank the staff at the University of Texas Press. First among these is my editor, Ali Hossaini, who fought for my manuscript at an awkward, early stage. I would also like to thank Heidi Haeuser for her enthusiastic encouragement of my involvement in the design process. Thanks too to Carolyn Wylie and Bob Fullilove for their expertise and patience with the copy edit. And a word of special thanks to Robert Dansby for his good-humored help in the final proofing stage.

Introduction

I can remember, almost to the day, when visual design first caught my interest. It was a chilly Sunday in 1972. Bathed in the golden light of a late fall, Cape Cod afternoon, I was sizing up a shot for a Super-8 film, in which one character was lying in wait to surprise another. When the second appeared, they were to have a fistfight. I had never had any luck in the past staging this kind of material. Fights had appeared across my cinema with staccato regularity, but they had all shared a desultory limpness that betrayed youth and obvious conceptual failure.

The scene was staged outdoors, on a sandy spit of land punctuated by bits of tall beach grass. By luck or intuition, I got the idea of placing the camera with the waiting character in one of the stands of grass. As soon as I looked through the viewfinder, I knew that this angle would work. The graphic impact created by the slightly off-center angle, the backlighting from the setting sun, the blades of dried grass intruding between the camera and subject created an immediately striking image—not the images *of* violence that I had created up to that point, but an image that in its formal qualities *was violent* (or at least striking). And just as I knew the shot was right the instant I saw it, I also knew that I would no longer be able to use the camera with the same casual incompetence that had marked my previous efforts.

As my filmmaking progressed, this happy accident changed into conscious plan, with two results. First, I ceased paying much attention to the literary content of most of the films I attended, except as it was embodied in the image. Filmgoing became a largely formal experience in which I pillaged the work of professional filmmakers for visual ideas. So, while I developed a taste for high-art *auteurs*, it was less because of their films' subject matter than because of the relative freedom these directors exhibited in exploring the potentials of the image. The existential inquiry of *The Seventh Seal* (Bergman, 1956), for instance, one of the favorite films of my adolescence, interested me far less than the striking images made possible by its me-dieval setting. With notable exceptions, this freedom with the image has been largely absent in Hollywood films, with their neurotic insistence on narrative-before-all.

The second result of my interest in visual design was more concrete. As I became more ambitious about my films' appearances, I began to haunt local thrift shops and antique dealers with an ever-more critical eye for the right costumes and props to dress my backyard epics. An area such as New England, with a past perhaps more glorious than its present, provided ample opportunity to treat history as a mine to yield precious, strange artifacts. While this process succeeded in making the surfaces of my films consis-tently attractive, something else happened as well: the realms of production and consumption merged. One of the purposes of production design, even at the homespun level, is to discriminate and select in order to create a plau-sible background to the narrative. Once this habit of enhancing a film's spa-tial reality is established, it is easy to start to view *all* space as something to be dressed and improved. So, I might say with little exaggeration that that shot in 1972 began not only my career as a designer, but also my adulthood as a consumer.

The curious part of design, whether of film or life, is that it works from deficiency. Curious, because if we think of design at all, we probably think of it in terms of *richness*. Yet like most aesthetic terms, richness is a rel-ative effect, created not so much by a glut of detail as by selective composi-tion leading to maximum impact. Film design works from the difference be-tween the physical world as it exists and the requirements of a particular narrative. This is another way of saying that the real world is *lacking*, is not good enough to provide an idealized, designed image. If the space in which a film is shot does not meet the story's needs, it has to be "designed" to fit the bill, so that, for example, the television antennas in the background of a pe-riod shoot have to be moved or avoided, and so on.

The second deficiency of film design derives from the image itself. The photographic image presents a compelling illusion of three-dimensional space. It nonetheless remains a two-dimensional surface that must be orga-nized to accentuate depth cues in order to maximize that illusion. The greater the success in creating this illusion the more difficult it becomes to juxta-pose shots in time, since the rapid alternation of space runs counter to daily, sensual experience. Stephen Heath's classic essay "Narrative Space"[1] de-scribes this phenomenon in terms of the need it creates for a unifying agent to cover these sensory disruptions. He finds this glue in the set of desires and expectations which narrative creates. These emotional interests allow the viewer to overcome or ignore the alterations to real space and experience.

The problem with Heath's argument is the limiting effect it has had on discussion of the image. Just as narrative directs attention to parts of the image at the expense of others, assuming that narrative has this capability has channeled discussion of the image *toward its narrative function*, regardless of whether or not such a discussion reflects the experience of a film. I would like to try to get around this scenario. I do not pretend to be indifferent to story and character, both of which figure in the following discussion. I merely question whether narrative has the power to focus my attention, channel my desires, and shape the way I view events *consistently,* whether the expectations a story may create can overwhelm interests I may have *outside* a film. While I cannot know if my reactions are typical, I am willing to insist that such a narrative-based definition of the image does not answer to my experience, is as needlessly coercive and limiting as narrative itself, and probably does not describe most spectators' relationship to the screen.

Despite the contributions Heath's essay has made, we may have to return to the theorist on whom he relies, Rudolf Arnheim, to avoid this prejudice toward narrative. Arnheim's *Film as Art* is one of the few works that confronts the representational inadequacies of the film image as a fundamental fact to be overcome. For Arnheim, the art of cinema comes not from a faithful mimicking of reality, but through the artist's triumph over the two-dimensional nature of the image. While we may no longer feel the need to defend cinema as an art in the manner that interested Arnheim, his basic observation remains as relevant to cinematic design as when he wrote it. Designers *always* have to overcome deficiency in order to create effective externals. The result may be the formalist play Arnheim advocated or the convincing duplication of spatial reality he disliked. In both cases, narrative enters as a set of *principles* to guide the design, not a set of *laws* to straitjacket the way we perceive it.

This supposed service to a story produces a fundamental tension in the design profession, a constant veering between artistic expression and the demands of the narrative. The first chapter of this work discusses the effects of design in terms of this tension. While I begin with production designers and their stated goals, for the purposes of this discussion, I view "design" in the sense of the *total* cinematic image. My discussion therefore encompasses not just the contributions of production designers, but also of cinematographers, directors, other visual technicians, and ultimately, the viewer. For it is in the heads of spectators that designed images come together, frequently in ways that have nothing to do with narrative.

The approach I have taken toward the image in Chapters 2 and 3, while acknowledging the power of narrative, focuses on the social, historical, and formal dimensions of design. These are what we bring to the image, a range of experience and knowledge that the film can exploit in order to function in narrative terms. By directing attention to alternative aspects of film design, I hope to establish a vocabulary that does not depend on narrative motivation. Such a discussion helps to fill in gaps of *rational* discussion left by the privileging of narrative. It cannot account for the pleasure we may derive from design.

The first three chapters deal with general issues about design; Part II specifically examines period design. Historical films provide useful examples of design because they obviously rely heavily on stylization. At the same time, despite this reliance, they rarely become as openly stylized as, say, the musical. This oscillation between realism and stylization provides a neat, condensed example of design's general tension between visible expression and invisible neutrality. Chapter 4 maps out some of the issues specific to historical design. Chapters 5–7 apply these observations to six films in detail. While these films were selected to provide a wide range of approaches to the historical image, I do not pretend to have exhausted the topic.

After examining some possible reactions to these films and their visual design, in Part III, I take the discussion into the larger social arena. To a certain extent, this final section is written to myself, in an effort to understand the interrelationships between my filmmaking, filmgoing, and taste in commodity consumption established in my adolescence. In order to balance this personal motivation with a more general discussion of the issues, I have chosen in Chapters 8 and 9 to discuss a particular consumption phenomenon in which I did *not* participate. I hope by this removal to perch myself between subjective expression and objective observation. My goal is neither to condemn nor to praise, but simply to understand in order to move on to something else.

Why this need to move on? I can answer that question with an observation not about film, design, history, or commodities, but about the state of academic media criticism. An uninitiated reader reviewing the bulk of academic criticism might be forgiven the impression that the people who write it hate cinema, or at best bear some kind of grudge against it for the pleasure it has provided them. At the same time, it is difficult to believe that critics would return repeatedly to a medium they despise only in order to point to the same villains and structures of dominance over and over again. They must enjoy *something*. The question then becomes, what perverse process makes us translate pleasure into displeasure?

Pleasure is blessedly irrational. All of the rational systems brought to bear to explain it—psychoanalysis, cultural theory, traditional aesthetics—fortunately fail to pin down a phenomenon that exceeds verbal description. Pleasure is the body's recognition of sensual truth. It is scarcely inferior to the mind's satisfaction at a logical proof or a penetrating insight, though it may be considerably more difficult to accept. Yet pleasure can be *understood* only by being accepted. At least one explanation for the disastrous academic alchemy that turns the gold of fun into the lead of drudgery is the insistence on imposing rationalist values on materials frustrating for their elusiveness, independence, and amorality. Put simply: the academic attitude toward mass media seems to be that if it is enjoyable, there must be something wrong with it.

Each critic must find his or her own values. For me, I prefer to admit to pleasure, to being able to enjoy the most reactionary texts (without "subverting" them), to recognize that I can be a willing participant in these cycles of power. I admit to this pleasure in order to develop a more affirmative, honest relationship to mass media. Design remains a powerful force in our lives. It obviously provides a great deal of gratification. That this pleasure frequently serves dominant interests in our society does not make the enjoyment less true. On the other hand, our satisfaction does not make the accusations of exploitation less accurate. We must therefore beware that in the effort to reclaim pleasure from moralists of the left we do not slip into supine exploitation from the right. For this reason, in Chapter 10, I suggest an alternative approach to these issues. This strategy acknowledges the problems and pleasures of design, confronts the inadequacies of either too negative or too positive an attitude toward consumption, and advances production in the service of personal needs and desires as a viable alternative. If this study opens up this possibility, it will have achieved some degree of success.

Part I

DESIGN

1

WHAT IS PRODUCTION DESIGN?

What do we mean by "production design"? From the standpoint of industrial practice, this is a relatively simple question to answer. Production designers supervise the overall "look" of a film, working in close collaboration with directors, cinematographers, and their own staffs. Designers are expected to have a thorough knowledge of a film's setting, from the basics of architectural style to the shape of a cufflink. As with any collaborative position, the designer's power varies according to the circumstance. A well-known designer working with a neophyte director may have more control over the final image. A less-established designer working for a director with a strong visual style may be little more than a functionary.[1] What remains true for all designers is their focus on the visual, physical realm of the movie.

Most designers have architectural or art school training, which is not surprising given their responsibilities. We might expect that given such a background production designers would stress the importance of the visual above all else. However, most would probably agree with the statement made by Charles and Mirella Affron in *Sets in Motion: Art Direction and Film Narrative*: "It all starts with the story."[2] Designers are hardly alone, of course, among film personnel in stressing the importance of the script to their work. Representatives of virtually every film craft repeatedly stress that they serve the story and characters. At the same time, the varying expertise that each of these professions brings to this service inevitably influences their notions of what "starting with the story" means. Indeed, to judge by the frequent laments of scriptwriters, the one thing that no one seems to care about is the script.

Another way to think of the production designer's task is to examine what he or she does. What distinguishes design from the other professions serving the script? This question returns us to the "look" of the film, that is, the final appearance of images when viewed by an audience. Narrative films may concentrate on story, but the medium depends on an illusion of taking place in space. French designer Léon Barsacq, in his important work *Caligari's Cabinet and Other Grand Illusions*, insists, for example, that "one of the fundamental requirements of the cinema [is] to give the impression of having photographed real objects."[3] The tie between film and spatial reality gives the medium an immediate hold on our imaginations. It also narrows expression to the external, visual, material, and spectacular and in the process puts filmmakers in an uneasy power relationship with reality. As filmmakers serve the script, they shape reality to fictional ends. The production designer sits at this conjunction between the world outside the story and the story's needs. The very label "production designer" (coined by David O. Selznick to describe the contributions of William Cameron Menzies to the production of *Gone with the Wind* [Fleming, 1939])[4] gives a key to the designer's function. Production, an industrial process, is shaped by a designer into aesthetically pleasing forms.

To a certain extent, this sounds like a definition of an "industrial designer," who is also responsible for shaping products into pleasant form. There are, however, important differences between the professions. An industrial designer trying to make a toaster attractive must design within fairly strict parameters. No matter how seductive the externals, if the bread does not come out toasted, the design fails. Production design, apart from its service to the script (itself a subjective, literary, artistic product), does not have to consider utility. Because the production designer works in a fictional realm, he or she frequently has tremendous freedom, even from the laws of physics. An architectural design that would fall apart in the real world must only "look right" in a film to fulfill its purpose, for example. The fact that tremendous effort goes on behind the scenes to create the illusion is unimportant to the viewer. The "toast" that the designed image delivers is its dramatic and visual impact, not its function in the real world.

These, then, are the two poles of production design: literary service and visual freedom. Left to their own devices, designers would probably choose to explore the potentials of visual expression. At least one way of looking at design would focus on how visible the design is, how much freedom the designer enjoyed in dressing narrative images. This is the approach taken by the Affrons in *Sets in Motion*, one of the few works to address design comprehensively. Their five categories chart an ever-increasing "design intensity," from merely descriptive, largely invisible sets (Sets as Denotation), through sets that serve occasional narrative significance (Sets as Punctuation), past those sets of which we are always aware, but that do not necessarily take over the story (Sets as Embellishment), to the Sets as Artifice category, in which sets are always visible and integral to the story's impact.

The Affrons are most interested in describing the relative power sets have in determining narrative effect. Thus, their fifth category, Sets as Narrative, is final less because of the visual impact of the design than because of the control such sets exercise over the stories that develop in their spaces. The Affrons suggest, for example, that the Sets as Embellishment category, in which design begins to assert itself as a value, requires "the spectator to read design as a specific necessity of the narrative."[5] The Affrons' work suggests that one criterion for understanding the "intensity" of a design would be the extent to which a visible set creates a sense of the "reality effect,"[6] the illusion of taking place in real spaces, despite the constructed, designed nature of the sets.

The Affrons' taxonomy systematizes a simple observation: some designs are more apparent than others. This relative visibility can profitably be related to the "reality effect." For example, by recognizing that the sets in *The Maltese Falcon* (Huston, 1941) and *Blade Runner* (R. Scott, 1982) do not function the same way, even though both are at some level detective stories, makes it possible to distinguish between the different *kinds* of attraction a film may provide. The narrative-centered sets of *Falcon* do not distract from the actors, and therefore contribute mutely to narrative development and identification. The assertive sets in *Blade Runner*, on the other hand, relentlessly privilege visual pleasure over emotional involvement.

However, there are at least two related problems in this approach. First, the wide range of service to a script demonstrated by the Affrons themselves throws into doubt the validity of basing too much on a script-based description. This limitation leads to the fallacy of explaining effect in terms of intention, since the only justification for describing sets on the basis of visibility is the profession's claim only to serve the script. It may well be that designers think they are only serving stories; that belief has only partial relevance to our perception of their work. Second, limiting the definition of "design" to set design, as the Affrons do, fails to account for other cues that may influence reception of the image. While it is certainly reasonable to discuss the effect of narrative on design, it is less reasonable to focus on narrative as the exclusive, or even primary, determinant of meaning. If Barsacq is correct that one of the purposes of film is to give the illusion of "having photographed real objects," those objects have meanings of their own exploited by the designer that have nothing to do with the script.

It may be profitable, therefore, to reexamine briefly the designer's supposed service to the story. Barsacq's discussion remains the most fully developed argument from the production standpoint.[7] He begins his overview of design with a distinction between the Lumière and Méliès traditions. He argues that Méliès's sets do not just record reality in the Lumière manner but also render the image greater density and depth, suggesting "the laws governing film sets: an illusion of depth; a judicious choice of the elements composing the set; their detailed, realistic execution; and, finally, their effective presentation."[8] By suggesting that the stylized fantasies of Méliès are an improvement over the Lumière tradition, not just a movement in another direction, Barsacq introduces design qua design as a value. A *l'art pour l'art* approach to film design, however, contradicts one of Barsacq's "laws" of design: "detailed, realistic execution."

With this contradiction, film design must be simultaneously realistic and stylized. Barsacq argues that film escaped its "primitive" phase not only when it had transcended the mere recording of reality but also when it moved away from backdrops à la Méliès to the use of three-dimensional sets and objects. This change required a shift from a scenic or graphic conception of cinematic space to an architectural one.[9] Barsacq thus introduces a tension to his argument that he never completely resolves, and which remains central to the design profession. Individual success depends largely on "the requirements of the production that should guide the designer in drawing up his plans"[10]—that is, on a relativist standard that subverts any design "laws." Recognizing those "laws" as arbitrary, in turn, exposes design's contradictory nature.

If we look at statements made by designers about their profession, this tension between a script's demands and strict realism infuses all of their work. For example, designer Ted Haworth notes about shooting on location that "what you see in real life starts to tell a story better than the script you're shooting. You go half-mad trying to get some of those things into the picture."[11] Ken Adam notes: "I find it dull to do a room as it is. I feel as a designer your function is to give a reality to the public that is real but departs from the dullness which is very often part of the actual place. . . . It is nearly always a heightened reality—stylization."[12] Albert Brenner, after the usual insistence that a design must be invisible ("If the audience comes out humming the scenery, you're in serious trouble"[13]), concludes, "You're always trying to get an emotional feeling out of the audience by what you do on the film."[14] Lawrence Paull, designer of *Blade Runner*, insists that "the key thing in film design is that the design works within the context of the story and who the characters are,"[15] then goes on to say, "I don't care if it's 1939 or 2019, the look and the style has to have a vision."[16] Without belaboring the point, it is clear that just as not one of these designers questions Barsacq's basic commitment to the script, neither do they overcome the profession's contradictory desire for visual distinction.

No doubt these designers would insist that the stylization in which they indulge is necessary to achieve the "deeper" reality of the story. This position accepts that cinema's capacity to record a space in time is insufficient. "Cinema" does not exist until reality has been dressed in a script's terms. In this process, the image acquires exchange value, which is to say that film's capacity to record is embellished with socially determined notions of worth as structured by a story.[17] As cinematic design exploits the relationship between the film image and reality, it suppresses any meaning that does not contribute to the story. In the process, design draws on, restructures, and produces meaning through association. Objects and spaces enter a narrative with preexisting associations of value; they leave the story changed by their use.

It is important to recognize that in order to achieve this added value, the image can never veer entirely from the realist pole. Value accrues only if, as Barsacq would have said, the film seems to have photographed real objects. Or, to put the issue in the terms developed by the Affrons, in order to achieve the "fiction effect," the sense of reality generated by a film story, the image cannot entirely deny the "reality effect," the relationship between the image and the world greater than the film.

The cultural background that makes the "reality effect" possible is powerful, but volatile. Powerful, because by establishing a point of reference far greater than the needs of the narrative, it can help to fill the vacant

Figure 1.1. *Knowing the Statue of Liberty in* Planet of the Apes.

spaces of the story. Since we bring this background with us, it is left to us to fill in the blanks imaginatively. For example, the surprise ending of *Planet of the Apes* (Schaffner, 1968) assumes that we will know that the broken-down monument on the beach is the Statue of Liberty (see Fig. 1.1). We can thus derive the proper conclusion from the image: that our world has destroyed itself, and that the "planet of the apes" is Earth. The dialogue does not have to discuss this; the social associations of the image are great enough and per-vasive enough to make underlining unnecessary.

This example also points to the potential volatility of relying on prior knowledge: social circumstances are unreliable and in constant flux. The unreliability can be demonstrated by a hypothetical viewer who does not know the importance of the Statue of Liberty. For this viewer, the ending of *Planet of the Apes* cannot work; the significance of its ruin must remain mysterious. Flux in association is no less potentially disruptive than igno-rance.[18] A viewer who had just seen *Planet of the Apes* would probably be less likely to feel the surge of operatic yearning signaled by the Statue's ap-pearance in *The Godfather, Part II* (Coppola, 1974), for example. Thus a de-sign that depends on the illusion of contemporary reality will be more im-mediately convincing, but will also date badly as the cultural environment around the design shifts in response to changing historical circumstance. Objects selected for their transparent resonance become opaque; those in-cluded as neutral filler find unexpected prominence within the obsessions of a new setting.

The interdependence of social and compositional meaning also im-plies that no narrative film can offer completely hermetic design. Even those with a tendency in that direction, such as *The Cabinet of Dr. Caligari* (Wiene, 1919) are relatively rare since, simply put, objects must be recognizable. "John's house" must read as a house before it can belong to John. (Or indeed, Caligari's cabinet must at least look like a box before we'll agree it is his cabinet.) A film design that relies too heavily on internal association runs the risk of meaninglessness. It can only achieve totally self-referential appearance if its makers are willing to venture into abstraction, a journey few narrative filmmakers are willing to undertake.

Regardless of the degree of verisimilitude intended, the set of meanings derived from both the film itself and the cultural context results in an unsteady mixture of associations. By opening the story to the outside world, imprecision becomes inevitable. This is one reason why restricting discussion of design to its narrative function inevitably distorts our understanding of the process. Such a restriction not only ignores the degree of knowledge the filmmakers expect us to have when we arrive but also valorizes the "fiction effect" over the "reality effect" despite the image's equal reliance on both.

Restricting a definition of "design" to set design furthers this distortion. We must try to understand the *totality* of the image and recognize the relationship between stories and the outside world as one of constant, mutual exchange and interaction. Objects exist independently of a story. In this state, they have their own string of associations. Once placed in a narrative, objects and spaces acquire meaning specific to the film. While the overriding goal of the use of these objects is to serve story and character, these narrational elements frequently can work at cross-purposes. These (and other) conflicts of intention, while not part of design's stated purpose, nonetheless affect the associations we take away from a film.

Story and character dictate what can be called a "level one" of design intention. In *Outland* (Hyams, 1981), for example, this first level is structured around a general story requirement to visualize the environment of a colony on one of the moons of Jupiter in the twenty-fifth century. The main character, O'Neil (Sean Connery), is a sheriff employed to keep a dirty business running smoothly. His private quarters present at least two "level one" design requirements. The first must continue to evoke the future while drawing on general, socially shared images of domesticity. Second, the quarters must display specific aspects of O'Neil's character without contradicting the general story requirement of the future. To underline his authority to survey the spaces of the station, for example, O'Neil's quarters are provided with

Figure 1.2. *O'Neil's power to survey in* Outland.

surveillance and communication monitors (see Fig. 1.2). To emphasize his masculinity, the color scheme is restricted to grays and blues (despite the fact that at least in the beginning, he shares the quarters with his wife and son).

Because the image of the future must rely on general, socially shared images in order to function, its appearance will inevitably be dated by the fashions and assumptions current during production. For example, although the story is set in the twenty-fifth century, most of the technology relies on High Tech stylistic conventions and indicators, such as exposed metallic tubing, microwave ovens, TV and computer monitors, and push-button phones (see Fig. 1.3). These design elements refer not to the 2400s, but to a vision of the "new" current in the early 1980s. Unintentionally, the film shows O'Neil not as a man of the future, but as a lover of antiques. These implicit associations are as immediately present as the image of the future. Another designer working on a film about an early 1980s upper-middle-class home might well select the same microwave oven, for example. In that context, it would be chosen for a dominant image of contemporaneity. The object remains the same; meaning, determined by narrative, changes.

Figure 1.3. *The antique/futuristic microwave in* Outland.

The microwave, then, can be said to have at least two contradictory associations: one, an image of the future; another, an image of the present. Since all objects have a similar range of meanings, there will always be a number of interpretative possibilities attached to them that have nothing to do with their narrative function. These latent meanings can then introduce semantic sour notes. Once the absurdity of placing a late-twentieth-century appliance in a twenty-fifth-century story is recognized, for example, it becomes difficult to see that object as neutral filler. It will stick out of the background every time it appears, because it is recognizably wrong. It may even appear funny, creating a response counter to narrative intention.

The richer realm of metaphor relies as much as ironic anachronism on the potential of implicit association. As Pier Paolo Pasolini described this situation: "'Brute objects'... do not exist in reality. All are sufficiently meaningful in nature to become symbolic signs.... the pregrammatical qualities of objects will have the right to citizenship in the style of a filmmaker."[19] Pasolini was discussing several films from the early 1960s that attempted to create figurative meaning from the "brute objects" of realistic space. Critical to these films is a complete identification between the filmmaker and his protagonist. The central character's emotional state thus provides a narrative excuse for distortions or stylizations of the physical realm. Chief among Pasolini's examples are the films of Antonioni, in particular *Red Desert* (1964), in which the heroine's neurotic condition motivates the director's stylistic aberrations and experiments.

Another example might be his film *The Passenger* (1975). When Locke (Jack Nicholson), an alienated Western journalist, goes into the African desert to interview a group of rebels fighting the local government, his car breaks down while returning. These desert sequences can be interpreted as a figurative expression of Locke's state of mind by taking associations from two directions. From the story, we know that Locke is undergoing some kind of crisis that reaches a head at the moment of the "breakdown." From the outside, we know that deserts are hot, parched, and unpleasant. Conjoined in the same space, these associations establish an equivalence between Locke's "empty" emotional state and the desert's physical emptiness.

At the same time, it is a desert. As Pasolini admits, "the filmmaker can never collect abstract terms. . . . images are always concrete, never abstract."[20] Thus, while the film can be staged and cut in a fashion that suggests a "something else" in the image, the extra meaning must remain vague, potential, never quite there in the same way that the desert as physical fact is there. And under the best circumstances, there is no control to link a particular vehicle to a particular tenor. The "something else" in the image can never be read except in terms of implicit, social associations; a metaphor can never transcend physical fact. Therefore, there is no guarantee that a visual metaphor will be perceived. It remains a hope, sighing at the edges of the frame, waiting for the sensitive viewer to supply the "as if." If we insist on seeing a desert as a desert, there is nothing in the image to prove us wrong, and quite a bit to prove us right.[21]

By definition, implicit meaning works at the edges and background of a film. In order to understand how design contributes to this meaning, we have to be willing to look at pieces of design that would normally go unnoticed. For it is just these silent witnesses to the narrative that give the designed image its power. They wrap stories and characters in plausible space. In a different context, each object might well resonate on its own. Just as workers may have talents and skills irrelevant to their employment, but integral to their lives, so too objects used for narrative cinema have existence on their own to which they return after a day's work on the set.

For example, *Barry Lyndon* (Kubrick, 1975) contains scenes in which characters drink alcohol, or in which glasses figure in the background decor. The variety of glasses changes from scene to scene, character to character, but none violates norms of eighteenth-century design or shows the surface perfection of machine-turned stemware. As these glasses help to fix the story in time and make it possible for characters to drink, they achieve their first level of meaning, the reason for their inclusion. Once present, however, they gather meaning from the narrative context that works with the external meanings that they brought to the film.

Having established that the eighteenth century was sufficiently developed for members of the middle class to make use of such glasses, the film produces the potential for a second level of meaning when they do not appear where we might expect them. For example, while Barry's relatively wealthy uncle is able to lay out a lunch spread with pewter, ceramic, and stemware (see Fig. 1.4), the German woman with whom he stays after deserting the army has only earthenware mugs (see Fig. 1.5). The relatively primitive conditions, in which an otherwise prosperous woman does not have glassware, do not have to be explained. "Things weren't as good in the past. Even the middle class didn't have glasses from which to drink," we might be led to think, as the social fabric revealed by the film unfolds.

This second level of meaning, in which the lack of stemware implies economic underdevelopment, can lead to a third level derived from accumulated association. The new association of "underdevelopment" can itself be exploited, so that just as there are shades of meaning in the glassware present, so too there can be shades of meaning attached to its absence. For example, rowdy carousing in the film is conveyed through a direct drinking from jugs, themselves noticeably premodern in form and material. This activity in the film is usually restricted to the middle and upper classes, who might otherwise be expected to have more elegant tableware. It therefore leads to a third level of association, between underdevelopment and dissipation. We *expect* members of the underclass to have no glasses; such a lack reflects their economic status. When more privileged members of society exhibit this lack, we have to explain the absence, and may therefore make this association.

More complications can occur when two narrative terms conflict, such as the competing demands of narrative clarity and outward expressions of character. As explicit and implicit associations interact, an unpredictable set of secondary meanings can result. If the narrative fails to motivate an

Figure 1.4. *The presence of glassware in* Barry Lyndon.

Figure 1.5. *The absence of glassware in* Barry Lyndon.

Figure 1.6. *Fascism and Symbolism combine to produce the office in* Batman.

object's presence adequately, if the design begins to rise to visibility without explicit thematic purpose, it can begin to act in relative autonomy, derailing the story's forward drive. If too many implicit readings get in the way, a dominant reading may become difficult if not impossible.[22] Joseph Losey complained about one such misinterpretation of his film *The Romantic Englishwoman* (1975):

> Here you can see the deceptiveness of the visual if you're not awfully careful. Richard MacDonald and I set out to make the ugliest house that we could possibly make. There's not one thing in that house excepting the Magritte reproductions that either Richard or I or anybody I know would want . . . yet the people who wrote about that picture spoke again about this lush and beautiful house of Losey. It was meant to be sheer nightmare horror![23]

For another example, consider the tycoon's office in *Batman* (Burton, 1989; see Fig. 1.6). The gray blue color scheme is traditionally masculine; the large desk evokes business offices and bureaucratic settings, while the symmetrical compositions and overblown scale of the space add a touch of Fascist pomp. These all lend fairly unambiguous associations to the image. Some details, however, are more problematic. For example, the murals, the Art Nouveau/Deco architectural accents, and Palance's dressing gown add to the wealth, power, masculinity triumvirate. They also contain implicit associations with the boudoir, Symbolist decadence, and taste for decor as an end in itself that work against the dominant meaning. These implicit meanings do not necessarily subvert the dominant. They can nonetheless thwart narrative, send it in directions it is not meant to go. (For more on how objects contribute to narrative clarity, see Chapter 3.)

It is this conflict of implicit meaning that leads to the possibility of figurative meaning derived from material objects. It is likely to be a figurative content unanticipated by the filmmakers even though the associations are implicit in the image. The play of meaning creates a formal irony, in which design works apart from the dominant. It is not so much a question of things not being as they appear, but because they appear that they are not what they seem. It is not surface yielding depth, but surface playing to surface and, in the process, obscuring what seemed perfectly straightforward.

And it is uncontrollable. Where narrative provides the framework for creating meaning and the rationale for design, no such watchdog guards implicit association. As a result, we are able to respond as the filmmakers intend, or not, depending on mood and circumstance. One person's metaphor is another's boredom; one person's passionate identification becomes another's reason for ridicule. There is nothing perverse in these responses; they simply fix on meaning that the narrative might otherwise suppress. Roland Barthes would call the details that catch *puncta* and describe the process they set in motion as a counterpoint of meaning.[24] I would call both part of the pleasures of *phronesia*, that is, prudence, discrimination, and practical reasoning.[25] In either case, the process is possible only because film design has captured the riches of the world and dropped them in our laps. It remains to be seen what happens when we try to pick them up.

2

CIRCLES OF FEELING

Do I look at a film or do I participate in it? The answer to this question determines every assumption and conclusion about cinema. If I look at a film, I assume it is an object, out there, different, alienated from me. Post-Brechtian theorists and, very differently, cinematic pictorialists, share this attitude toward the image. If I participate in a film, cinema becomes a temporal, aleatory process of emotional identification, drive for closure, that wraps me in an empathic envelope. Both traditional narrative cinema and theorists seeking to understand it share this definition of the medium.

In fact, I both look at and participate in a film, and do neither at the same time. By this paradox, I mean simply that while narrative cinema may attempt a seamless stream of images, it is incapable of achieving that flow unless the spectator allows it. Cinematic viewing is better seen as a contest between identification, denial, interest, indifference, participation, derision, understanding, confusion, and surprise. And most importantly in this context, savoring, lingering imaginatively over preferred images, moments, phrases, and sensations. In that connoisseur's moment, the image freezes into an object.

To emphasize the objective, spatial qualities of the cinematic image is not to deny its existence in time. Indeed, to understand the differences between cinematic and other forms of design, it is impossible to ignore time and narrative. Nonetheless, as much as possible, we should try to isolate design from its narrative purpose in order to understand the image's impact beyond story. In order to do so, we must have a theory that assigns spaces and objects pride of place. Architectural theory is triply appropriate for this purpose, since many film designers started as architects, the rules of architectural depth are ground into film lenses, and production design requires a knowledge of architectural practice.

Architect Christian Norberg-Schulz's *Existence, Space, and Architecture* provides one means to begin this process. Norberg-Schulz, deriving his ideas from the developmental psychological theories of Piaget, describes architecture and space as a series of ever-widening affective circles extending from the human subject.[1] He proposes five basic categorical circles: graspable objects, furniture, the house, the street, and landscape. We can adapt this theory to cinema (if we add two categories) because of film's capacity to persuade that it occurs in real space and because of the frequent strategies employed to put the spectator in a position of spatial identification with the camera. The two additional categories sit at opposite ends of the scale: before grasping the thing next to us, we wear design in clothing. At the far end of the scale, cosmic space moves beyond architectural, but not cinematic classification.

Costume, Makeup, and Jewelry

Costuming is the first circle of cinema's affective space. Yet it creates an immediate problem. If our bodies are the center of the space set in motion by cinema, we feel our clothing while looking at characters whose attire may differ considerably. This contradiction becomes heightened in those moments when we are placed inside a character's perspective. During such moments, our bodies are the characters' bodies, but we know our clothes cannot be their clothes. The more substantial the difference between the film's costumes and our own, the more critical the disjuncture between what we see and what we know. Costume, makeup, and jewelry thus become the most apparent trace of stylization because they occupy a point in space so intimately close to the skin as to be part of it, moving difference from the visual to the tactile.

This difference between our clothing and a film's costumes is fundamental to the viewing experience. Jane Gaines, for example, suggests that although costume is made to serve narrative, the relation between the two is actually "antithetical" because of costume's ability to distract from the story.² Léon Barsacq insists further that any film set earlier than the nineteenth century is doomed to a sense of strangeness because the male attire will differ too greatly from today's dress.³ George Custen, examining the Hollywood biopic's temporal and spatial prejudices, supports this proposition.⁴ Barsacq's observation raises an interesting question, since it assumes a closer scrutiny of male than of female appearance. Trained to objectify women, to view them as constantly changing surfaces, we judge actresses' costumes less critically than those of the actors. Male attire must justify its stylization by answering to a higher level of verisimilitude.⁵

As a result, a story with a setting too far removed in space or time from modern Western male attire must compensate for the odd appearance of the men. Deviations from this norm challenge the capacities of cinematic representation. For example, in *A Passage to India* (Lean, 1984), the Indian Dr. Aziz seeks to be accepted by the British colonial elite. That desire ends when he is accused of raping an Englishwoman. Once cleared of the charges, the filmmakers signal Aziz's change of allegiance by having him abandon his Western clothing in favor of traditional Indian dress. In doing so, he removes not only his thematic ties to British imperial values, but the cinema's bridge between spectacle and spectator. His new attire heightens conceptual, sensual difference between image and point of observation. Such moments foreground design, stopping narrative flow for the non-Indian spectator to allow him or her to revel in the objective strangeness of the image.

A Passage to India represents a thematically explicit example of a general phenomenon. Most films dress their characters differently from the audience. Costume, makeup, and jewelry are therefore the first, fundamental steps in anthropocentric design. They must be similar enough to the audience's appearance not to rise to the level of awareness, but also different enough to answer a narrative's specific needs. In the process, costume design creates an exchange value based on these contradictory, simultaneous experiences of emotional identification and objectivity.

Objects

Graspable objects form Norberg-Schulz's first category. Objects close to us in space contribute toward the construction of the sense of a center and personal territory.⁶ For this reason, apprehensible objects, overlooked in order to privilege narrative, ground the viewer in a set of details easily

Figure 2.1. The frustrated spectator in Bergman's Persona.

understood because of their comforting smallness. Implicit in this description, however, is the possibility of picking up the object if we desire.

Barsacq reminds us that "one of the fundamental requirements of the cinema [is] to give the impression of having photographed real objects."[7] Only the impression, of course, because film objects remain elusive. Like the boy at the beginning of *Persona* (Bergman, 1966; see Fig. 2.1), anyone who reaches up to touch a film is doomed to frustration. The emphasis produced by magnification gives film objects a vivid presence that *almost* substitutes for the tactile and olfactory. Since we cannot actually touch the object, we remain like beggars outside a bakery, forced to consume only with the eyes and ears what remains tantalizingly tangible, yet inadequate.

To compensate, filmmakers must embellish visually to suggest olfactory or tactile appeal. The care lavished on the presentation of blueberries, cream, pears, wine, and cheese in *Elvira Madigan* (Widerberg, 1967; see Fig. 2.2), for example, or the shimmer of silk and damask in *The Innocent* (*L'innocente*, Visconti, 1979; see Fig. 2.3) obviously are meant to heighten visual appeal as a substitute for taste and touch. As we enjoy these sensual moments for themselves, these objects are given inordinate emphasis,

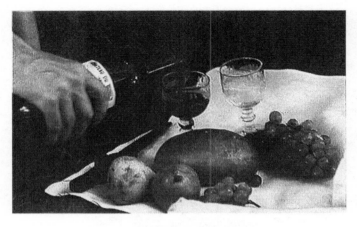

Figure 2.2. *Stimulating the olfactory in* Elvira Madigan.

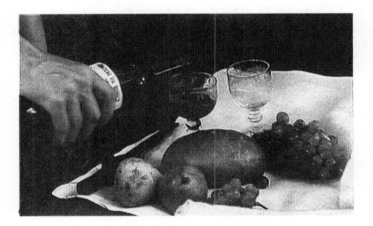

throwing the stories off balance and reversing traditional narrative values, leveling actors and objects to the same significance. Even when motivated by character desire (nested in a point-of-view sequence, for example, to demonstrate interest), the object's visual appeal cannot completely be contained by narrative. Indeed, such magnifications are frequently based on visual fascination *apart from* narrative. As the filmmakers pause to linger over an object, to revel in its surfaces, they put a temporary roadblock in the narrative's forward journey. More fundamentally, once a cigarette lighter, for example, becomes as significant visually as the man using it, it becomes difficult to insist on the special status of the latter.

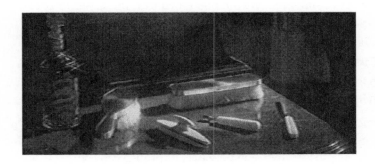

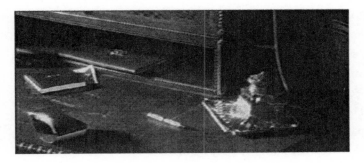

Figures 2.4–2.11. *An eight-shot sequence from* Last Year at Marienbad.

An eight-shot sequence from *Last Year at Marienbad* (*L'année dernière à Marienbad*, Resnais, 1962; see Figs. 2.4–2.11) provides vivid evidence of the power of objects. In close-up, "A" (Delphine Seyrig) moves her head. At the completion of each movement, there is a cut-in on an object. By the conclusion of the series of shots it is unclear which shots are motivating which. Is A looking at the objects, or are they looking at her? Seyrig's change in expression, from impassivity to a conventional display of fear, suggests some horror. Yet what produces her reaction? At least one plausible explanation for this paranoia is that objects have come alive through their extreme emphasis. Certainly the commodities are photographed with the same glossy care as Delphine Seyrig.

Marienbad represents an extreme example, in this case a direct expression of its writer's ideas.[8] More everyday examples of object emphasis are in some ways more radical, since they do not announce their deviance. For example in *Charlie Chan at the Race Track* (Humberstone, 1936), Chan's shots in one shot/reverse-shot sequence are framed so that his face occupies equal space with a Chinese vase sitting behind him (Fig. 2.12). Slightly out of focus, the vase has an assertive, odd presence. Its probable purpose is to add a layer of ethnicity to an image weakened by a white actor playing an Asian character. In this underlining, however, the vase rises to visual prominence, momentarily becoming equivalent to the character. And although the framing, in traditional terms, would be considered a medium angle, the shot becomes a close-up since it focuses attention on a particular portion of the image. It just happens that attention is fixed on the vase, rather than the actor.

Such emotionally directed close-ups contradict not only the relative importance of the human subject, but also the spatial classifications based on that subject. If a shot composed around an actor takes in his body from head to foot, for example, this is described as a "full shot." If a shot of a vase about the size of a human head is framed in its entirety, we refer to it as a "close-up" *not* because of any affective relationship to the object but because the framing roughly corresponds to the space that would be occupied by a human subject *if it were there*. In architectural terms, such a shot might be more accurately described as a "full shot" of the vase, since it preserves its wholeness. Perhaps an ungainly label like "emotional close-up, spatial full shot" would best fit the bill. The awkwardness demonstrates how traditional cinematic spatial classifications answer to only one measure and inherently bias description toward human-centered narrative.

Figure 2.12. *The strangely visible vase in* Charlie Chan at the Race Track.

Yet virtually every major theorist of the cinema, including Eisenstein, Pudovkin, Bazin, and Arnheim, has noted the importance of objects. This importance de-emphasizes the human center, implying that objects have equal claim to our attention. Substituting vision for the tactile or olfactory heightens prominence because the visually embellished image stimulates interest in a commodity outside the requirements of the story. As films satisfy eye and ear, while frustrating skin, nose, and mouth, they become the perfect medium for the commercial.

The visual conventions used to suggest the unrepresented senses derive from other art traditions,[9] such as still life. In *Looking at the Overlooked: Four Essays on Still Life Painting*, art historian Norman Bryson defines still life painting overall as everyday, small-scale, and modest in ambition.

It can, however, through sheer skill of execution, provide the heroic depiction usually associated with genres such as history or religious painting. Technical virtuosity lavished on trivial subject matter signals the effort to make an image seem more than it appears. This description of heroic still life suggests that commodity depiction in film can also be heroic to the extent we are aware of technical skill. If so, any definition of cinematic spectacle must include the small-scale as well as the large. In other words, details matter.

And if, as Mies van der Rohe once said, "God is in the details," there is also an implicitly religious component to this heroic depiction. In describing the still life paintings of Juan Sánchez Cotán (1561–1627), for example, Bryson notes:

> Cotán makes it the mission of his paintings to reverse this worldly mode of seeing by taking what is of least importance in the world—the disregarded contents of a larder—and by lavishing there the kind of attention normally reserved for what is of supreme value. . . . the result is that what is valueless becomes priceless.[10]

The Transcendental Materialist stare encouraged by such artists as Cotán tries to make the image yield more than the illusion of a simple physical fact, to find religion in the everyday. (This label may not be so paradoxical as it first appears. Marx meant the commodity fetish metaphor in religious rather than psychological terms.[11]) When filmmakers perpetuate this tradition through aesthetically heightened object close-ups, they simultaneously create the security of Norberg-Schulz's enveloping object world while partially placing the origin of that security outside the image. Technical virtuosity becomes the means to view a transcendent world. It also suggests that transcendence is possible through the artist's heroic exertions. Technique becomes both a gift from and means to God.

Furniture

Norberg-Schulz's next circle of space centers on furniture. From an architectural perspective, it makes sense to move from graspable objects to furniture, since tables, chairs, desks, and lamps are the things we are most likely to touch after letting go of the objects that fit in our hands. Yet, while real furniture contributes to architectural effect, film furniture is rarely used as anything other than a passive backdrop to events. Though it must "look right" for a particular narrative, it serves almost purely as filler, or at best as literal support for characters and objects. Objects can be made to serve character desire; cinematic furniture remains largely impersonal.

To understand why furniture should work relatively impersonally, consider two possible design objects, an expensive cigarette lighter and an ostentatious chair. Both have been selected to reflect the tastes and economic status of their owner. Their functional differences lie in the lighter's portability. We know it can be taken easily by a person moving in space. Thus, if the protagonist, having visited a poor family, forgets his lighter, it becomes a marker of his presence. Out of "character" with the family's surroundings, the lighter is in "character" for the protagonist. He does not have to be present for his visit to register, nor do we have to see him entering or leaving the space because the lighter's portability implies the potential for movement.

The chair, on the other hand, cannot be used outside the protagonist's immediate surroundings. If sitting behind his desk at work, for example, it would be just one of many details used to describe his wealth and taste. It would be difficult to establish the link between the chair and the character so easily established with a portable object like the lighter unless a dramatic action were connected to it. On the other hand, if the chair appeared in the poor family's room, its presence would have to be explained through action or dialogue. For it to appear without explanation would raise too many questions. Too big to ignore, too rich for its impoverished setting, its background function in the office would change to a foreground function in the family's room.

In those sequences where furniture figures prominently in the action (such as the proverbial Western barroom brawl), its participation is almost always negative and destructive. The furniture acquires significance because it is used for a function (such as a weapon) for which it was not designed. Even the numerous beds that could be cited to demonstrate the importance of furniture to cinematic narrative rarely have much function beyond their support of sex, illness, or death. The rare occasions when they resonate almost inevitably hinge on exceptional, even outlandish appearance.

In *American Gigolo* (Schrader, 1980), for example, where the protagonist's bed is central to his profession (prostitute), we have little sense of how it looks. In *The Rise to Power of Louis XIV* (Rossellini, 1966) the extended sequence of Cardinal Mazarin's death provides no full view of the bed on which he lies. On the other hand, the more obvious Pope's bed in *The Agony and the Ecstasy* (Reed, 1965), revealed when Julius II is at death's door, is ridiculously huge by contemporary standards. It is so encrusted with elaborate carving it cannot fail to register with the viewer. The aspect of character it expresses, however, is the social exceptionality of the Pope's position. It is his *impersonal* authority that makes it possible for him to sleep so sumptuously. Michelangelo, the focus of the story, sleeps on a bed little better than a wooden cot that we never see in full. Even the consistent exception of the films of Ozu helps to prove the rule: traditional Japanese furniture is light, flexible, relatively mobile, and therefore easier to move about in the story.

Western furniture is too big to be used as anything other than a support, obstruction, or proof that the design fills the frame.

In order for a piece of furniture to acquire associations from the story, it must be made clear that it is the furniture that is the point of emphasis. Since furniture is geared to the human form, it cannot be photographed without also showing a person occupying it. For example, the patriarchs' empty chairs at the end of *The Long Gray Line* (Ford, 1955) or the beginning of *The Godfather, Part II* evoke the presence, through absence, of their previous occupants. In neither case would the chairs acquire their emotional weight if they had not been previously shown supporting particular characters. The chairs function as direct extensions of their owners' bodies.

Framing and scale also affect shots of unoccupied furniture. A shot framed to photograph, say, an empty chair would be just wide enough to include a fair amount of its surroundings. Attention would be diffused, the focal point ambiguous. As a result, even though purportedly under the control of the character whose tastes dress the set, the usual purpose of cinematic furniture is first to fill the background (that is, to fulfill the production requirement for a full image), second to reflect character taste, and only rarely to call attention to itself. In this regard, cinematic furniture differs considerably from real furniture, since the latter offers some of the most obvious, immediate expressions of individual taste.

The Livable: The House/the Set

With Norberg-Schulz's next level, "architecture" appears. Cinematic architecture gravitates toward two poles: the location, or the soundstage set. A location exists before the film, with all the inconveniences of a preexisting space. As such, it exercises greater control over the film than is exercised over it. While presumably selected for what it can add to the story, its selection also closes off opportunities available on a soundstage. It nonetheless provides what Barsacq describes as "the absolute authenticity of the setting,"[12] a presence that cannot be faked.

If an interior set is meant to be read generally, a location may be not just sufficient but preferable, since it will provide Barsacq's "absolute authenticity." If the space must express more specific qualities, such as a character's way of life, the greater control of space and camera position would make a soundstage set more desirable. Barsacq described the impact of character upon decor as a means of selecting detail that outwardly expresses individual psychology, to move beyond minimal narrative function.[13] For example, designer Paul Sylbert described how one character shaped the look of an apartment in *The Prince of Tides* (Streisand, 1991):

> We made a long list of adjectives that represented this man: European, international, cosmopolitan, polished, elegant, powerful, fascistic, talented, domineering. Then opposite to the column are all the materials and styles that would match this list.[14]

When sets reflect a particular character's emotional, material, physical state, we can call it "Expressive Decor"—this room is expensively furnished because the man who owns it is wealthy, for example. This definition, of course, relies largely on internal story dynamics for motivation, which is to say that the resulting set may express character, but do little to catch our attention as viewers.

It is the attention-catching aspects of the set that the Affrons discuss in detail. The Affrons describe sets on a sliding scale of "design intensity" calculated on their visibility. "Visible" sets call attention to themselves; invisible sets remain in the background. The Affrons' approach can be incorporated into a body-centered reception theory, with the recognition that some of the results may contradict the authors' original classification. (They suggest, for example, that their Sets as Embellishment category, in which design begins to assert itself as a value, requires "the spectator to read design as a specific necessity of the narrative."[15] Such a privilege of narrative and intention restricts response to planned meaning, ignoring the contribution of the outside world and our personal histories.)

We can assume that any set that imposes its presence works against narrative flow and forces us momentarily to become aware of the image as an image. A second consideration would be the extent to which a visible set creates a sense of real space, or in the Affrons' terms, the "reality effect," and thus invites projection into the image. This projection can work both with and against narrative, depending on the circumstances. A set that tends toward the embellished or artificial is unlikely to invite projection since we are more inclined to try to grasp an objective image than to move into it. On the other hand, a set that effaces itself is more likely to encourage projection into the image as a real space.

The overriding factor in the oscillation between visible and invisible sets may be the extent to which the image and design rely on social associations rather than those created by the narrative. For example, in *Blade Runner*,

Figure 2.13. *The empty apartment in* Last Tango in Paris.

which the Affrons include in their Sets as Artifice category, the sets have a strong presence that "create[s] new realities." [16] The Affrons seem to suggest that these new realities are created by the image generated by the narrative. However, this compositional reality is possible only because the film self-consciously dresses its sets in a socially shared image of an unpleasant environment: constant rain. The stylization, among the strongest in the history of cinema, nonetheless gets buried under a realistic downpour. The cumulative effect is not to objectify the image, despite the sets' artifice, but to invite projection into a physically palpable atmosphere.

As we noted in Chapter 1, even when films create a self-referential reality, their stylizations must maintain some tie to reality. Physical space can at best be ignored, never overcome. If necessary, spaces must appear habitable. Both *The Scarlet Empress* (von Sternberg, 1934) and *Ivan the Terrible* (Eisenstein, 1944, 1949), for example, offer stylized visions of Russian history. Neither attempts realistic verisimilitude. Still, when Catherine charges up a staircase on horseback or when Ivan broods in the shadows of an archway, stairs or arch do not threaten to collapse. Both have fulfilled Barsacq's dictum, however elaborately: the films seem to have "photographed real objects."

Sets in *Last Tango in Paris* (Bertolucci, 1973) occupy a more typical middle ground where many of the issues around Expressive Decor crystallize. We can interpret the apartment in which Paul and Jeanne meet first as an ex-

Figure 2.14. *The bourgeois apartment in* Last Tango in Paris.

pression of character. Its initial emptiness can be seen as a metaphor of Paul's emotional bankruptcy at the moment of their meeting (though since theirs is a struggle between equals, it is arbitrary to ascribe the apartment to a projection of Paul's psyche). Their relationship develops with the increase in their furniture and objects. Despite Paul's desire that they remain strangers, the apartment reflects the growing complexity of their affair (see Fig. 2.13).

How "intense" is this set? The photographic style and framing are self-conscious enough to encourage recognition of the image-as-image. The apartment's emptiness also encourages a nonrealistic, subjective interpretation of the space since emptiness in cinema is exceptional (see Chapter 3). At the same time, the lighting also elaborately maintains the conventions of single-source illumination; the costuming reflects the characters' income, period, and social standing. The selected objects are banal, and thus the more effective in weaving a realistic tapestry of architectural background. In short, these images contain equal tendencies toward artifice and reality, image-as-object and image-as-space.

On the other hand, when the film depicts Jeanne's parents' apartment for two scenes, the space must "read" quickly, therefore, more generally (see Fig. 2.14). The apartment's dark colors, somber lighting, clogged bookshelves, overstuffed furniture, and frames telegraph a simple message of "bourgeois prosperity." When Paul chases Jeanne to the apartment, he notes that it has "a lot of memories," binding its clutter to thematic significance. Thus, the first apartment can be read as a subjective projection partly because the parents' apartment has been explicitly thematized. That thematization depends on immediately recognizable, socially shared images of middle-class life that then contrast with the empty apartment. If the parents' apartment is an image of impersonal affluence, the empty apartment becomes an image of personal expression.

It seems as if even in the most stylized, artificial environments, there is likely to be some play with and to generally accepted images of reality, if for no other reason than to heighten difference. The Realistic norm works behind the scenes, giving the most "embellished" set its ability to display itself, the most "expressive decor" its license to visualize the subjective.

The Walkable: Streets

When Norberg-Schulz moves outside, he abandons the individual, personal focus of the closer circles and enters the social realm. "The urban level (which comprises sub-levels) is mainly determined by *social interaction*, that is, by the common 'form of life.'"[17] The street set begins to show the limits of production design, for two reasons. First, the social interaction required by a street set presents the designer with an ever-larger space to control. Second, streets' social values clash with the character-centered ideology of classical narrative.

Like any other set, a street can be built, or developed on location. However, even someone as committed to the designed set as Léon Barsacq admits that "apart from special kinds of films such as ballets or musicals, exterior sets are ill adapted to stylization or simplification."[18] Perhaps this bad fit results from the street's social aspect. It is relatively easy to justify objects, furniture, and rooms as logical reflections of a character's economic status, and so on. The social realm of the street, however, is a stage for conflict. A street set cannot be designed as the expression of a single character since, by definition, a street expresses a reality greater than individual desire or taste.

For example, in *Doctor Zhivago* (Lean, 1965) several scenes are staged on a Moscow street set outside Zhivago's family home (see Fig. 2.15). This set is a space of social negotiation. All of the major characters, as well as a protest march and massacre, conscripts leaving for the First World War, and proletarian Christmas celebrations, are shown at various points on the street. The

Figure 2.15. *The street set from* Doctor Zhivago.

street set expresses a public function through a scale large enough to stand in for the Whole and a visual appearance that serves none of the characters specifically. While the design could have made the set reflect the heterogeneity of the script and characters, to have done so would have undermined the social image of a period street. Instead, the film abandons heterogeneity in favor of general images of "Russianness" and "turn-of-the-century-ness."

The alternative—to use a real street for *Doctor Zhivago* and thereby incorporate the social by the act of production—submits the script to the tyranny of circumstance. At best, a preexisting street expresses a script imperfectly. The street will read as itself before it reads as a particular street in a particular story; that is the purpose of using a location, to achieve lived, social recognizability. However, if recognized, the location brings the narrative to a halt, as the space as physical fact triumphs over narrative service. Such danger of recognition always exists because of the design's need to connect to external reality.

Doctor Zhivago's budget allowed the construction of designed streets, but the set does not have the authenticity of a location. In none of the film's street scenes is there a fully unencumbered view; the wide angles tend to look down on the action, so blocking the vanishing point. Even the largest sets lack the vitality, variety, and chaos of an average urban street. In contrast, the aerial perspective provided by location photography lends the period physical environment in *The Godfather, Part II* a tangibility lacking in *Zhivago*'s streets. This relationship is most obvious and powerful in a shot when the young Vito Corleone crosses the street. As the camera travels with him, the shot momentarily widens out to reveal the street receding to the horizon. Siegfried Kracauer describes the affinity between film and the street as one based exactly on its chaos:

> The affinity of film for haphazard contingencies is most strikingly demonstrated by its unwavering susceptibility to the "street." . . . Within the present context the street . . . is of interest as a region where the accidental prevails over the providential, and happenings in the nature of unexpected incidents are all but the rule.[19]

As soon as movement and life become designed, they lack the immediacy of an untouched location. The social dimension, the purpose of a street, is inevitably reduced.

Landscapes

With the street we are forced to confront the social. With Norberg-Schulz's next category, landscape, we must deal with the suprahuman. "The landscape level results from man's *interaction with the natural environment.*"[20] This distinction between man and the natural environment implies a fundamental difference and independence. Nature, shaped by forces outside human control, determines that which architecture is not. Norberg-Schulz notes further, "The place is experienced as an 'inside' in contrast to the surrounding 'outside.'"[21] This distinction conflates "nature," beyond the perception of any single person, and "landscape," the view of nature from a fixed point in space. Architecture in effect creates landscape by fixing human space as a point looking out onto nature.

Cinema similarly embraces nature as a space to be controlled by human perception, and in the process renders nature as landscape. What by definition is greater than a single person gets reduced to the visual demands of an individual occupying a point in space. In doing so, perspective distorts space, both through the geometric formula it applies and the human-centered position it duplicates.[22] Even as the film image widens, it provides nothing that a human eye could not perceive. (Wide-angle lenses prove, rather than disprove, this point, since they introduce noticeable distortions to normal perspective.) Though editing provides multiple perspectives, nature always exceeds the ability of the eye or the lens to perceive.

While all photography contains this prejudice, anyone who has tried to take a photograph of the Grand Canyon knows that large-scale subjects elude the camera's capacity to record. They do so to the point that photography becomes a stylization. The lens reduces to human scale what is inherently beyond that scale by confining it to the retreating lines of perspective. The impact of the space—its enraptured totality, its seemingly boundless opening onto the inconceivable—can be conveyed only through secondary devices, such as narrative. Emotions generated by a story substitute for the visceral effect of real space long ago described by Edmund Burke as "the Sublime."[23] These responses may equal the sensation experienced in the space photographed. They are nonetheless different responses, since they depend on the introduction of human material foreign to the space.

Cinema is not the first Realistic art to confront the distorting aspects of perspective. Robert Rosenblum has demonstrated how nature acquired the transcendental affect lacking in Protestant theology in the work of such artists as Casper David Friedrich.[24] Of course, paintings are static, and invite the contemplative gaze that provokes the sublime. The observer is invited, expected to linger, to allow imaginative projection to open the depicted field onto limitless potential. A painting's stasis is its greatest asset. Narrative cinema must move forward, and can only approximate the sublime in a story's terms. When it does not, the effects can be risible. For example, at the midpoint of *The Agony and the Ecstasy* Michelangelo acquires directly divine inspiration by seeing the Sistine Chapel ceiling composition in a cloud formation. The reduced scale of perspective perception makes it impossible to experience the space as anything other than a constructed image, leaving nothing but the visible effort to provoke the reaction.

The relationship between narrative and landscape will always be edgy because film landscapes are almost always gratuitous in narrative terms. As something apart from (though used by) the narrative, landscapes also hint at a visually based value system beyond dramatic need. As the landscape shot appeals to this external set of values, it offers an impersonal perspective beyond character or narrative control, and thus can work against the narrative as much as with it. In *My Darling Clementine* (Ford, 1946), for example, Monument Valley lends visual richness to the story of Wyatt Earp. The story gives the inadequate representation of space some emotional resonance by linking Monument Valley to its events. At the same time, the location dwarfs an underdeveloped story out of scale with the physical environment.

Even as narrative helps landscape imagery to overcome the emotional limitations of perspective-based representation, nature repays the loan by the visual authority it gives the narrative.

Cosmic Space

Norberg-Schulz stops with landscape, which is understandable since his theory is based on a body- and ego-centered conception of space. He overlooks religious architecture, which has consistently sought to transcend ego-centered experience, evoking, if not containing the cosmic. Filmmakers have no less often tried to merge cosmic and cinematic. Yet any attempt at creating cosmic cinematic space is founded on a fundamental limitation, the materialist approach to representation involved in the film image itself. As with landscape, in order to achieve cosmic affect, cinema must resort to a combination of techniques, including an evocation of its architectural origins.

The most consistent attempts to represent cosmic, transcendental space in film occur in the genre most removed from the everyday material world, science fiction. (I am concerned here with religious affect, not subject matter. Most Bible Epics fail to generate religious response precisely because they view religion in literary, rather than formal, terms.) The reasons for science fiction's religious component are not difficult to understand. With subjects frequently set in outer space, science fiction is often literally cosmic in outlook. Moreover, in a materialist age, science fiction comes closest to expressing our age's self-image, since it displays, revels in, flaunts that in which we "have faith": technology. Without resorting to the banality that science is a modern religion, empirical method remains a bedrock of faith on which all ideas are expected to be built. Technology, as the most direct product of that method, is therefore a highly appropriate subject for any attempt to evoke the religious for the modern viewer.

Science fiction also embodies one aspect of the religious when its special effects encourage a double sense of wonder: "how wonderful," and "I wonder how they did that?" The question is critical, since it implies that we perpetuate the scientific inquiry depicted in the stories with a consciousness running counter to the illusion. This awareness is simultaneously the article of faith that makes the illusion possible. This is one reason why it is possible to speak of a transcendental response to the cinematic cosmos, but not to the cinematic landscape. Cinema's outer space is manufactured, unreal, part

Figure 2.16. *Retreating to infinity in 2001's Star Gate.*

of the materialist system it seeks to transcend through trickery. Nature, indefatigably nonhuman, exceeds any human effort to control or duplicate it.

While there are dystopian exceptions, most science fiction films set in space struggle to achieve the sense of awe that can only be called "religious." Although *2001: A Space Odyssey* (Kubrick, 1968) is the most obvious example of finding religion in outer space, others include the *Star Wars* trilogy (Lucas/Kershner/Marquand, 1977, 1980, 1983), the first *Star Trek* film (Wise, 1979), and *Forbidden Planet* (Wilcox, 1956). All of these films attempt to evoke the cosmic through the same device borrowed from Baroque painting: exaggerated perspective. (And one of the few dystopian visions of deep space, *Outland*, does not resort to transcendental perspective techniques in its otherwise technically complex special effects.) In *2001*, the Star Gate, which gives Bowman access to the infinite, is created by two planes receding rapidly to a point at the center of the screen (see Fig. 2.16). In both the *Star Wars* and *Star Trek* films, the filmmakers signal that velocities greater than the speed of light have been achieved when space blurs into lines of light rushing to the vanishing point. In *Forbidden Planet*, the achievements of the superhuman Krell are shown as a series of architectural wonders so huge in scale that they retreat to the vanishing point.

One-point perspective, the material source of this technical and religious affect, starts in Renaissance architecture. The ordered, simple forms of Renaissance churches heighten religious affect through abstract, ideal models of the cosmos. Art historian Heinrich Wölfflin described the Italian Renaissance as an era of "perfect proportion" that stood in for the presence of God.[25] Rudolf Wittkower, in *Architectural Principles in the Age of Humanism*, argued that this Renaissance architecture nonetheless expressed a contradictory worldview. Wittkower agrees with Wölfflin that the perfect form of the Renaissance church was an example in small of the perfection of the cosmos, an analogy for the universe. He nonetheless argues that perfection was achievable only as an idealized view as perceived from the station point of a man in space.

Therefore, these evocations of religious architecture and painting contain a double contradiction. The trick of infinitely receding space would not be possible without the mathematically based empiricism that more often than not works against religious faith. Furthermore, perspective itself requires an individualist, fixed conception of space and experience that contradicts a religiously structured cosmos. Whether these contradictions reinforce or subvert each other will depend on the context in which individual images exist. Will an image appear more "cosmic" or "human"? The answer to that question will depend on the degree of obviousness in the perspective construction. To be obvious, the image must be at least partially static, or move only along lines that maintain a single vanishing point.

It is interesting that this religious affect should most often occur in those cinematic spaces—the apprehensible and the cosmic—lying slightly outside standard cinematic form. Classical cinema is built on middle distances, the cutting patterns of spaces calculated to human scale. While the apprehensible is within human reach, the framings necessary to achieve it shift emphasis to materials. The cosmic acknowledges the human only as the perceiver of the gateway to God, and depends on the overwhelming of response to evoke the transcendent. Scale and distance fundamentally determine our emotional relation to the image. And yet cinematographic scale itself is achieved through conventions designed to exploit the frame and resolution of the cinematic image. To understand our relationship to the image, then, it is not enough to chart our distance from the subject; we must also take into account those other rules that contribute to our perception.

3

IMAGING

Up to this point, we have discussed production design as if the objects and spaces it creates were real. They are, of course, images governed by rules that influence our perception as much as the associations carried by the design. In this chapter, I would like to examine some of the techniques and conventions related to this "imaging" of spaces and objects. This discussion restores visual grammar to centrality and lays the groundwork for detailed discussions in later chapters. Implicit in this overview is the assumption that cinematic design primarily provides a means to organize a delimited picture space. Limitation is necessary, of course, for without some boundary the designer's work would never finish. As he or she abandoned the image to embellish the real world, production design would return to architecture.

Charles Altman has noted that there are generally two metaphors used to describe this delimited space: the cinematic image as "frame," or as "window." As Altman points out, the frame metaphor is derived from art-historical practice.[1] It is so persuasive that it is easy to forget that the film image has no frame in the same way that a picture on a wall may. It has instead a picture field that can be more accurately described as "on camera" or "off camera." The "window" metaphor stresses the film image's illusion of depth by using compositions that move *away* from the center of the image toward the edges of the field, frequently in loose centrifugal organizations. "Framed" images move *toward* the center of the image in centripetal organizations that emphasize the picture plane, rather than the illusion of depth.

Rudolf Arnheim has suggested that the picture frame originated in the post-and-lintel architectural setting of art in its original, religious context.[2] This frame served to make the artwork appear as a window looking on the outer world, thus mixing the frame and window metaphors. In *Film as Art*, he argues further that the cinematic frame is essential:

> The limitations of the [cinematic] picture are felt immediately. The pictured space is visible to a certain extent, but then comes the edge which cuts off what lies beyond.[3]

> The limitation of the image is as much a formative tool as perspective. . . . Moreover, a frame is an absolute essential if the decorative qualities of a picture are to be displayed; one can only consider the filling of the canvas, the allotment of space, and so forth, if there are definite limits to act as framework for the pictorial design.[4]

Arnheim's ideas can stand in for all those theorists (including, in addition to Arnheim himself, Eisenstein, Pudovkin, Nöel Burch, and Jean Mitry) who define the essence of cinema on the basis of the plastic qualities of the image.

In contrast to the centripetally organized frame, the window metaphor suggests that the camera's selection of material is arbitrary, that the world on-screen is merely what *is* shown, not all that could be shown. The most famous advocate of the window metaphor is André Bazin, for whom cinematic space is inherently open and centrifugal. Moreover, "the screen is not a frame like that of a picture but a mask which allows only a part of the action to be seen."[5] While Bazin's position has influenced many (particularly such writers as Andrew Sarris, Charles Barr, and very differently, Gilles Deleuze), it has proven equally controversial, not least because of its fundamentalist insistence on open space as cinema's true purpose.

Leo Braudy's more balanced position notes that the open/closed metaphor describes not only graphic organization but an entire view of cinema and the world:

> The aesthetic motion in a closed film can be described as a burrowing inward, an exploration of inner space, an effort to get as far as possible into the invisible heart of things, where all connections are clear. . . . an open film is more dialectic, an interplay between artifice and the reality that refuses control, which escapes interpretation not by its mysteriousness but by its simplicity.[6]

While Braudy offers an important attention to objects and spaces ("What does the filmmaker and the cameraman love the way the writer loves words? . . . the most characteristic element in any film is the way it presents all its objects—animate as well as inanimate"[7]), his model nonetheless falls short for discussing cinematic design because of his need to narrativize. Criticizing both semiotics and formalist film theory, he states that "the methodology of film criticism must finally be brought into the world of story, whether fiction or nonfiction."[8] Braudy makes this assertion despite his own recognition that "the different efforts to control and order the elements of a film must constantly face the knowledge that facts escape, that objects have another life outside the film which feeds the life within."[9]

In order to discuss design, it may be necessary to return to the source of the distinction between closed and open form: art historian Heinrich Wölfflin. In *Principles of Art History: The Problem of the Development of Style in Later Art*, he defined the difference between open (window) and closed (frame) organization in the following terms:

> What is meant [by closed form] is a style of composition which, with more or less tectonic means, makes of the picture a self-contained entity, pointing everywhere back to itself, while, conversely, the style of open form everywhere points out beyond itself and purposely looks limitless, although, of course, secret limits continue to exist, and make it possible for the picture to be self-contained in the aesthetic sense.[10]

Wölfflin's conclusion relates directly to cinematic design: "The final question is . . . whether the figure, the total picture as a visible form, looks *intentional* or not."[11] Wölfflin discusses the subjects of open or closed organizations only as they express an attitude toward the boundary. The classic style accepts the boundary as a given limitation, and concentrates attention on the included. Open organization effaces the boundary through compositions that seem at most an unintentional limit on an otherwise boundless field. Wölfflin sums up the differences between the two approaches as both a matter of style—the closed organization is more architectural—and as a matter of worldview. The closed organization offers a static, enduring vision of the world; the open form stresses movement and change.[12] He also recognizes that the open form, whatever its pretenses to "happening" upon its subject, derives from intention and convention as much as does closed form.

Wölfflin's description recognizes that open form emphasizes movement, and suggests that we can equate camera stasis with closed (framed) form and camera movement with open (window) form. Therefore, as a first step in understanding cinematic design, we can examine the degree to which camera movements make us forget the boundary and encourage the illusion of looking at real space. For example, pans embrace space, implying a rotating totality. In the hotel lobby sequences of *Death in Venice* (*Morte à Venezia*, Visconti, 1971), the 360-degree pans around the space give a strong sense of reality and tangibility, dissolving the frame so that, as Altman described Bazin's window metaphor, "we feel that if we could move to the left or the right a bit, we would be able to catch a glimpse of the objects and people masked by the screen's border."[13] Pans thus work as strongly centrifugal movements, while encouraging the imaginative construction of a space outside the frame.

Despite the effects of pans, however, a simple equation between camera movement and open form would be mistaken because camera movement frequently works centripetally.[14] For example, a camera movement can establish the object as a static point in space emphasized by the motion, as in the "statue" shots of *Contempt* (*Le Mépris*, Godard, 1961), where the camera tracks and pans around statues fixed at the center of the frame. The camera can also move centripetally along a visible or easily imaginable architectural line. For example, in much of *Last Year at Marienbad* the camera tracks along architectural perspective lines or decorative details. Hitchcock's camera movements work similarly, particularly his signature subjective movements down corridors. In such emphases, the perspective construction leads the movement, pulling the camera along the lines receding to the vanishing point. In fact, tracking shots generally create linear, architectonic movements, since they use literal tracks (lines) across space.

Moreover, camera movements frequently assert themselves as production traces, making them an unreliable glass to fill the window of invisible, open form. Elaborate camera movement is usually synonymous with the work of "baroque" stylists like Max Ophuls, Bernardo Bertolucci, and Federico Fellini. While these directors provide frames with porous boundaries, their images impress less for their mimetic faithfulness to space than as virtuoso form that calls attention to its singularity.[15] For example, *Lola Montes* (Ophuls, 1955) and *The Last Emperor* (Bertolucci, 1987) open with shots that opulently caress space with combined tracks, pans, and tilts. To achieve this flow of space, however, the movements rely on architectural details (lowered chandeliers in *Montes*, a train and passenger platform in *Emperor*) to lead camera and eye into an appreciation of the bravura technique.

Figure 3.1. *Movement to either edge of the picture produces an expectation of space outside the field.*

A more direct use of movement to efface boundary is simply to have characters move in and out of frame, in centrifugal movements away from the center, as in any film by Renoir or Robert Altman. In Figure 3.1, for example, note how the body position of the man to the left and the movement of the woman climbing the stairs lead the eye out of the picture to either side, suggesting a world not only outside but before and after as well. These positions manage this effect despite the strongly architectonic nature of the overall composition. In Robert Altman's *McCabe and Mrs. Miller* (1971), for example, much of the "reality effect" produced in the gambling scenes results from the movement of characters in an out of frame, bouncing off the central card-playing action.

Yet in Altman's case, these porous boundaries are at least to some extent contradicted by the director's self-conscious use of the zoom lens. The zoom, not so much a camera movement as a lens movement, changes spatial relations without either subject or camera having to move. It is an assertive gesture that constantly readjusts perspective, deforming space.[16] Alone, the zoom is an assertively centripetal movement since it moves into or away from the center of the image. Combined with another movement, such as a pan, the zoom is less assertive, as the center constantly repositions. In *McCabe and Mrs. Miller*, the zooms squeeze and mold the space invisibly

Figure 3.2. *Actor movement dissolves boundaries in* McCabe and Mrs. Miller.

Figure 3.3. *The composition reestablishes centrality.*

Figure 3.4. *The zoom reasserts importance through centripetal emphasis.*

with the help of pans and character movements, while occasionally asserting themselves for directorial comment (for example, zooming into the hands of a character picking on a violin; see Figs. 3.2–3.4.)

On the other hand, when combined with noticeable architectural details, the zoom becomes almost impossibly assertive to the point of disorientation. For example, in another shot in Visconti's *Death in Venice*, a combined zoom back, lateral track right, and pan left punctuated by a row of columns in the foreground turn the central character's simple walk across St. Mark's Square into a dizzying, virtuoso spatial display. Hitchcock's famous "Vertigo effect"—the combination of a zoom in and a track back—similarly relies, at least in its initial use, on the strong architectural spatial cues of the staircase seen from the point of view of the central character.

These examples suggest that while camera movement can work to heighten the illusion of a boundless space, it can work at least as often as authorial assertion. When combined, different kinds of camera movements work at cross-purposes. They can enhance the sense of an invisible window onto an expansive space. At the same time, they can hint at a strong directing personality obviously guiding the image in particular directions. Even strongly "open" movements like pans can be mitigated by other types of motion. Movements that involve architectural details are among the most frequent of these contradictions to the "open" image.

Only the reframe, the slight movement left or right, up or down, frequently in response to an actor's movements, works consistently to efface the boundary. While most obvious in the films of Renoir and Altman, reframes are nearly ubiquitous in narrative cinema. Like shot/reverse-shot editing, the reframe effaces form, limiting camera movement to a descriptive rather than expressive function. By panning, however slightly, the reframe sets up the illusion that the designed space exists beyond the edges of the image. At the same time, by motivating the camera movement with an actor's action, reframes exploit the conventions of centripetal organization, maintaining a fixed center and subject while effacing boundaries. Centered on actors, reframes prop up narratives, fixing the human subject as the focus in an otherwise dissolving world.

Editing and design share other characteristics besides this negative similarity. Editing fractures space *over* time; design arranges space *in* time. Editing juxtaposes images in a flow, either in collision (Eisenstein, Godard, commercials, MTV) or in construction (Pudovkin, classical narrative cinema).

Design juxtaposes in a pictorial field, overlapping a range of objects in a single image. In the famous Kuleshov experiment, the expression on an actor's face was perceived to change because of the content of an intervening shot. If juxtaposition in time can affect meaning, we might expect it to do the same in space. Just as shots can collide or flow, pieces of a design can work in harmony or dissonance. If so, the orchestration of meaning should become ever-more complex with each added detail, just as editing organizations can add layers of meaning through accumulated impact in time.

Gilles Deleuze has in fact suggested that the open/closed distinction is secondary to a consideration of what and how much the image contains.[17] The visual field only has significance as a subset of a totality that we know exists, but that can never be encompassed. Deleuze thus argues first to consider the saturation or rarefaction (fullness or emptiness) of the image.[18] He argues further that the frame will tend to be more geometric in appearance if the organization is closed and more organic or physical if the organization is open.[19] (This geometrical/physical distinction is echoed by Wölfflin [126] and Arnheim [*Film as Art*, 74]). This distinction in turn will be more apparent depending on the materials photographed.[20]

Combined, Deleuze's and Wölfflin's observations provide four basic attitudes toward the frame, all at best relative: open/empty; open/full; closed/empty; closed/full. The combinations chart tendencies, not truths, exhibited to greater or lesser degree from shot to shot, moment to moment, film to film, always complicated by movement. Interestingly, the "empty" side of the equation appears infrequently. When introducing the idea, Deleuze has recourse to only a few examples (two from Hitchcock, a general reference to Antonioni).[21] This paucity of rarefied *mise-en-scène* suggests that design is an additive process, a matter of filling the frame.

Joseph Losey, known for his attention to production design as well as his debt to Brechtian theatrics, claimed that Brecht taught him the need for "the stripping of reality and its precise reconstruction through selection of reality-symbols."[22] These comments support the idea that design is an additive process: first, an emptying out, then a movement back toward saturation, within the governing terms of the conception. This tendency to fill, rather than to empty, accords well with production design's economic function, to provide value through product differentiation. An economic definition of saturation and value, it suggests that the more a frame contains, the "richer" it will appear because of the accumulated value of the contained objects.

Figure 3.5. *An empty space invites filling.*

In Figure 3.5, for example, we have an "empty" space, waiting to be filled by furniture and people, to *anticipate* narrative and value. Only the blank walls and paneless window create an explicit association, with Modernism, thus dating the space as no earlier than the twentieth century. Beyond this dating function, only the broom offers imaginative possibilities by stirring a physical expectation. The broom is presumably present because the room needs cleaning, or was just cleaned. If the latter, it must have been left by someone, and it thus creates both a *before* the image, and potential human presence. These possibilities reinforce the *temporary* nature of the emptiness, since it provides a hint that the moment lies between moments of habitation.

As the frame begins to fill, two basic approaches are likely. The first, most common in Hollywood classicism, fills the image with redundant reinforcements of the basic space. (This approach more or less conforms to the Affrons' first two categories of denotation and punctuation.) Under this principle, the empty space in Figure 3.5 would be furnished with Modernist artifacts to harmonize with the decor, and thus to form a relatively passive backdrop to the drama enacted in the space. Decorative emphasis could

Figure 3.6. *Contradictions between decor and space.*

occur only to the extent that individual objects acquired significance, either through narrative emphasis or through odd visual appearance.

A more complex approach is provided in Figure 3.6, in which the decor contradicts the Modernist space around it. While momentarily contradictory, this visual tension can still be exploited by narrative. We noted in Chapter 2 how the decor in the similarly contradictory apartment in *Last Tango in Paris* was "contained" by contrasting it with otherwise full spaces and by attributing its exceptional appearance to character. Presumably, the contradictions in Figure 3.6 could equally be explained by character taste and desire. If, for example, the space belonged to an antique dealer, the presence of such furniture would follow logically from the story. (Just such a justification of discordant space and furniture occurs in Resnais's *Muriel* [1963], for example.) The visual impact of the design, muted and justified by character motivation, is able to function as filler. In this sense of filling the frame, the decor remains impersonal, since it has no direct relationship to the character's body.

Decor becomes personalized when props are introduced that allow characters to interact with the space. In Figure 3.7, for example, the contradictory Modernist/Empire design is complicated by the introduction of contemporary props (briefcase, hat, overcoat, keys, scarf) easily imagined as *usable* by the owner. While none of these objects accords with the furniture, to the extent that they are grounded in a character's actions (the owner has

Figure 3.7. *Character details contribute to "optimal saturation."*

just returned home from work, for example), they help create a realistic texture of objects.

As they express specifics, such objects set characters apart from the environment in the same way that narrative emphasis removes them from the social texture around the story. Moreover, once accepted as belonging to an individual character, such objects bring associations of their own that can be exploited (as discussed with the glassware in *Barry Lyndon*). The overcoat and scarf suggest a cold climate without showing one; the keys imply an automobile, even if one never figures in the action, and so on. In fact, not all the objects have to be used by a character so long as it is plausible they *might* be. The keys do not have to be put in a lock, for example, since their presence alongside the briefcase makes some degree of sense. Assuming that one of the objects is motivated, the others follow logically from the context in which they are embedded. In turn, the objects' presence contributes to an "environmental unconscious" of plausible detail *around* a character and story.

An image like Figure 3.7 has reached a point of optimal saturation. Even if the objects in it conflict with one another at one level, by being attributed to a character's tastes, they work together toward an overall impression of convincing, material detail. It "works" as a designed image because the number of possible associations has been limited and structured. Optimal saturation occurs when objects and design contribute most to the dominant meaning, and conflict as little as possible with it or each other.

Figure 3.8. *When saturation goes too far, meaning gets murky.*

However, if the economic model of value is correct, there is still plenty of space that could be filled by other objects, and thus ample opportunity remains to increase the value of the image. The problem with this model is that as more objects are introduced, more ambiguity has to be clarified. Figure 3.8 demonstrates some of the problems that can arise when an economic definition of value is accepted too literally. In economic terms, it is "richer" than 3.7, since there are considerably more objects. The image nonetheless fails to achieve the same degree of value since the contradictions between the objects begin to raise gratuitous questions. Why are there *two* vases? Why is the CD tower placed so that we cannot see the picture behind it? What is that strange black box at the edge of the table? Even such details as the oddly placed overcoat and hat that we might have accepted in Figure 3.7 as expressing a particular narrative moment ("they are hanging there because the owner came home and started work in a hurry") here are more likely to register as simple clutter. In short, we are thrown out of the narrative rationale into a consideration of the image-as-image.

The fact that these objects in fact do belong to a single person, myself, only demonstrates the relative impoverishment of designed images. As Alain Robbe-Grillet pointed out, classical and Realistic notions of "character" define individuality on the basis of a limited range of "characteristics" that have little relation to the richness of human expression.[23] These characteristics limit experience in dramatically convenient, if experientially suspect, ways, by *rationalizing* it. In this sense, Figure 3.8 is the truer image to the extent that its complicated clutter reflects a range of uncontainable contradictions and multiple meanings. It nonetheless is less likely to register as a "rich" (or valuable) image because of its lack of *narrative* clarity and purpose.

The contribution of saturation to image value also depends on the frame's openness. Deleuze notes that closed frames can never reach completion. "Every closed system communicates";[24] every visual field is a subset of a larger set, the ultimate whole of which can never be apprehended. So as the closed frame attempts to create a self-sufficient system, it will tend toward saturation in order to include as much as possible to approximate the infinity of the whole. Thus, the closed/full frame will probably be a tantalizing subject because its centripetal organization sucks the gaze toward a center embroidered with the lapidary excesses of material production. The objects in Figure 3.8, for example, are rather casually placed and structured. More carefully arranged, they would no doubt have much greater legibility, and thus greater potential for visual fascination.

The open/full frame encourages a different illusion. Its centrifugal organization succeeds as a Realist device because its pretended disregard for boundaries creates a notion that the boundary *can* be ignored. The centrifugal frame, by presenting a "random" angle, exploits conventions of representation in order to suggest its connection to a world it acknowledges but which it excludes as much as the closed frame. As a result, open, like closed, organization saturates the image to stand in for the excluded field's infinite richness. The results are nonetheless different. As the closed image creates a self-sustaining world, it objectifies itself and invites scrutiny as an image. This is the key distinction, the degree to which the tendencies of open, closed, full, and empty combine to encourage the spectator to contemplate the image as an object. In the process, the seduction traps the gaze for proper, frustrated appreciation, stimulating our bodies to touch, taste, or smell objects, while failing to deliver.

Deleuze's comments suggest further that these tendencies will be accentuated in a widescreen image because "the big screen and depth of field in particular have allowed the multiplication of independent data."[25] This increased saturation of widescreen images was noted early on by Charles Barr. In "Cinemascope: Before and After,"[26] Barr tried to show how widescreen processes shifted filmmaking away from montage aesthetics, toward saturation and selection. John Belton, developing Barr's argument further, suggests:

> Cinerama and CinemaScope, in particular, effectively transformed the notion of frame, expanding the horizontal angle of view to such an extent that there was, for all intents and purposes, no sense of any borders at the edges of the frame.[27]

Belton argues further that this increased image size was naturalized in narrative terms by use of genres like historical spectacle, with the consequence that traditional narrative values were slightly displaced in favor of visual display.[28] If these authors are correct, "widescreen," as a general, descriptive term will suggest rich spectacle and saturation. By implication, this greater saturation requires more design control in order not to overwhelm the narrative,[29] because the more space to be filled, the more "independent data" to be introduced and therefore the greater the chance for narrative imprecision. Consequently, the cumulative density of the widescreen image may create imagery well beyond the absorption capacity of either story or viewer.

Besides narrative considerations, there is a production logic to this emphasis on saturation and visual control. A Hollywood studio would be unlikely to stake a major investment in a widescreen spectacle and leave the visual style to chance. The capital-intensive nature of early Cinemascope productions all but guaranteed that technicians would try to use the new screen space as artistically as possible—that is, within culturally acceptable terms. If true, this attempt to legitimize the Cinemascope image, combined with the new problems of directing attention in a wider range of space, offered a greater likelihood for self-conscious framing, since a closed frame would accentuate the image's "art" value through centripetal emphasis.

An extensive use of camera movement might have overcome the self-conscious framing; however, Leon Shamroy, cinematographer of the first Cinemascope production, *The Robe* (Koster, 1953), noted how the widescreen image, far from inviting camera movement, encouraged exactly the opposite: "Cinemascope is most effective if the characters, not the camera, do the moving. If the camera is moved too much it wastes the ability of our lens to see more at once than ever before."[30] To this greater stasis can be added an affinity for a static subject, architecture. As Lyle Wheeler, supervising art director at 20th Century Fox during production of *The Robe*, noted: "Thanks to CinemaScope, sets will play a more integrated part in the picture

Figure 3.9. *Two kinds of "obsessive framing": architectural excess in the widescreen epic* The Fall of the Roman Empire.

than ever before. Just as on the stage, width, not depth will represent the typical setup."[31] Even Barr acknowledges the affinity of the Cinemascope frame for horizontal composition. "Scope automatically gives images . . . more 'weight,' and it also of course enhances the effect of lateral movement."[32] Such an affinity for lateral composition is simultaneously an affinity for line, of exactly the variety linked by Deleuze, Arnheim, and Wölfflin with closed framing. Thus, although Barr argued that widescreen composition offered viewers a greater range of choices, in fact, the insistent horizontality of the widescreen frame inspired greater, not lesser control of the image, since it made designers think in terms of line (geometry, architecture) rather than space.

With the widescreen image presenting so many problems, it is hardly surprising that the generation of filmmakers working after the appearance of Cinemascope should develop what Pier Paolo Pasolini called "obsessive framing," a concentration on the film image as "pure, absolute significance as picture."[33] This "pure significance" occurs when the narrative halts to allow appreciation of an image for its plastic, design values. While Pasolini was interested in demonstrating the unique characteristics of films made by Modernist *auteurs*, the process he described is not restricted to their work. To the extent any film invites detached observation of its surfaces, whether in Pasolini's terms or through self-consciously artistic composition, its images can be said to be "obsessively framed."

In fact, the widescreen epic and the Modernist drama *visually* have a good deal in common (Figs. 3.9 and 3.10). Both are very self-consciously

Figure 3.10. *Alienated commodities in* Blow Up.

composed. Both use objects, spaces, and decor as integral parts of their content. Even the commodities necessary to fill historical widescreen sneak into their "poetic" counterparts. They are not utilized in the same ways, since the widescreen spectacular usually uses commodities as impersonal background filler, while the Modernist drama tries to render the material world personally significant. Both genres nonetheless begin with a separation between commodities and characters. In the case of historical films, this separation occurs in favor of ideological precision. In the case of Modernist dramas, the separation is frequently thematically motivated as the protagonist's "alienation" from his or her surroundings.

To the extent that it enables us to make connections between genres not usually discussed together, saturation must be recognized as one of the most important aspects of cinematic design. How important will depend on the attitudes of the filmmakers. Some may consciously choose to saturate the image. Others may use techniques that deviate sufficiently from the classical norm to force attention on objects as objects, such as the extra beat of emphasis on object close-ups in Losey's films, or the ponderous movement of actors into and out of depth in Welles's, or the lugubrious pace of Sirk's melodramas. Or the precise execution itself may mark authorial presence, as in Antonioni's evocative compositions, or in the perfectly timed

Figure 3.11. *Self-conscious composition: "presence through absence."*

edits of Resnais or Hitchcock, implicitly acknowledging the presence through absence of the means of production.

As the author's presence rises to the surface, the economic model of saturation becomes more valid. Except that the terms of the image's value move from the objects in the frame to the image itself, to "visual style" as a mark of artistic personality. (Antonioni has had frames from his films exhibited as still photographs, for example.[34]) Even an image as simple as Figure 3.5 can be "dressed up" with only a slight change of angle. In Figure 3.11, the relatively casual, uncomplicated image now becomes self-consciously posed by the flattened space and deliberate centering of the vanishing point. With this self-consciousness, the image maker becomes a ghostly, unacknowledged presence outside the frame. Whereas the broom in Figure 3.5 introduces narrative possibilities beyond the moment of the image, the composition in Figure 3.11 produces an awareness of plan and artistry, and with that awareness, distance.

This objectivity is produced by the supposed neutrality of the photographic act obviously *mediated* by an eye that refuses to show itself. As a result, the broom (already prominent because of its contrast with the otherwise empty frame) acquires an existential significance beyond physical fact. If it is waiting to be used as part of a narrative in Figure 3.5, it has *already* been used in the second image (Fig. 3.11) by being posed and photographed by the image maker. Or, to put it differently, the emptiness in the first image reads as a lack to be filled by narrative explanation, and thus to be *forgotten* or *overlooked* once so grounded. The emptiness of the second is *complete* as composition and thus to a certain extent independent from narrative significance.

The visibility of such techniques will be determined by the degree to which they are motivated by the story. So long as the designer has successfully organized the image to enhance rather than overwhelm the narrative, story and design work in relative harmony. At the same time, as we have seen, both narrative and design work in an edgy exchange with the culturally and historically specific moment. Even if the design achieves a successfully neutral realistic image, that neutrality cannot be expected to work invisibly as the codes of realism change. As time shifts, each moves further and further away from the other, and it is debatable which has the greater staying power. "Datedness" may be only that moment when the film's physical environment reacquires presence and visibility.

For design is always a process of distortion, even if the goals are realistic. Consumed at a point in time close to its production, this distortion will read as "true" because the assumptions and attitudes of filmmakers and audiences overlap more than they differ. As time progresses and attitudes change, the film remains a static record of a particular moment as expressed through artifacts. Images designed to evoke "chic" after time inevitably do nothing more efficiently than date their production period. Walk-on appearances by actors who later became stars fix the gaze on documentary evidence of a body's appearance at a particular time, forcing character into the background. Characters crossing an urban street to further the story get lost in the jumble of once trivial details now fascinating as historical record.

A dramatic example of the capacity for history to change an image's meaning is provided by *Charlie Chan at the Olympics* (Humberstone, 1937). At one point, Chan rides the airship *Hindenburg* from New York to Berlin. The film includes two brief newsreel shots of the *Hindenburg* in midair that fascinate as a record of the ship before its famous crash in Lakehurst, New Jersey. In the story's terms, the ship is included as an example of state-of-the-art transportation. The image stops the narrative flow, however, because of the object's vivid role in history.

An explicitly ideological image provides an even more interesting example. In at least one print of the film, the swastikas on the tail fin of the

Figure 3.12. *The menace of Nazism in* The Hindenburg. *Copyright © 1975 by Universal Studios, Inc. Courtesy of MCA Publishing Rights, a Division of MCA Inc. All Rights Reserved.*

Hindenburg have been scratched out.[35] In 1937, before the symbols of National Socialism had become synonymous with a new demonology, the swastika would have served as verification of the *Hindenburg*'s national origins. At some point, history caught up with the sequence, and the swastika's potentially disruptive effect had to be removed. The power of the image drastically exceeded narrative requirements as a result of a shifting context. The newsreel shots obviously were included as filler, proof that because the dialogue had raised the *Hindenburg* as a mode of transport, the film had the means to show it. The political world around the airship (and the film) would have been a nonissue. History has shown the failure of such an attitude, however, and evidence that a film from this period could offer a neutral image of Nazism must therefore be suppressed.

To put it simply: *Charlie Chan at the Olympics* is not about Nazism; history suggests it should have been, and we become aware of the blasé attitudes of the filmmakers through the documentary evidence of the swastika. When *The Hindenburg* (Wise, 1975) was made, the swastika on the tail became *de rigeur* because the script explicitly raises Nazism as an issue, albeit at not much greater depth than *Charlie Chan at the Olympics*. Political repression remains little more than a threat hovering around the characters, proven physically by the swastika overhead (see Fig. 3.12). What must be removed for its ability to exceed a story in a documentary image must now be present because it has been neutralized by narrative into a decorative detail that "proves" the production's ability to create an encompassing environment. Because we know at some level that the swastikas in *The Hindenburg* are part of a design safely manufactured in Hollywood rather than a record of a political reality, they can be included as "neutral" filler.

Since an explicitly stylized film admits to an alienation between its images and the reality it dramatizes, it is better suited to weather these changed expectations of realism. One of the consequences of this alienation, of course, is a fascination of the gaze at the moment of self-conscious spectacle. The composition arranges space and directs the gaze, based on a set of culturally agreed upon notions of value. So long as those codes do not shift perceptibly, so long as there remains a fixed notion of what constitutes the "artistic" image, designed films guarantee at least some degree of continuing cultural worth.

These attitudes are more fixed than narrative hooks of realistic representation. The "Realistic" acting of the 1950s, for example, may look grossly self-indulgent today; but films with glossy production values from that period still maintain most of their luster, despite the equal datedness of individual objects or fashions. This truth tends to be hidden by an ideology that insists on the "deeper" resonances of human identification, yet the fact remains that films' surfaces endure better than their "depths." Even though period style changes, notions of physical verisimilitude remain fixed. Acceptable stories shift with ideological winds, but a 35-mm lens ground in 1925 could still be used to record a story from 1995 on film. (Or, to put it differently, while we frequently have to be coached and guided through silent film narratives, we have no difficulty in recognizing the objects they record, unless it is a particularly bad print.)

Since emotional or thematic depth, and the narrative trappings designed to reveal them, are subject to ideological fashion, they are more superficial than surface, the physical product of a survival need. Surface is therefore more fundamental than constructed notions of intellectual and emotional process. Perspective and the representational systems deriving from it enable us to abstract surroundings into a persuasive, if limited, substitute for spatial depth. Until an alternative means of representation is developed that addresses those survival needs more adequately, the surfaces of a film can be expected to have a longer life than the stories they contain. Long after stories fade, images remain.

And so, in order to move on to specific examples of design, to examine in detail its function and effects, we should look at films with a distance between style and subject. This alienation can best be detected where the optical rules of perspective are most consistently followed, the architectural heritage and the appeal to traditional notions of cultural importance most flagrantly obvious, political and religious discourse and form frequently conflated, the excesses of production most obviously marshaled for the purpose of saturated spectacle, frequently within the widescreen frame. This Conservative Stylization, more or less active in all narrative films, becomes most explicit and necessary in the History Film.

Part II

HISTORY

4

HISTORICAL DESIGN

To a certain extent, to attempt to prove the importance of design to the History Film is unnecessary and pedantic. Every filmgoer expects a film set in the past to have higher-than-average production values. George Custen has demonstrated in *Bio/Pics: How Hollywood Constructed Public History* how that expectation can be used to sell a film. And every production designer working on a period film knows that, whether striving for the invisibly realist background or the assertive, spectacular foreground, he or she must confront difference as the overriding quality of the historical image. Even filmmakers self-consciously using an anti-illusionist approach to the past must face this expectation as a convention to be fought, subverted, ignored, or evaded.

While Barsacq and other designers discuss the problems raised by History Film as central to their profession, film critics have paid little attention to the question. Only Sue Harper, Leger Grindon, and the Affrons have discussed the issue comprehensively, and only Harper addresses it as a central concern.[1] (Grindon provides several detailed formal analyses, but with the aim of thematizing visual spectacle as a form of historiography.) Even Harper's otherwise positive efforts to describe the British costume film in design terms founder on a reverse prejudice. Arguing that working-class and feminine pleasures frequently worked against dominant notions of historical respectability, Harper valorizes the blatantly artificial and Expressionist. This approach has the unfortunate consequence of equating visual pleasure with display. Questions of realist visual pleasure become almost moot.

Aside from these efforts, most critics disregard History Films' surfaces altogether. At best there is a grudging description of these spectacular images as something to be gotten past in order to get at the "really important" material—history. For example, in his influential work *The Film in History: Restaging the Past*, Pierre Sorlin outlines the five components necessary for a film to make an audience believe it is witnessing the past. Incredibly he does not even include decor or costume.[2] There is something to be said for this attitude. By stripping away the spectacular wrappings, a critic can reveal how cinema shapes and is shaped by ideology. Focused particularly on history, such an approach demonstrates how we use the past as a relatively neutral battleground to discuss contemporary issues. However, to pretend that somehow the viewer (or the critic) does not take surfaces as an *integral part* of the historical message is self-deceiving, and ultimately damaging, since at least one consequence of the designed historical image is to make the past appealingly pretty.

Arguably, those writers on History Film who downplay design do so from the perspective of a Realist ontology of the image. Their criticism (or overlooking) of cinematic spectacle derives from a belief that the image should be invisible and serve ideas. There is, of course, an insurmountable contradiction in this attitude. Implicit in the Realist ontology is an identification of reality with space and vision, which is to say that truth can be revealed by the camera because it shows surfaces and appearances. However, we know the past did not look the way the present does. We know this because other disciplines equally dependent on surface appearance—art history and archaeology—lay substantial claim to our sense of historical truth. The equation of visual appearance with truth and the knowledge that appearances have changed over time conflict in any attempt at Realistic historical re-creation. Our knowledge of past style requires that a Realistic narrative be dressed in a fashion that answers to that awareness. At the same time, our knowledge that our reality does not appear as it does on-screen immediately marks the historical image as stylized, thus fictional. The attempt to bridge these two "realities" results in the stylized image that makes the bitter pill of history easier to swallow. (The fact that the visual design usually is exponentially more accomplished than the scripts it serves only exacerbates this problem.)

What the Realist position may be reacting against is the air of unreality that pervades many costume dramas, the sense that history matters only to furnish an exotic backdrop to cheap, hackneyed stories. Whether this mood is deliberate or the result of incompetence, it is clear that not all historical films invest the same energy in historical verisimilitude. There are a number of ways to address this issue. Harper, for example, suggests:

> It is necessary to recognise at the outset that it is inadequate to deal only with films which represent real historical events; we are more likely to construct a map of popular taste if we concentrate on costume dramas. These deploy recognisable historical periods, but not necessarily major events or personages. Historicity is differently nuanced in them, and they fulfill a heterogeneous range of functions.[3]

By this definition, any film that is set in the past becomes "historical." The problem with this approach is that it runs the risk of undervaluing content to the point of meaninglessness. While historical accuracy may be secondary in the costume film to visual impact, historical content is not neutral. Custen argues that "in lieu of written materials, or firsthand exposure to events and person, the biopic provided many viewers with the version of a life that they held to be the truth."[4] A viewer restricted to *Nicholas and Alexandra* (Schaffner, 1971), for example, will probably have a very different view of the Russian Revolution than someone who has seen Eisenstein's *October* (1928), or who has read Trotsky's *History of the Russian Revolution*. And one need only look at the controversies surrounding the "fascist revival" films of the 1970s to recognize the problems in an approach that values style apart from historical events.[5]

We might, then, combine Harper's attendance to style with Custen's attention to historical events. Even this definition of History Film, however, encounters difficulties, not least of which is Custen's equation of fame with biography. To be more precise, because Custen wants to demonstrate how Hollywood created the past in its own image as the preserve of Great Men achieving great results, he argues that there was an inevitable equation between "history" and "fame." At first, this concern was expressed in political biographies, but emphasis eventually shifted from political movers and shakers to entertainers and fine artists.

Unfortunately, to concentrate on a person's fame rather than on what the person is famous *for* skews our experience of cinema's view of history. Do we respond to, say, a *Juarez* (Dieterle, 1939) the same way as, say a *Lady Sings the Blues* (Furie, 1972) just because both are "biopics"? Probably not, and probably because the explicitly political content of the former is accentuated over its melodrama. In artist and entertainer biographies, on the other hand, political content rarely distracts from the artist's emotional turmoil. Custen ignores these contradictory purposes of political and artistic biography. The relationship between such melodrama and history, in fact, has been described most aptly by Ellen Draper as an "aversion."[6] According to Draper, melodramas must appear to happen here and now to create an emotional response. Historical illusion requires a sense of viewing events as if in the past. If in fact an "aversion" exists between melodrama and History Film, it almost certainly lies in the relative importance given to emotional response and to social identification and values.

Draper's observations provide a negative, first step in understanding historical design since melodrama emphasizes individual problems at the expense of social engagement. Its decor is also structured around character expression rather than more generalized backgrounds. With this basic distinction in mind, we can see that if not all costume films are History Films, neither are all biopics because the latter frequently concentrate on melodramatic response at the expense of history. Therefore, as much as a combination of their approaches clarifies cinematic history, we need refinement beyond Harper and Custen to take into account the explicitly social address of History Films' content and imagery. Most helpful in this regard would be Leger Grindon's assertion that

> the historical film is fundamentally concerned with the association of the individual and the state and the relationship between personal experience and the extrapersonal forces shaping history. In essence it is a political genre. . . . This tension between private and public life is expressed in the generic motifs of the romance and the spectacle.[7]

Grindon's "tension" helps us to recognize that because some biopics concentrate on affect rather than politics, they fall outside History Film. On the other hand, those that begin with characters that György Lukács in *The Historical Novel*[8] (in a phrase borrowed from Hegel) called the "World Historical Individual" are more likely contenders. World Historical Individuals are people famous from history whose names and images are synonymous with particular historical moments.

Lukács introduces the World Historical Individual in discussing the Historical Novel, in which such characters play peripheral, if important, parts. He then contrasts this form with the Historical Drama, which differs fundamentally from the Historical Novel in focus and, by implication, in politics. These differences arise from their formal solutions to similar expressive aims. Each medium seeks the most effective means to achieve a "totality of life."[9] For the novel, the goal is achieved through a broad social depiction, in which a mediocre hero embodies the relevant social conflicts. In drama, because of the need for condensation and economy, historical forces are best represented by those World Historical Individuals who embody them already by their place in history. Since drama relies entirely on external action to reveal character, and since character is the only means of providing the historical collision, the World Historical Individual emerges as the most efficient means of heightening historical representation.

Since film derives from both the novel and the drama, it is clear that the Lukácsian model raises two fundamental issues: first, the relative importance of the World Historical Individual in a film's story; and second, the means used to provide the "totality of life" that Lukács sees as the shared aim of Historical Novel and Drama, and which we can assume is a shared goal of History Film. Film, of course, also introduces prerequisites of its own, created by its photographic roots, that must be taken into account. Not least of these is a greater emphasis on objects in film than in either novels or theater.

Physical environment is not something with which Lukács deals extensively except to condemn when it takes over. Criticizing Flaubert's *Salammbô*, he notes:

> [Flaubert] chooses an historical subject whose inner social historical nature is of no concern to him and to which he can only lend the appearance of reality in an external, decorative, picturesque manner by means of the conscientious application of archaeology.[10]

The "external, decorative, picturesque manner" Lukács derides in Flaubert is certainly an accurate description of cinema's historical re-creations. Even more relevant is his description of such history as "a world of historically exact costumes and decorations, no more than a pictorial frame."[11] This criticism is based on the assumption that the purpose of a historical novel should be to reveal the "Totality of Objects" of an era, as defined by Hegel. These objects are not the physical representations from a period, but the social mores and structures of a given place and time.

Extending Lukács's argument, the History Film mistakes this socially defined "Totality of Objects" for literal objects. While Lukács's condemnation of this tendency in historical novels is problematic, for our purposes, we should recognize that he does not criticize historical novels for having *any* physical description. It is only when the physical environment takes over that he sees decadence setting in. Without sharing the moralism of the assumptions, we can easily see a parallel in the History Film's crowded frames, cluttered with objects divorced from social significance.

Lukács's comments suggest that we should consider a History Film's saturation while discussing its melodramatic content. Sue Harper's description of the British costume film persuades that, like historical novels, not all History Films treat objects and design the same way. The Affrons' classification scheme suggests further that one way to systematize those differences would be to discuss the decor's visibility. Decorative frame saturation, the visual equivalent of Lukács's "external, decorative, picturesque manner," in turn might be one reason for design to assert its presence. In short, just as a story may direct attention to particular parts of the image at the expense of other parts, a saturated design may work against this direction to establish visible design as an end in itself.

Aside from those films that self-consciously evoke art-historical styles as part of their narrative purpose, the most consistent means to achieve a convincing image of history is through the saturated frame.[12] The "objects" in that frame may be not just commodities but human beings since Lukács insisted that the World Historical Individual embody larger social and historical movements. Such a protagonist interacting with the public produces the *social* by motivating a *spectacle*, since the most "economical" way to represent the social visually is with a crowd. The crowd scene simultaneously proves the hero's ability to gather an assembly, thus to participate in social history, as well as the production's ability to gather and dress extras. Exotic objects are not enough; History Films must embrace large-scale action that serves as a partial stand-in for the Whole. Both punctuate History Films with a rhythm of spectacle as dependable and regular as production numbers in a musical or, indeed, sex scenes in pornography.

These mass demonstrations, battles, and riots make conspicuous consumption of production resources into an aesthetic. As Walter Benjamin pointed out:

> The shooting of a film, especially of a sound film, affords a spectacle unimaginable anywhere at any time before this. It presents a process in which it is impossible to assign to a spectator a viewpoint which would exclude from the actual scene such extraneous accessories as camera equipment, lighting machinery, staff assistants, etc.—unless his eye were on a line parallel with the lens.[13]

Just as the parade of valued objects saturates the past with material production, large-scale set pieces, the wide-angle equivalent of the precious apprehensible, display the machinery of industry at work.

Thus, to achieve the saturated frame, historical *mise-en-scène* concentrates on two extremes of space. At one end, exotic apprehensible details provide confirmation of the production's ability to corral the precious. At the other, large-scale set pieces staged on streets and landscapes create images that by their scale mask the necessarily partial representation. The middle regions of the house and the set are developed only to the extent that they (1) serve as display cases for exotic apprehensibles; (2) motivate a movement outdoors, from the intimate into the public and social; or (3) are themselves exotic objects that further prove conspicuous consumption, such as, for example, a palace interior. Spaces scaled to the human form are not lacking in History Films, but they are secondary to large-scale reconstruction of the past. The space of history, wrapped in the pretense of a totality achieved through materials, subsumes personal motivation.

In this dual concentration on the small scale and the wide angle, the History Film again positions itself against the melodramatic aesthetic. As Thomas Elsaesser described the latter in his influential essay "Tales of Sound and Fury,"

> [In melodrama], lighting, composition, decor increase their semantic and syntactic contribution to the aesthetic effect [there is] a sublimation of dramatic conflict into decor, colour, gesture and composition of frame.[14]

This melodramatic aesthetic produces imagery that displaces emotions beyond literal depiction on to a physical environment, producing a hothouse narrative world that creates meaning through the string of associations generated by the film. Connections with the outside world are suppressed in order to create empathy with the protagonist's problems interacting with other people. Since these interactions are most efficiently conveyed through middle-distance framings, the medium shot can be equated grossly with melodrama, and might be said to be the spatial building block of the genre.

The History Film keeps decor and character figuratively and literally separate. No effort is made to make space reflect emotions. While the profusion of commodity close-ups cut objects from *character* possession even as they heighten *spectator* desire, the long shots dwarf characters in transcendent space. Historical decor functions as a general background of familiar cultural props that convey importance and lend impersonal significance. This impersonality proves the narrative's social and historical validity, since the space is not controlled by the potentially petty concerns of individuals, but by the larger, social forces of history.

Consider, for example, the use of Empire chairs in *Imitation of Life* (Stahl, 1934) and in *Conquest* (Brown, 1937), a biopic based on Napoleon I's affair with Marie Walewska. In the former, the chairs express individual taste and economic status, the successful entrepreneur as social arriviste. Their presence is motivated by a character whose proximity and emotional attachment to the furniture are ours. In *Conquest* the economic status expressed by the chairs is the *production*'s power to corral the objects together; the taste expresses the *designer*'s ability to measure the image against the past. *Conquest*'s chairs first express their "Empireness," their place in history.

This call to impersonal significance requires a knowledge of archaeology to reinforce the film's temporal setting. The image must register immediately as antique, measured against the moment of consumption. At the same time, in order to succeed, this impersonal, historical decor depends either on an *inadequate* knowledge or on a tacit agreement with the viewer not to recognize the deficiencies of re-creation. The quest for archaeological accuracy must stop somewhere—usually, the edge of the frame. This deficiency can be overcome partially through the style itself. Foster Hirsch, among others, has noted the relationship between cinema's vision of history and nineteenth-century painting.

> The Hollywood epic presents a conservative view of the ancient world. Its sense of the past is based on visual conventions borrowed from Victorian paintings, Nineteenth-century stage design, the *decor* in the early Italian epics and in the pioneering work of Griffith and DeMille.[15]

A nineteenth-century aesthetic is recognizably outdated, stylized. As such, it creates an immediate distance between the viewer and the spectacle that compensates for our awareness of the essentially artificial nature of the undertaking. The nineteenth-century Academic painting tradition is not supple or fluid; it provides ideal, uniformly smooth and glossy views. Its measure of quality is not the level of perception of the frequently remote subject but the extent to which the painting answers to Academic standards of depiction.

Furthermore, most nineteenth-century Academic artists were trained in the public, didactic ideals of neoclassical theory, first introduced during the French Revolution.[16] The work they produced usually contained a moralizing impulse that survived long after the revolutionary energies of the bourgeoisie, an impulse that arguably survives in the public character of many History Films.[17] And the virtues instilled were of a particular type:

> The virtues [commissioned history paintings] celebrate are those expected of the nation at large—courage, sobriety, continence, respect for the laws and, above all, patriotism. Their aim was not to reflect the glory of the Crown but to educate the people.[18]

To this similarity of purpose can be added a similar form of composition. Both neoclassical history paintings and the History Film are usually organized around the closed frame. A closed organization provides the benefit of a self-referential space, in which the external world can be ignored. Everywhere pointing back to itself, denying an out-of-field that would destroy the illusion of the past having been re-created, the closed form provides the History Film with an efficient means to achieve the Totality of Space. Therefore, the History Film should be seen as a particular kind of decor in a specific use of the frame.[19] Composed for static values, the shots in History Films have trouble moving along, making them equally a rhythm of editing and camera movement, as shots composed as independent wholes bump and grind awkwardly across the screen.

Despite these similarities, however, there is a major difference between the work of such high neoclassical artists as Jacques Louis David, François Gérard, or J. A. D. Ingres and History Film composition. Movies move, and the primary means to motivate their movement is narrative. Thus it was probably the reign of Louis Philippe (1830–1848) rather than the Revolutionary or Napoleonic periods that had the greatest artistic influence on the development of cinema's visualization of history. During this time the rules of traditional history painting were beginning to break down to allow more familiar, genre scenes. In *Painting Politics for Louis-Philippe: Art and Ideology in Orléanist France, 1830–1848*, Michael Marrinan argues that French art of this period wedded the rhetoric of history painting to the propaganda aims of the bourgeois monarchy. The particular expression that history painting acquired during the era of Louis Philippe resulted from the contradictory nature of the regime, historical circumstances, and a shift in artistic fashion.[20] During the July Monarchy

> a new kind of image—the *genre historique*, with its modern history subjects, authentic costumes, and entertaining episodes rendered in a style of precise, clearly readable forms—came to center stage as the most appropriate picture for the modern collector. *Genre historique*, like most viable art forms, had more than a stylistic history; it emerged as the necessary product of a complex set of social, political, and technological changes.[21]

This change in history painting came about at a time when the genre's traditional aristocratic and clerical sponsors were on the wane. The rising middle classes, however, could not afford to purchase the huge canvases associated with the genre.[22] In order to serve this potential market, artists began to produce paintings that combined a new mixture of history and genre scenes on easel-sized canvases. These paintings also introduced a new, looser form of compositional organization made possible by changes in expectation created by popular prints.[23] These looser compositions frequently resulted from narratives dispersed across the frame, with multiple points of interest, rather than the centralized drama of classical art.[24] This new "middle-class History" was given final sanction by the king's taste for such familiarized, domesticated history.[25]

Given the moment at which it appears, it is easy to understand why *genre historique* is materialist without being Realist. It derives its power from the illusion of surface reality provided by the manipulation of line and color, but continues to focus on history as a series of idealized or sentimentalized moments. There is thus a discrepancy between the means employed and the subject depicted since the technical virtuosity required to render realistic detail seems excessive lavished on frequently banal subject matter. Marrinan suggests that this discrepancy results from the confused expectations raised by merging genre and history painting.[26]

That very contradiction serves cinematic history perfectly, since History Films themselves sit uneasily in a compromise between surface verisimilitude and historical knowledge. For this reason, to concentrate exclusively on the artificial aspects of historical design, as Harper does, misses a primary component of historical pleasure: the sense of the past having been re-created in *physically tangible* form. The genre must be understood as a complex of relations between its idealized, public subject matter and its materialist appearance.

Therefore, in evaluating and attempting to define History Film's *mise-en-scène*, we must take into account all of the following:

(1) The degree to which the filmmakers attempt to create the Realistic, plastic illusion of witnessing the past. This factor also assumes that

(2) The historical content of the story will at some level be taken seriously. That is, the purpose of a historical setting moves beyond providing the excuse for visual spectacle into at least a cursory attention to history as a subject.

(3) History as a subject must be defined in explicitly political terms. Historical melodrama does not qualify because its primary address will be to emotional response rather than social identification. (Included in the "explicitly political" would be those films with religious content, such as 1950s Bible Epics, that maintain the style of traditional History Films.)

(4) Because of the social address of political History Films, their design is best understood as a means of providing physical backdrop to ideological drama.

(5) Films that do not rely on an illusionistic representation of historical space but that nonetheless seek explicitly political discussion can be considered, if not as a subgenre, then as a viable alternative to traditional historical design.

Thus, *The Birth of a Nation*, not *Gone with the Wind*; *Ludwig: The Mad King of Bavaria*, not *Lola Montes*; *The Last Emperor*, not *The Sand Pebbles*; *Juarez*, not *Vera Cruz*; *Edvard Munch*, not *Lust for Life*; *Colonel Redl*, not *Letter from an Unknown Woman*, and so on.

In the process, we can add to Lukács's and Hegel's "Totality of Objects" in the epic and novel, and the "Totality of Movement" in the drama, the "Totality of Space" in History Film. Where the novel reveals the dense tapestry of social relations, and the drama heightens political conflict through the clash of major historical actors, a classical or late classical History Film provides the illusion that the world extends indefinitely beyond the field of view. It is historical re-creation defined and activated by physical detail acting as historical capital.

Therefore, in order to understand the relative "intensity" of the decor in historical films, I propose three categories of historical design: Realist

History, Designer History, and Didactic History. Like any classification, these labels ultimately are a matter of descriptive convenience, thus banal. They exhaust neither design generally, nor History Film specifically. In no way are History Films unique in their reliance on stylization; however, they are, with science fiction, uniquely obvious in that reliance. By concentrating on how History Films exploit design, I hope to lay the groundwork for a broader discussion of the topic that takes into account the complex relationships between narrative, design, the spectator, and physical reality.

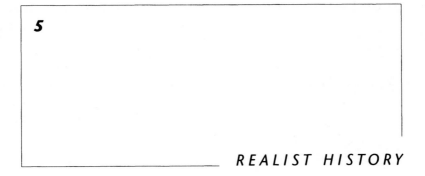

5

REALIST HISTORY

Whatever their differences, *Nicholas and Alexandra* and *The Leopard* (*Il Gattopardo*, Visconti, 1963) share the Realist aim of convincing that they have successfully re-created a Total Historical Space. Realist History is the easiest to describe, since it unproblematically assumes that the truth of history lies in its surfaces. The closer one mimics those surfaces in the service of a narrative that does not veer too greatly from chronology and plausible causation, the closer to historical truth one comes. Both *Nicholas and Alexandra* and *The Leopard* assume that the best way to understand the past is to visualize it through convincing period details spread across saturated widescreen frames. Their differences lie chiefly in the graphic means used to present those details and in the effects they have on the viewer.

Closed Organization—*Nicholas and Alexandra*

Nicholas and Alexandra provides an excellent example of the History Film's stylistic mean of closed, saturated frames. The film's sharp, high-key photography parallels the *genre historique*'s depictive style. Its compositions are Academically perfect, and as a result, the editing relies heavily on point-of-view sequences and eye-line matches to motivate movement from one shot to another. What little movement there is within the frame is usually motivated by action. While the film's origins in a straight history book might lead to an expectation of greater historical accuracy than usual, the film in fact has a strong melodramatic component. Whatever truth Robert K. Massie's *Nicholas and Alexandra* may provide, both book and film subsume history in favor of visual pleasure and emotional response.

The film's melodrama presents a perfect example of the consequences meted out in History Films to political figures who allow personal concern to triumph over social obligation. In this regard, the film is merely faithful to Robert Massie's intentions: "Since the day . . . that my wife and I discovered that our son had hemophilia, I have tried to learn how other families dealt with the problems raised by this unique disease."[1] At the same time, of course, the Romanovs were not just any family. They were "one family whose struggle with the disease was to have momentous consequences for the entire world."[2]

This convergence of melodrama and history can be viewed at least two ways: as complementary (we feel history as "deeper" by personalizing it); or contradictory (the travails of one family are meaningless against large-scale events). Massie relies heavily on letters and diaries to construct his interpretation. The reader is assumed to know about the larger historical currents at work, which the author abandons in favor of biographical portraiture. For example, Massie writes of Nicholas that

> his own best qualities were gentleness, kindliness and friendliness. . . .
> [his] diary was identical to that of his cousin King George V; both were
> kept primarily as a catalogue of engagements, written in a terse, monoto-
> nous prose, and regarded as one of the daily disciplines of an ordered
> life. Curiously, Nicholas's diary, which lacks the expressive language of
> his private letters, has proved a rich mine for his detractors.[3]

By labeling the criticisms of Nicholas as "curious," Massie reveals his own investment in personalizing the lives of the powerful. Trotsky, for one, put a very different gloss on the diaries.[4] Even a recent coffee-table book devoted to tsarist splendor describes Nicholas as having "no political strengths or weaknesses at all. He was not trained in politics . . . [and] was completely unprepared for the task."[5] Massie's blindness to Nicholas's flaws results in a history based on an excess of depiction. Large-scale social movement exists in the background to the imperial family's personal problems, which are wrapped in satiny material detail, such as "Alexandra wore white or cream silk gowns embroidered in silver and blue and worn with diamonds in her hair and pearls at her throat."[6] (Just how successful Massie was in his "personalist" ignoring of historical currents is attested to by two articles in the trade press that announced production of the film based on Massie's *novel*.[7]) As Massie's book invites identification with royalty in moments of trial, it stimulates visual imagination through the description of objects, establishing a precedent for an "archaeological" view of history.

As a result, Massie's descriptions split the monarchs' "true," psychological selves from their sumptuous surroundings. The efforts to personalize the imperial family are done entirely on the basis of their human failings. Their extraordinary wealth is always something separate. Objects become general indications of the past and originate outside. For example, the phrase "cream silk gowns embroidered in silver and blue and worn with diamonds" may produce flights of fancy, but it is unlikely to be lingered over when presented impersonally, as a substitute for history. Nor does the verbal description have the power to arrest a narrative that an image of "cream silk gowns embroidered in silver and blue and worn with diamonds" possesses. Massie's descriptions cover the book's lack of historical analysis by stimulating visions of the commodity. Images of these objects serve the same function in the film, substituting for a broad historical canvas of European politics, but with a major difference. The film's physical re-creation always runs the danger of overwhelming the narrative in a way that Massie's descriptions do not.

Furthermore, a book's length is dictated by the author's interests. A film's duration depends on the audience's willingness to sit through it. While a film can easily capture the viewer's gaze with "cream silk gowns embroidered in silver and blue and worn with diamonds" it cannot depict a broad historical environment without considerable narrative time. Given the breadth covered by the film (1904–1918) it is clear that the filmmakers must fit a lot of information into three hours. Yet, aside from the parade of well-known historical figures, there is very little to connect the story to events. The only large-scale historical moment depicted in detail is the Bloody Sunday massacre of 1905. This absence of historical incident no doubt results from the melodramatic attention to Nicholas's family.

At the same time, production has a reality that moves beyond aesthetics. The cost of reproducing an imperial past with scrupulous attention to detail makes it impossible to produce a film like *Nicholas and Alexandra* inexpensively. (The film was budgeted for $8 million in 1970, a tidy sum to invest only in a story about one boy's hemophilia.[8]) Even with no large-scale moments, the film still would have required a large financial return for

Figure 5.1. *The crowd as geometric mass in* Nicholas and Alexandra.

success. Without such large-scale moments, profit would prove elusive in a genre dedicated to display. In short, generic conventions and expectations dictate large-scale staging, even if artistic sense argues against it.

The Bloody Sunday sequence is critical in understanding the film's attempt to address these contradictory goals, since it is a historical event defined by the imperial couple's absence. According to Massie's book, the tsar was not in St. Petersburg the day of the demonstration, making it impossible for him to receive the list of grievances presented by protesting workers and the police spy, Father Gapon.[9] The film motivates this absence by a hemophiliac attack on the infant Tsarevich. The sequence thereby becomes a condensed incident that illustrates the imperial couple's failure to engage their people and their secretive handling of the Tsarevich's affliction. Melodrama extracts the imperial couple from history.

The sequence, typical of History Film's architectonic space (the sequence was directed by production designer and second-unit director John Box), builds three actions in three locations: (1) the petitioning crowd (marching from left to right); (2) the soldiers guarding the Winter Palace (moving in a single line from right to left); and (3) the imperial quarters at Tsarskoe Selo as the Tsarevich recovers from his hemophiliac attack. The imperial couple appear only in this third space, which seems to have been included in order to be able to intercut it with the riot for dramatic contrast.

Token efforts to personalize the crowd through the characters of Petya, a factory worker, his wife, and their child and to historicize the march with the presence of Father Gapon are largely gratuitous since Gapon falls out of the story after the sequence, Petya has only one more brief scene, and

Figure 5.2. *Soldiers as line in* Nicholas and Alexandra.

his wife is killed. Instead, the first shot of the full crowd reduces the mass to a formal echo of the railway shed behind them, turning both into near abstractions, two opposing triangles (see Fig. 5.1). This elegantly spare formality is typical of the entire sequence. Figures in the crowd remain impersonal, almost literally faceless, even when emphasized through occasional long-lens shots. Movement is channeled by architectural detail—railway lines, urban corridors, the rectilinear courtyard of the Winter Palace—not by personal desire.

In contrast to the crowd's geometric mass, the soldiers defending the Winter Palace walk in a straight line across the palace courtyard, parallel to the architecture behind them (see Fig. 5.2). When an unidentified soldier precipitates the massacre by lowering his rifle to fire directly into the crowd, the action becomes a single movement of line, in which the suddenly horizontal rifle contrasts with the diagonally raised ones behind it (see Fig. 5.3). Historical tragedy becomes a conflict between line and volume, rigidly framed toward the center.

In the third location, the imperial couple rush to Alexis's bedroom after he recovers from his first attack. The Tsar and Tsarina are centered in the shot; their importance is underlined by a combined pan and zoom. They attract the camera, in a double movement that briefly opens the frame as the Tsarevich's nurse extends her arms to give the baby to the Tsarina, who then carries the baby in her outstretched arms to her husband, who embraces both in his arms. The apprehensible envelops the space in a ballet of gestures that encourage us to enter the softly sensuous mauves of imperial space, a comfortable inside, against that dangerous outside of history.

Figure 5.3. *Graphic violence between diagonals and horizontals in* Nicholas and Alexandra.

Against these caresses, the static grays, browns, and whites of the riot offer chilly formality, framed at the level of the street. The framing ties the action to the illusion of a large-scale social reality tidied by abstraction into geometry. Realistic settings are selected to serve as physical alibis for the historical re-creation; the number of extras proves that the enacted conflict moves beyond individual into social and historical concern. Turning the crowd into geometric shapes, while filtering the scene through the prettiness of winter, maintains the stylization, that sense of period strangeness, that reads as historical re-creation.

The design in this sequence works as part of the film's overall emphasis on melodrama over history. Still, a large-scale film about public, historical characters must occasionally show those characters in large-scale situations, even at the threat of overwhelming the intimate portrayal. To minimize that risk, the moments selected to show the imperial couple's social function are largely gratuitous. In all those large-scale scenes in which the Tsar and Tsarina appear, virtually nothing happens.

For example, just prior to the Bloody Sunday sequence, the imperial couple bless departing troops from a railroad platform filled with soldiers, officers, and clergy. Aside from news of the Tsarevich's health (which is told, not shown) the scene lacks narrative significance. It exists sheerly as spectacle, proof that the film is capable of restaging the past on a large scale. At the other extreme, when Nicholas and Alexandra attend the dowager Empress's birthday party, the sequence begins on a tight close-up of a Fabergé egg, held by the dowager (see Fig. 5.4). There is a cut to a medium angle as Alexandra and the Tsar's mother kiss, then a cut to a wider angle to take in

Figure 5.4. *Gratuitous spectacle in* Nicholas and Alexandra: *the Fabergé egg.*

the full spectacular revelation of dresses, uniforms, plates, silverware, marble floors, columns, flowers.

The narrative moment is trivial: the dowager serves little dramatic function; the space, the Grand Duke Nikolasha's palace, never appears again in the film. Indeed, the Grand Duke later complains that he wants to sell it. Only Alexandra's introduction to Rasputin in an adjoining, intimate anteroom has any importance in the story. The triviality announces itself through the Fabergé egg, setting the sequence immediately into the literally apprehensible, held by the dowager, but also the fantastically rich, the realm both of a vanished imperial past and of the movies.

The Fabergé egg has a narrative gratuitousness equivalent to its social uselessness, suggesting that aristocratic extravagance and cinema have in the case of *Nicholas and Alexandra* become one. In a press packet, producer Sam Spiegel boasted that the marble used in the film's sets is real, because it was cheaper to use the real thing, guaranteeing that people who attended *Nicholas and Alexandra* will get their money's worth of spectacle.[10] (The filmmakers also originally tried to shoot in the real Russian locations, but politics intervened. They were perhaps lucky, since the telefilm *Rasputin* [1996], which did have access to the real spaces, was overwhelmed by them.) The significance of Spiegel's statement lies not in his assertion that the marble is real (who could tell?) but in his implied promise that the filmmakers have attended to a desire for opulent surroundings. In this sense, the story of *Nicholas and Alexandra* exists only to motivate the spectacle, the real subject for a late-twentieth-century consumer. The events are not neutral, since they encourage us to think of pre-Soviet Russia as a sequence of artfully composed

Figure 5.5. *Establishing shot of the corridor sequence from* Nicholas and Alexandra.

Figure 5.6. *POV of the Emperor and Empress.*

Figure 5.7. *Reverse-angle full shot.*

Figure 5.8. *Imperial POV.*

Figure 5.9. *Full shot of the corridor.*

Figure 5.10. *The imperial couple pass a line of guards presenting arms.*

images and exotic objects. Historical or political insight is merely an excess derived from those images, not the other way around.

History's secondary status is no more dramatically obvious than in the Tsar and Tsarina's departure for the dowager Empress's birthday party. No significant action takes place, and the spatial transition, from the palace to the party, could be accomplished in a simple cut. There is also little new narrative information. The sequence consists of six shots:

(1) Full wide shot: Nicholas, in uniform, appears camera right, emerging from an elevator. He crosses to the middle of the room, joining the Tsarina. Bidding their daughters good night, Nicholas and Alexandra move toward the foreground, the Tsarina complaining about having to go to the party. Their conversation is cut short by the appearance of Count Fredericks. They return his bow, a music cue begins, they look forward. (Fig. 5.5)

(2) Point of view of the imperial couple: A pair of ornate doors are opened invisibly, revealing a long corridor lined with uniformed guards, who salute with their swords. (Fig. 5.6)

(3) Reverse angle, full shot: The imperial couple walk through the doors; guards bow as they pass. (Fig. 5.7)

(4) POV of the imperial couple: The camera tracks forward down the center of the corridor. (Fig. 5.8)

(5) Full shot of the corridor: The imperial couple reach a corner and change direction. (Fig. 5.9)

(6) Wide angle overhead: A large room lined with guards presenting arms; the imperial couple walk between them. (Fig. 5.10)

If the narrative content is minimal, as spectacle, the sequence makes sense. While later scenes in the corridor will be far less positive, here, before the revelation of the Tsarevich's hemophilia, the space reads as "triumphant," even "exultant," laid out as experienced by Nicholas and Alexandra at their emotional high point. This exultation is produced by placing the viewer in a position of centered spatial identification with the monarchs, in shots 2 and 4, allowing us to possess the objects, servants, and spectacle as they do. The materials photographed produce both a sense of rich display and a direct effect as the corridor extends into depth, invoking the ecstatic response of transcendental perspective. The monarchs (and we) not only possess the space; we have the point of view that leads directly to God. The visual devices converge to produce a stylized omnipotence, a drastically privileged moment of intimacy (we occupy the monarchs' bodies) made spectacular.

The sequence's mixture of the spectacular and the intimate therefore creates a cinematic history based on material production. Historical events are of little importance; social, economic, or political change is of even less consequence. The spell of commodities colors the past; it is through a nostalgia for a time when (at least some) people could possess limitless wealth that we are made to sympathize with actors impersonating Nicholas II and the Tsarina Alexandra. The actions are mere backdrop to the tantalizing array of the nearly attainable, the fantastic just out of reach, ordered for our delectation.

Later, when Nicholas returns from the front stripped of rank and privilege, his walk down the corridor acquires an irony built on the earlier sequence's exultation. Instead of the precise organization offered by the saluting guards, only hostile workers and soldiers lounge about in random disarray; instead of Nicholas moving on a straight line to infinity, he must negotiate a slow, unsteady movement toward a door he has to open for himself. No longer master of luxury, Nicholas becomes pitiful. This pathos derives almost exclusively from our sense of "loss" of the palace spaces, since almost nothing happens in any of these corridor scenes. Nicholas's fall from power and status is expressed in physical, material terms as his, our, lack of control over spectacle.

It is, however, a loss only of a particular *kind* of spectacle. The scenes of decline gather as many resources as the exultant ones. What they lack is the architectonic ordering of men and matter toward the transcendent vanishing point of late imperial excess. The revolutionaries in the corridors are a disruption, a slovenly intrusion dispersed across the frame. The liveried servants the revolutionaries replace are part of the decor. Their uniforms match the carpets and furniture. Each is paired to a Corinthian column in servile postures that attune as much to the architecture as express their social position. The line of guards exists to be a line, visible evidence of both the Tsar's and the production's ability to order human activity to spectacular ends.

Open History

Nicholas and Alexandra suggests that a History Film with a closed frame organization objectifies the image and produces a desire for its contents. When combined with a narrative that encourages viewers to identify emotionally with characters, the closed organization reconstructs history as a series of exquisitely dressed, atomized, personal incidents. Is this overvaluing

Figure 5.11. *Father Pirrone enjoys a snack in* The Leopard.

of commodities inevitable? Does an open organization produce a different emotional response?

Luchino Visconti's film of Giuseppe di Lampedusa's *The Leopard* shares a strong melodramatic plot line with *Nicholas and Alexandra* and an equally elaborate physical production in the service of a Realist (external, archaeological) historical reconstruction. Also like *Nicholas and Alexandra*, Lampedusa's novel evokes the past through trivial details. For example,

> [The Prince of Salina] climbed the stairs again, crossed rooms in which his daughters sat chatting with friends from the Holy Redeemer (at his passage the silken skirts rustled as the girls rose), went up a long ladder, and came into the bright blue light of the observatory. Father Pirrone, with the serene air of a priest who has said Mass and drunk black coffee with Monreale biscuits, was sitting immersed in algebraic formulas.[11]

This passage describes a brief transition; neither it nor the scene that precedes it appears in the film.[12] The scene in the study, however, is dramatized in detail great enough to contain a trace of the transition, tucked into the edge of medium shots of Father Pirrone (Fig. 5.11).

A still life of coffee pot, cup, and presumably "Monreale biscuits" is casually placed at the edge of the frame (see Fig. 5.12). Both written description and visualization ground the story in intimate space. Minor, trivial details seduce emotionally by inviting physically with apprehensible, delectable objects. It is, of course, possible to see the film and miss these few objects in an environment so saturated with details that they even appear off-camera. (In an interview regarding the 1983 rerelease of the film, for

Figure 5.12. *The still life (detail).*

example, Burt Lancaster recounted how he opened a dresser drawer on the set to find it filled with silk shirts. When Lancaster asked Visconti why they were there, since they could not be seen by the camera, the director replied that they were there to help him realize his character.[13]) Any of these details could be removed without wreaking havoc. Remove them all, however, and you cease discussing *The Leopard*.

Lampedusa has an advantage over Robert Massie by writing a work of fiction. Massie describes historically determined objects to evoke the physical environment of the Tsar's court. He does so in order to provoke sympathy for the monarchs by depicting their lavish way of life removed from social consequences. In both book and film of *Nicholas and Alexandra*, this description serves as substitute for social evaluation. Lampedusa, writing fiction, has merely to motivate the coffee and cookies through character desire. They are not alienated objects impersonally verifying period, but materials directly used by a character.

However, while this process suggests another attempt to make viewers identify with characters, it is important to recognize that food's primary appeal is social, since it is based on a shared experience, hunger. Food images make viewers identify sensually, not emotionally, with characters, placing our bodies in the frame by senses other than sight. For Walter Korte, this emphasis on details leads to a process of "fantastic enlargement . . . of things that Lampedusa saw as depleted or corrupt."[14] The director

> expands the novel's attention to detail, as if taking a meticulous inventory. His contemplation of the textures and colors of objects, of

movements and symmetry, impoverishes the events, which, in some scenes, are only ornamental memoranda for papier-mâché characters.[15]

Korte's problematic condemnation does not detract from its phenomenological accuracy. The film clearly elevates the Sensuous Event to the status of history. The question remains, does such an elevation "impoverish events" or enrich them? And does this emphasis on detail contradict the film's Marxist historical critique or simply vary that critique? It was, after all, Marx who wrote:

> To say that man is a corporeal, living, real, sensuous, objective being full of natural vigour is to say that he has real, sensuous, objects as the objects of his being or of his life, or that he can only express his life in real, sensuous objects.[16]

This passage suggests that Visconti's emphasis does not so much betray Marx as attempt to depict a world in which human beings possess a direct relationship to their sensual life. That this world is available only to the aristocracy is part of the critique.

The source of Korte's condemnation is Marx's description of the commodity fetish. Marx exposed the mystification of exploitive relations that encourages us to view commodities as a series of disembodied things, rather than as the product of alienated labor. Stripped of the fetish, the commodity will cease to have any value beyond utility. The problem arises in equating utility with productive utility, which leads logically to a puritanical aesthetic since sensuality is seldom considered productive. As the passage from Marx cited above suggests, however, the emotional value of a commodity cannot be measured in such narrow terms. In fact, to express oneself in "true, sensuous objects" suggests being able to enjoy commodities for their nonproductive *uselessness*.

A utilitarian critique of *The Leopard* can point to the attention lavished on coffee, cookies, skirts, and tablecloths and suggest that such sumptuous presentation distracts us from social inequalities. On the other hand, these objects do not cease to have a utilitarian value for the characters (and by extension, for us as viewers). The question then becomes to what extent does utility express emotional attachment, and what debt does such a tie owe to a willful disregard of social reality? Understanding this issue will help to clarify the History Film norm.

Clearly *The Leopard* saturates the image with objects for the same reason as *Nicholas and Alexandra*: to convince that the past has been re-created through details that evoke period through appearance. These appearances include not just period-correct details, but large-scale action that broadens the space out to the level of the street. The Battle of Palermo, for example, includes a number of events calculated to reveal the larger historical tapestry of the Sicilian rebellion. Even when Tancredi (the Prince's wily, farsighted nephew) appears, the framing provides a consistently long view.

The affective circle of the street and this distant perspective combine to produce a double sense of historical reality. The story connects events to the illusion of a larger social fabric by commingling central characters and representative groups (vengeful peasant wives, Bourbon officials, etc.) on the street. Yet, by staging the action in a consistently long view, the street as social space becomes more the center of attention than the characters. That Tancredi becomes no more important than anyone else has obvious political significance. The effects on historical re-creation may not be so obvious. The absence of close-ups not only de-emphasizes the hero, it discourages the apprehensible. The viewer cannot imaginatively participate in events through character *or* space. The wide framing helps render the image quaint, removing it slightly from a contemporary perspective. Outside the action, the camera's spatial distance equals our temporal distance from the real events.

Thus *The Leopard*'s total composition moves beyond cookies, coffee, skirts, and tablecloths. Accumulated details remain key to the film's success, but it is difficult to claim that *The Leopard* offers a quantitatively more saturated frame than the norm (however we would measure it). Rather, these details combine with the open frame and camera movement to produce the illusion of a Totality of Space and the Sensuous Event. Of course, the film's "casual" framing and pretended willingness to abandon perfect organization are anything but accidental. They represent a highly organized imitation of nineteenth-century paintings whose historical importance lies in their relatively undesigned composition.

The film's visualization relies less on the French *genre historique* than on mid-nineteenth-century Italian art. In *The Body in the Mirror: Shapes of History in Italian Cinema*, Angela Dalle Vacche has suggested that the battles in Visconti's other film set in the *risorgimento, Senso,* were inspired by the paintings of Giovanni Fattori (1825–1908). Fattori and the group of which he was a member, the Macchia, had strong connections with the Italian struggle for unity and independence, a connection that makes them logical models for films set during the period. In *The Art of the Macchia and the*

Risorgimento: Representing Culture and Nationalism in Nineteenth-Century Italy, Albert Boime argues that the Macchia's work should be evaluated in terms of its articulation of a new nationalist consciousness. For example, after discussing the rise of the Italian historical novel in the early nineteenth century, Boime notes regarding the work of Francesco Hayez (1791–1882):

> As in the case of the historical novelists including D'Azeglio, Hayez's painting progressed in the direction of fidelity to the Italian environment. The incorporation of Italian landmarks that function as synecdoches for Italy parallels the historical novelist's topographical nationalism.[17]

Hayez makes the radical move of depicting real Italian landscapes in history painting. The Macchia extended this logic further by painting the contemporary world. In contrast to aristocratically privileged "view" paintings of Italian cities produced for foreign tourists, however, the Macchia's view of the world was distinctly bourgeois. Boime notes that "the Macchiaioli push from the scenic to the participatory, from the privileged to the liberal view, from watching the spectacle to taking part in it."[18]

However persuasive this equation of bourgeois perspective with engaged involvement, Boime introduces a contradictory note when discussing the work of Fattori as "breathtakingly detached and low-keyed as the newspaper graphics."[19] After equating detachment with the aristocratic and the participatory with the rising middle class, Boime glosses over the potential class component of Fattori's "detachment." Like Visconti committed to a progressive cause, the artist nonetheless maintained a "detached" perspective on events. His work is thus both temporally and temperamentally suited to *The Leopard*'s simultaneous involvement in and distance from historical events.

Of course, a difference remains: Fattori's detachment was toward contemporary events; Visconti's was toward history. Thus, to imitate Fattori in a re-creation of the past is no longer a question of style—the inevitable expression of artistic personality—but of stylization—the selection of a mode that differs from the neutral norm. And since Fattori is appropriate only to the battle scenes, *The Leopard* must have recourse to other art traditions—Neapolitan genre, Winterhalter, Corot, Tissot, and so on—to create an eclectic pastiche.

Indirectly, style reproduces its period's view of the world, but only because *The Leopard* is set in the eclectic nineteenth century. For the Victorian era did not just freely borrow from the past; such borrowing was seen as a legitimate means of understanding history. Among the most influential philosophers of eclecticism, Victor Cousin advocated a method that looked to history as a means of discovering Truth through emulation of the best of the past.[20] Three aspects of his theories are relevant to the evolution of the style of History Film generally and *The Leopard* specifically: (1) beauty can be apprehended through a historical appreciation of styles; (2) borrowing freely from all styles is legitimate to the extent that such borrowing reveals a unity of purpose; (3) random imitation is not legitimate; it must be done with the goal of discovering a greater truth embodied in the original sources.

The evocation of Fattori and others in *The Leopard* is rarely achieved through direct imitation of particular paintings. One can, for example, sense Fattori's *Garibaldi à Palermo* (*Garibaldi at Palermo*, 1860–1862) in the battle scenes in *The Leopard*, but no frame duplicates it exactly. The filmmakers emphasize aspects of Fattori's form analogous to cinematic expression, which is to say, Visconti finds ways to visualize in time the static, privileged moment created in Fattori's painting.[21]

In his description of the painting, Boime notes how "catching" the background debris in midaction contributes to the painting's "nearly documentary" effect.[22] This observation links Fattori to the popular print sources Boime cites, to Marrinan's *genre historique*, and to photography. It also introduces motion as a possibility. It is the sense of a moment having been caught by the painter as revealed by objects in motion that heightens its momentary specificity, and thus its "realism." The debris withers the privileged moment with an implicit before, after, apart, outside different from the field of view. From where did the debris come? Who threw it? Where are they? Such questions expand the field by acknowledging the image's partiality and imperfection, while threatening the primacy of the foreground narrative.

Debris falls in the Battle of Palermo in *The Leopard*, but it is not used to dissolve the frame since movement in and out of the field and of the camera's view does the same work. While the camera glides slowly along a drive under the opening credits in strongly centripetal movements, such motions are relatively rare in the film. The film normally employs centrifugal, nearly constant motion that nonetheless does not distract as motion for its own sake. Most often, the camera continually reframes spaces, stopping short of a full 360-degree description but, by its movement, creating the illusory possibility of continuing. During the trip to Donnafugata, for example, the camera does a series of graceful pans of the landscape that strongly evoke a sense of place. Or, during the Battle of Palermo, the camera begins on the bodies of victims of the Bourbons, pans slowly to the right to show a child walking down the empty street, then gradually reveals the arrival of the Garibaldini, "casually" entering the frame from out-of-field.

This use of the out-of-field to dissolve the frame is *The Leopard*'s chief "movement strategy." For example, in the sequence after the credits, as the Salina family bustles about after receiving news of Garibaldi's invasion, several of the characters simply leave or enter the frame, extending the film's space into the out-of-field, beyond its actual re-creation. During the ball sequence, such movement is combined with the increasing fixity of the Prince as he moves through the space, expressing the "distance" between him and his surroundings.

For even as these strategies work to heighten the illusion of reality through false casualness, the film simultaneously creates a spatial, temporal, and kinesthetic detachment. Combined with the film's art-historical references, the camera always presents an impossibly perfect view. Korte describes this aesthetic distance invidiously—his "slightly over-aesthetic veil of unreality." Arguably, however, it is this combination of the distant and the picturesque that enables *The Leopard* to produce its strong sense of historical reality. Recognizing the stylization is part of the process of historical re-creation, since such recognition adds to the emotional distance between viewer and event. By acknowledging graphically that distance is the reality of historical re-creation, the wide frame and the open composition paradoxically make possible a stronger bond between audience and film. By recognizing our recognition, the film shares our perspective, implicating each in the other. Three distances—spatial, temporal, emotional—combine to create a strong sense of *presence*.

The Sensuous Event caps this paradoxical presence, by moving identification from the emotional to the physical. We identify not so much with the look of the space, as with its feel. Unlike the corridor sequence in *Nicholas and Alexandra*, where identification is achieved through traditional strategies of spatial placement and the alternation of objective and subjective shots, *The Leopard* produces identification through sensual analogy, using the mixture of sights and sounds to stimulate touch, taste, and smell.

To the extent that this identification with space encourages the viewer to indulge in the commodity fetish, criticism of Visconti is valid. By wrapping events in aristocratic *risorgimento* splendors, the film arguably encourages us to wallow in a guiltless luxury divorced from material means. Yet this argument overlooks those parts of the film in which sensual evidence

Figure 5.13. *Tancredi gives Concetta a cooling handkerchief in* The Leopard.

presents a far from glamorous evocation of the past. The look of the picnic sequence during the trip to Donnafugata, for example, may encourage sighs of nostalgic regret. The tangible discomfort created by the period clothing, however, is not likely to make a contemporary viewer envious. Precisely because the film so effectively forces identification between the viewer's senses and the story space, these scenes are as likely to produce a parallel displeasure in the viewer as a desire for the commodity.

For example, the brief moment when Tancredi gives Concetta a moist towel to cool her forehead is almost completely palpable as tactile relief (see Fig. 5.13). The squalid conditions of the roadside inn in which the Salina family find themselves in the following sequence will not attract contemporary tourists; Father Pirrone and the peasants with whom he converses sit in spaces less revolting than the filthy bedrooms occupied by the Prince's family. (This was among the sequences cut for the shortened American release.) Even the heavy sensualism of the famous ball sequence works at least equally to exhaust the viewer as to exalt the voluptuous surroundings; certainly few movie balls have shown so much *sweating*.

"Contradictory" political views; aesthetics based on sensuality; emotional, temporal, and spatial distance; and the resources of a large production combine to heighten the affective relationship between people and things. This heightening does not, however, lead automatically to the overvaluation of materials. Instead, it restores to those materials some of the historically determined specificity they are usually deprived of by narrative. The Sensuous Event offers a privileged moment when the relationship between ourselves and material production becomes the subject, when, however briefly, humanity "has real, sensuous, objects as the objects of [our] being."

In this direct connection between body and space, the open organization of *The Leopard* differs from the more objectified frame of *Nicholas and Alexandra*. The films share a richly pleasurable design in the service of a Realist approach to historical representation. Both take their history seriously, but it is difficult to insist that the images suffer as a result. The very care lavished on the physical environment in both films assures a high degree of visual pleasure only tangentially dependent on obvious display. Because of the contradiction involved in any Realist history, the *mise-en-scène* never fully disappears from either film. The desire to prove the "truth" of the presentation requires a massive investment in exotic details from the past. In such films, design and history are in roughly equal balance. When design takes over, the results are rather different.

6

DESIGNER HISTORY

The design in Realist History has one major purpose: to provide a physically plausible backdrop to a narrative setting. Once achieved, that space may be used to underline political discussion, heighten emotional identification, or both. The design may well rise to visibility because of the effort involved in its creation, despite the presumed aim of a relatively neutral backdrop. Realist History's commitment to serve the story through spectacle results in a constant tension between display and effacement.

Designer History works from a different premise: to create a self-sustaining artifact. Historical references become secondary to design, although they are never entirely absent. For example, an exaggeratedly stylized film like *The Scarlet Empress* makes short shrift of Russian history. Its director, Josef von Sternberg, prided himself on the unrealistic qualities of the images he produced.[1] Even so, the film takes pains to evoke an essence of eighteenth-century attire. Women dress in elaborately hooped skirts; men wear powdered wigs and characteristic three-cornered hats. Such Designer History Films go only so far in contradicting the audience's historical expectations. Having named characters "Catherine the Great" or "Grigory Orlov," the filmmakers apparently felt some obligation to provide an image of eighteenth-century Russia.

As Designer History maintains just enough of a tie to the past to allow freer exploration of formal potential and as it plays down the historical and political significance of its events, it does not revert to melodrama. In *The Scarlet Empress*, for example, although there is an almost exclusive focus on Catherine's affairs, and little attention to her political ability, there is no attempt made to make the viewer identify with her emotionally. Quite the contrary, the film self-consciously poses Marlene Dietrich as the center of a spectacle for which the only justification is the visual impact it creates. If politics takes a back seat to spectacle in Designer History, it shares it with pathos.

Designer History creates a chilly vision of the past, as it combines the apolitical focus of costume melodrama with the impersonal affect of traditional History Film. The past becomes a movement of empty forms and exquisite objects, with politics chosen as a subject largely for its inability to involve a spectator emotionally. Instead, the spectacle of power rattles in a sparkling shell, a series of moves and countermoves by mannequins fighting over nothing beyond the quality of the tailoring. That very emptiness becomes the fascination of these films. When they succeed, they no longer need their historical references. They have become their own justification, a series of perfect poses, staged against the void.

Stavisky . . .

Few History Films so self-consciously avoid the "historical" as does Alain Resnais's *Stavisky* . . . (1974). In a published interview, Resnais noted that this avoidance was a deliberate choice resulting from the central paradox of realistic historical depiction:

> The problem for me in making a film that isn't contemporary is that it seems to call for a suspension of disbelief. The creation of an illusion you know is false. But [screenwriter Jorge] Semprun and I were in agreement right from the start that *Stavisky* . . . would be an anti-illusionist film.[2]

It is reasonable to assume that at least a second reason to avoid a Realistic portrayal was the controversy still surrounding the real Stavisky, a charming con man whose schemes contributed to bringing down the French government in the early 1930s.[3] Having selected this approach, however, Resnais and his collaborators proceeded to construct a self-referential, ahistorical artifact à la von Sternberg.

> What I am striving for in a film is to try to construct a kind of compact object in which all the pieces or elements interrelate, but in isolation

seem irrational. What I'm trying to create are different kinds of harmonics, which taken together will make an emotional impact.[4]

This emotional impact presumably derives at least in part from the sympathetic portrayal of the central character, a sympathy underlined by the casting of Jean-Paul Belmondo in the part. These "harmonics" of sympathy and charm, however, point to the problems the film faced when released. For example, Pauline Kael's somewhat insulting description of Belmondo's performance nonetheless concisely describes the film's effect: "The audience accepts [Belmondo], I think, as charming, sexy Belmondo; he goes well with the furniture."[5]

Although Kael's reaction was more negative than most, many reviewers stressed the film's sets and visual beauty. In a production report that perhaps set the terms for response to the film, Jonathan Rosenbaum reported in his first paragraph about "a gargantuan neo-Lubitsch set comprising Stavisky's office complex . . . that took forty people a month to build, even though it'll only be used for a relatively short part of the film."[6] Jan Dawson, reviewing the film for *Film Comment*, noted that "like *Marienbad*, *Stavisky* is concerned primarily with facades. . . . Isolated images still have a frozen, 'tableau' quality."[7] Reviewing the film's rerelease in 1991, Michael Wilmington of the *Los Angeles Times* noted, "It's a real *objet d'art* film."[8] The anonymous reviewer for the *Independent Filmmakers Journal* commented, "It doesn't make for great audience identification on an emotional level, but in this case, Resnais has loaded the film with exquisite trappings."[9]

Positive or negative, these comments consistently distinguish between visual beauty and emotional participation. Implicit in this division, of course, is the familiar separation of objects and people, with the assumption that the latter should take precedence. We have seen, however, how objects can take on a life of their own, particularly when photographed with extreme care. Resnais, the director of *Last Year at Marienbad*, is responsible for one of the most radical instances of this magnification, but *Marienbad* has the advantage of being an openly deviant film. *Stavisky . . .* , on the other hand, remains a largely traditional narrative, structured on character desire. To receive the emphasis the objects do disrupts expectation. We do not so much expect Belmondo to go well with the furniture, as expect the furniture to complement Belmondo.

That this disruption occurs in a History Film further aggravates the situation since, as we have seen, the tacit assumption with historical design is that *precisely because it has the power to take over the image through spectacular appeal*, the designer should make the decor work in the background. It is not only all right, but necessary in traditional classical/realist terms for a film version of the life of Serge Stavisky to include Art Deco decor and other expressions of 1930s style. It is not all right for the decor to come first, to serve as the film's primary appeal. To do so threatens every assumption about film design, narrative, and human significance.

If we agree that the film overpowers narrative and character and subordinates star personae to the clothes they wear and the chairs they sit in, it remains to be seen how that effect is achieved. Despite the strong commodity fetishism in *Nicholas and Alexandra*, for example, the viewer is unlikely to feel as "chilled" by it as by *Stavisky . . .* What produces this effect? Especially given the participation of such well-known actors as Belmondo, Charles Boyer, François Perier, and Michel Lonsdale, we would expect it, not *Nicholas and Alexandra*, with its unknown leads, to be the more likely film to appeal emotionally. That it does not suggests a "design" in the largest sense that works against participation.

It is difficult to describe how the film's chilly effect is achieved since, given Resnais's "harmonics," any one element of the composition is unlikely to impart the air of unreality achieved by the film. We have to examine the film's intricate kaleidoscope of pieces in dynamic relation to each other in order to understand how the overall effect is created. For example, nothing about the set design announces deviance. Quite the contrary: each set and object has a pronounced Realistic presence, clearly selected for its ability to contribute to an image of "1930s France." While the almost exclusively wealthy setting undoubtedly contributes something to the impact of the film's surfaces, we need only look at similar films (such as *Reversal of Fortune* [Schroeder, 1990], for example, or the film to which *Stavisky . . .* is often compared, *The Great Gatsby* [Clayton, 1974]) to recognize that an upper-class milieu need not be immediately striking, appealing, or glacially cool.

The photography is more explicitly stylized, with a strong use of diffuse light and cross-screen filters that transform highlights into a series of crosses dancing over the surface of the images. The use of neither technique, however, can solely explain the effect of the film. Diffusion is a common cinematographic technique, and was particularly popular in the mid-1970s. It would have been familiar to the art-house market, having been popularized by the work of Bo Widerberg (*Elvira Madigan* and *Adalen 31* [1969]), Geoffrey Unsworth (*Murder on the Orient Express* [Lumet, 1974] and especially

Figure 6.1. *Male display in a production still from* Stavisky . . .

Cabaret [Fosse, 1972]), and Vittorio Storaro (*The Conformist* [Bertolucci, 1971] and *Last Tango in Paris*). Cross-screen filters, though less common, were used in *Cabaret*, *The Betsy* (Petrie, 1978), and other costume films from this period. In short, generic convention in the 1970s would have prepared viewers for this type of photography. *Not* to have employed such techniques might have been more eye-catching, particularly for a film set in the 1930s.

The thirties setting also mitigates the possibility of strange male attire (see Fig. 6.1). The film in fact revels in male sartorial elegance: Belmondo seems constantly to be changing clothes, between a silken dressing gown and a sharply cut, wide-lapelled day suit, from a disguise as a modest bourgeois into a tuxedo with accompanying, iridescent white scarf. Charles Boyer creates the Baron Raoul's pronounced style not only through elegantly cadenced delivery, but by the unself-consciously turned-up collar to his woolen overcoat and the canted brim of his Panama hat at the casino in Biarritz. Even the young Gerard Depardieu, in a walk-on performance as an earnest young inventor, is described at least as much by his slightly ill-fitting, not-quite-polished woolen suit and leather briefcase clutched possessively to his chest as by his actions and dialogue.

However, when we look at *female* appearance, some of the reasons for the film's effect begin to suggest themselves. The only female role of note in the film is Arlette Stavisky, who is chiefly defined on the basis of what she

Figure 6.2. *Cars and clothes to sell* Stavisky . . .

wears. She changes clothes even more frequently than her husband (Anny Duperey's wardrobe was designed by the well-known couturier Yves Saint-Laurent), and her first appearance is as a model, emerging from and posing next to a vintage Hispano-Suiza. In a sense, she never leaves that position since her role consists primarily of poses. (The film's poster included a picture of Belmondo and Anny Duperey standing next to a Rolls-Royce; see Fig. 6.2.) After her entrance at the car show, her next appearance is on the golf course (viewed by the Baron Raoul through binoculars), where she poses theatrically. The night Stavisky's empire begins to collapse, she, the Baron, and her husband go to the opera. Her appearance is structured explicitly as an entrance, and the Baron reacts accordingly: "Arlette! How lovely, that ermine wrap! You are the harbinger of winter, of the joys of long snowbound nights when friends can get together!"[10]

Arlette's posing imposes at least one rhythm of spectacle on the film, but it is not the rhythm of punctuating set pieces usually associated with historical spectacle.[11] In most History Films, the self-conscious appeal to visual values is based on the large-scale moment staged in the circles of the street or the landscape. While there are crowd scenes in *Stavisky . . .* , most notably at the car exhibit and in the very brief scene when a group of people await Leon Trotsky's departure from Barbizon, they are secondary to the middle distances of shots like those of Arlette's entrance. Yet while the film largely uses the middle distances associated with melodrama, it fails to deliver on the emotional interaction associated with such spaces. It is thus not coincidental that Kael should remark on Belmondo going well with the furniture since the scale of the human form and the scale of furniture are virtually the same.

If *Stavisky . . .* lacks the usual rhythm of large-scale set pieces, it shares with traditional History Film a rhythm of spectacular apprehensibles. Just as the Fabergé egg in *Nicholas and Alexandra* is introduced as a direct extension of the dowager Empress's grasp, precious commodities in *Stavisky . . .* are usually held by hands in the frame. Even in this similarity, however, there is a slight difference. The Fabergé egg, gratuitous to the story of *Nicholas and Alexandra*, is pure spectacle. The diamond necklace conned by Stavisky from a provincial woman and then given to his wife participates directly in the story. Even one of the apprehensible close-ups that might seem to appeal to viewer delectation, an extreme close-up on Arlette's ermine wrap as a few drops of Stavisky's blood sprinkle on it, has a narrative significance produced by the Baron's earlier comments and by a dream related by Arlette earlier in the film.

The rhythm of commodities is probably the less important of History Film's spectacular displays. Certainly *The Leopard*'s success in re-creating the past suggests that a History Film need not emphasize objects in order to achieve the effect of "history." It is interesting, therefore, that *Stavisky . . .* should choose to emphasize the commodity over the wide-angle set piece, and even more revealing that, unlike a *Nicholas and Alexandra*, these commodities should largely be grounded in character or narrative significance. It would suggest that while the filmmakers work within the formal expectations of melodrama, they refuse to deliver the melodrama's emotional pay-off. A detailed examination of the film's spatial strategies reveals how the form can be melodramatic with nonetheless chilly results.

Two sequences highlight the film's subtly "irrational" *mise-en-scène*. The first is the opening sequence, which breaks into three parts: the credits, the arrival of Trotsky, and Stavisky's first appearance. These three parts also establish the contradictory stylistic impulses of the film: the relative realism of the Trotsky scenes (Resnais says of these sequences, never fully ingested into the main story, that "we were looking for a subplot . . . which would situate the time and the world in which Stavisky's actions were taking place" [12]), the stylization of the main story, and the mixture of the two in the credits sequence.

The credits begin with a disclaimer as to the historical truth of the film about to follow. This rather extraordinary device immediately undercuts any faith in the subsequent images. The disclaimer simultaneously has the peculiar reverse effect of *re*establishing faith in the film, since it was obviously made by people with the integrity to proclaim the fictional nature of what follows. The main titles only heighten this uncertainty. Stephen Sondheim's somewhat wan and thin theme, scored for saxophone and strings, is not exactly standard "epic" music. Moreover, its insistent 4/4 rhythms are underlined by the timing of the lines of type that appear and disappear with the beat, thus once again drawing attention to the stylization at work.

The graphic design is no less double-edged. On the one hand, we have the simplicity of white on black type. On the other hand, the cutting to the music and the use of the "**BROADWAY**" typeface to evoke Art Deco graphics are stylistically self-conscious. The typeface also places the film in the matrix of other films from the period—*The Conformist, The Fortune* (Nichols, 1975), *Chinatown* (Polanski, 1974), *Murder on the Orient Express, Day of the Locust* (Schlesinger, 1975), *Mr. Klein* (Losey, 1976), *The Betsy*—that use the same or similar typeface to evoke the 1930s. Whether this repeated type style added to the "reality effect" or detracted from it is difficult to say. For the 1970s viewer it would at least have been familiar, especially given the decade's Art Deco revival. To a contemporary viewer, the type is more likely to read as explicit stylization. At least we can plausibly suggest that by using the " $\mathbb{BROADWAY}$ " typeface, the filmmakers were exploiting generic precedent as much as historical reality to place the film in time.

After this contradictory credits sequence, the film enters its relatively realistic opening sequence. The first twenty-four shots largely conform to the norms of standard cinematic space, including wide-angle establishing shots of locations, medium angles to fix characters in space, facial close-ups to motivate glances, and nested point-of-view shots. In fact, the viewer unfamiliar with the film might be forgiven wondering if reels had somehow been misplaced. What started with a disclaimer about the reality of the artifact and segued into a very deliberate credits sequence settles into traditional space and representation. This sense of error is compounded by the concentration on Trotsky ("Was the title *Trotsky* or *Stavisky?*"). Only one cut in the sequence—a cutaway to an allegorical bust of France as Inspector Gardet says to Trotsky, "The French Government, considering the very exceptional circumstances in which you find yourself, and wishing to make a humanitarian gesture . . ."[13]—violates the norms of traditional classical space, and that in muted fashion since the line of dialogue motivates the use of the iconographic statue.

Having established this traditional style, the film allows the viewer to settle back into the passive enjoyment of two vintage automobiles moving slowly through a Côte d'Azur townscape. Until, that is, an inexplicable cut to a blank sky with cheery, salon-style music in the background throws us out of the image. After the cut, the camera tilts down to reveal the Claridge Hotel, a nineteenth-century baroque building completely at odds with the architecture seen in the earlier shots. A subtitle reads, "Meanwhile, in Paris . . ."[14] There is then a cut to the interior of the Claridge as Stavisky and a minor character glide downward in a glass-encased elevator.

After these cuts, we may expect to remain in Paris and enter a new phase of the story, but instead we return to the shot of the cars moving through the streets of Cassis, with the realistic background sounds of a small city, the automobiles, and no music. This jolting intercut completely disrupts expectation, even the expectation of the unexpected, since, after establishing the Claridge and Paris, the film returns to Cassis. The disruption continues when there is yet another cut to the elevator of the Claridge, the salon music continuing in the background—but *not* from where it cut away in the outside shot of the hotel, but from the point in the music where it would be after allowing for the intervening shot from Cassis (see

Figure 6.3. The streets of Cassis in the opening sequence.

Figure 6.4. The Claridge Hotel in Paris.

Figure 6.5. *Stavisky in the elevator.*

Figs. 6.3–6.5). In other words, even the music, which is frequently used in disjointed cutting sequences like this to help smooth visual transitions, here is used to *accentuate* cuts, rather than to mask them.

This back-and-forth cutting proceeds for another three shots before the film remains with Stavisky in the elevator. Like many openings, this one works to establish expectations for what follows. However, most openings first establish a narrative situation, second a space, and only third the style in which to expect both to continue. *Stavisky . . .* radically alters these presentation priorities first by disrupting the reliability of the story through the opening disclaimer; second by establishing that rhythm and form will be of paramount importance through the opening credits; third by beginning the story with a nonparticipant (Trotsky), establishing spatial contiguity only to disrupt it through unmotivated cutaways; and finally by finding the major character of the story, some eighteen shots into the opening. The only guarantee of coherence we have in this sequence is the skill with which these pieces are juxtaposed.

Thus, to say of *Stavisky . . .* that it is about style is not so much to point out the obvious attention to fashion and hardware as to recognize that *only* style makes the film hold together as it disrupts expectations. For example, in an early scene, Stavisky asks the Baron to describe Arlette's appearance at the Biarritz auto show to him. The Baron begins his story, and there is a cut to what he describes, only to have Stavisky interrupt the description in order that he might savor it later. And while the Baron eventually does finish his story, and we see it visualized, it turns out that there is more to it than the Baron reveals to Stavisky. The Baron apparently witnesses a conversation on the golf course between Arlette and her suitor, Juan Montalvo. The Baron's voice-over makes it clear he could not hear what was said between the two. ("What is she saying to him? Arlette looks absolutely entranced."[15]) After establishing this limited point of view, the film then proceeds to give the viewer access to the whole conversation—even though the scene has been nested in a flashback from the Baron who can*not* hear the conversation.

Resnais's ability to impart a rhythmed grace to these thwarted expectations derives from his editing skill, an ability that includes both the jolting cuts of the opening sequence and more traditional cutting. Yet, in the film's elaborately calculated design, even the most traditionally edited sequences show subtle deviations. For example, in an important, late sequence in the Barbizon forest, there is an extended series of glance cuts that, on the face of it, seem to conform to the logic of standard narrative editing. The subtle disruptions the sequence in fact contains demonstrate how even in the most traditional of structures, Resnais is able to keep the overall "harmonics" in balance.

Stavisky, Arlette, the Baron, and Juan Montalvo have enjoyed a day in the Barbizon forest. They are about to get into their car to return to Paris when the Baron notices a young woman, Erna, across the street, who had figured briefly in the story earlier. He calls Stavisky's attention to Erna, then crosses to speak with her. During the Baron's brief conversation, there is a chain of glances to underline the emotional dynamics we already know are at work. (Arlette is devoted to Stavisky, but afraid she'll lose him; Stavisky has already made a pass at Erna; Juan is looking for any opportunity to steal Arlette from Stavisky.)

The sequence begins with an unambiguous point-of-view triad, starting with a two-shot of the Baron and Stavisky (Fig. 6.6). The Baron notices Erna off-camera and directs Stavisky's gaze to her. There is an insert POV of Erna from their position (Fig. 6.7), and the camera returns to the men in a tighter two-shot (Fig. 6.8). After reminding Stavisky who Erna is, the Baron crosses in the direction of their gazes, and Stavisky continues to look in that direction.

In the next shot (Fig. 6.9), the Baron crosses the street, presumably from the angle from which he and Stavisky had seen Erna. This one cut already undermines the reliability of the sequence. The angle is motivated in story terms by the Baron's noticing of Erna, but since the shot is framed for both him and Stavisky, it is unclear when the Baron enters the shot if what we are seeing is his perspective or Stavisky's.[16]

To a certain extent, this question is resolved by the fifth shot (Fig. 6.10), a close-up of Stavisky looking in the general direction of the Baron and Erna, retrospectively grounding the previous shot as his gaze. This supposition is reinforced by the sixth and seventh shots (Figs. 6.11–6.12), a repetition of the angle of shot 4 and yet another close-up of Stavisky. Once again, however, an ambiguity gets introduced when, in shot 8 (Fig. 6.13), the angle returns not to the same as in shots 2 and 4 but to a close-up of Erna looking in Stavisky's direction. While in emotional terms this close-up makes some sense as an extension of Stavisky's point of view (his increased interest in Erna is reflected graphically by the increased scale of her image), in spatial terms it does not make sense at all, since Stavisky has not suddenly crossed the street. (In fact, Erna and Stavisky never share the frame in this sequence).

Erna's close-up begins a seven-shot exchange of glances. In shot 9 (Fig. 6.14), Arlette, who until this point has been uninvolved in the sequence, appears in a medium close-up. She glances in the direction of Stavisky, sees that he is occupied, then follows his gaze in Erna's direction. Her smile immediately disappears. When it does, there is a cut to shot 10 (Fig. 6.15) as Juan recognizes her displeasure. On his glance to Arlette, there is a cut to her, now in tight close-up (Fig. 6.16), as she again looks at Stavisky. In shot 12 (Fig. 6.17), a medium close-up of Stavisky, he clearly looks down to her, smiling. There is a return to Arlette (Fig. 6.18), who again changes the direction of her glance, back toward Erna. In the last close-up of the sequence, shot 14 (Fig. 6.19), Erna returns Arlette's stare.

The exchange of glances in shots 7–14 provides a textbook example of narrative and character-motivated cutting. The fastidious attention paid to the direction of glances, camera position, and timing seamlessly advance the story. Had the sequence ended with these seven shots, it could be cited as a largely unambiguous use of traditional identification techniques. Shot fifteen (Fig. 6.20), a repetition of the wide angle seen earlier in shots 4 and 6, complicates matters. When the camera returns to this position, it seems to be motivated largely to reestablish the space in which Erna sits—that is, as a moment directly after her close-up in shot 14, and a continuity cut that reestablishes the space in which she sits. If so, however, something is wrong, since the Baron no longer stands in the shot.

Figure 6.6. *The Barbizon forest sequence from* Stavisky . . . , *shot 1.*

Figure 6.7. *Shot 2.*

Figure 6.8. *Shot 3.*

Figure 6.9. *Shot 4.*

Figure 6.10. *Shot 5.*

Figure 6.11. *Shot 6.*

Figure 6.12. *Shot 7.*

Figure 6.13. *Shot 8.*

Figure 6.14. Shot 9.

Figure 6.15. Shot 10.

Figure 6.16. Shot 11.

Figure 6.17. Shot 12.

Figure 6.18. Shot 13.

Figure 6.19. Shot 14.

Figure 6.20. Shot 15.

Figure 6.21. Shot 16.

Shortly after returning to the angle, the camera begins to move and we belatedly realize that there has been a temporal jump. As the camera retreats further, and Erna's boyfriend enters the frame, the gap in time seems to have been longer than at first anticipated (Fig. 6.21). It also seems as if the angle, previously grounded as the point of view of the Baron and/or Stavisky, was in fact unreliable as either, since the camera now moves in what was presumably a static space. In the last shot of the sequence, a medium close-up of the Baron looking backward from the rear window of the car (Fig. 6.21), the previous shot is once again retrospectively grounded as a point of view. The effect is not so much to reorient the space as to disrupt everything that has come before. What had been reliably established as Stavisky's perspective has been returned to the Baron. What was supposed to be an angle viewed from across the street is now revealed to have been *in* the street. The coup de grâce to the sequence's reliability occurs later when we learn that the Baron remembers this episode as the high point of his relationship with Stavisky, casting the whole episode into the doubt of a sentimental memory.

This constant play with subjectivity and emotional response and the film's exquisite texture give *Stavisky . . .* its "chilling" effect. At one point, Dr. Mézy (Michel Lonsdale) expresses this feeling: "In order to understand Alex, you sometimes have to forget the files. You have to dream about him, try and imagine what his dreams are." [17] Pauline Kael, again more negatively than we have to accept, suggested that "if we dream after this movie it's of hardware and fashions." [18] Yes and no: if we dream after this movie of clothes and Rolls Royces, we do so not for themselves, but as part of the play of surfaces, the reverie of constantly shifting facades, the appeal and sparkle of an exquisitely perfect diamond held up to light.

Henry V

Stavisky . . . successfully creates a tantalizing object. *Henry V* (Olivier, 1944) is less successful in this regard. This failure raises significant issues about design's contribution to cinema, and is what makes the film interesting. *Stavisky . . .* represents a successful blend of "harmonics" to create a new whole; *Henry V* never quite gels, despite, or perhaps because of, equally sophisticated design.

Shakespeare's play has been subject to a range of interpretations. Olivier's production builds on a tradition established in the nineteenth century that emphasizes the play's militaristic and heroic qualities.[19] The film is probably therefore less famous for its interpretation of Shakespeare than for its division into three distinct sections and styles. The first and last sections are staged in Elizabethan dress in a reconstructed Globe Theater. The second section, which includes the bulk of the play, is staged in early-fifteenth-century costume on blatantly painted, artificial sets, derived in style from medieval manuscript painting. The third, briefest section, the Battle of Agincourt, is staged realistically on location.

This division into distinct styles immediately establishes a distance between the viewer and the image equivalent to the difference between contemporary speech and Shakespeare's period poetry. As Olivier expressed the purpose: "I didn't want the eye to quarrel with the ear; what the eye saw had to bolster the seeming reality of the language."[20] Though perhaps extreme in its solutions, the film's design confronts the standard problem of adapted theater: the competition between image (cinema) and word (the stage). This competition was well described by André Bazin: "in the theater the drama proceeds from the actor, in the cinema it goes from the decor to man."[21] Whereas in film, "the decor that surrounds [the human subject] is part of the solidity of the world," the specifically theatrical effect of plays "is not their action so much as the human, that is to say the verbal, priority given to their dramatic structure."[22]

Bazin suggests that a fundamental component of an adapted play is the relationship between the dialogue and the surrounding decor. Film, by its photographic heritage, exposes the spatial artifice central to theatrical performance. The solution to this problem lies in coming to terms with that artificiality, finding cinematic expression that serves the theater. *Henry V* addresses this issue by creating one of the most purely artificial theatrical environments in the history of cinema. With the possible exception of the Agincourt sequences, we are never in danger of forgetting the film's theatrical origins. It is this combination of theatrical space and blatant artifice in *Henry V* that creates its unique form of Designer History.

The Affrons classify *Henry V* as an example of Sets as Artifice and suggest that the stylized settings contribute toward a naturalizing of the otherwise off-putting Shakespearean dialogue.[23] Sue Harper, after acknowledging the considerable effort and expense expended on the film's design, nonetheless concludes that "the skills required from the audience [to understand the images] are quite other than those needed for popular historical spectacle."[24] She suggests instead that the film's success and reputation should

Figure 6.22. *The opening model shot from* Henry V.

be attributed to official semisponsorship and the sense of status implied in being able to "enjoy" the film.

Whether such a description is accurate or not, it is clear that the film's design is central to its impact. What may be less clear is the degree to which the mixture of styles contributes toward the film's *dissolution* and the uneasiness that results from their juxtaposition. Raymond Durgnat provocatively suggests that "the shifting stylizations of *Henry V* oddly prefigure Godard's use of the non-realistic, the non-conviction of life seen through the filter of an art which distorts (the medieval perspectives)."[25]

While it is probably too narrow to place all of the film's difficulties on the use of medieval perspective, Durgnat's comments point to some of the issues raised by the film's stylization. The depth of a cinematic image always results from the perspective of the lens used for the shot and that of the objects photographed. In realistic photography and cinematography, these will largely match. If the items photographed do not have realistic perspective, the lens will merely reproduce the distortions of the object; the shot will realistically record deviance. Thus, when the designers for *Henry V* paint medieval depth onto their backdrops, the camera picks up the reality of their stylization. The film itself does not suddenly acquire medieval perspective. It is the very *inability* of the camera to record in such manner that the filmmakers exploit as they photograph the painted medieval perspectives. There is thus a contradiction inherent in the images themselves.

The film continues to exploit these contradictions. The Affrons note about the opening shot (Fig. 6.22), for example, that it moves from "palpably a model of Elizabethan London" to "a quite authentic reconstruction of the Globe Theater." [26] They do not, however, consider the perceptual jolt such a juxtaposition might create. Indeed, the opening shot itself slides in reliability. While *at first* it reads as a model, by the end of the shot the illusion becomes much more persuasive. When this shot is followed by an obviously real flag raised against the sky, we find ourselves shuffled quickly through at least two levels of stylization. Model shots in general complicate our relationship to objects and spaces. The reality of the space, its toylike availability, must be suppressed for its imaginary, narrative purpose, to fool as a landscape. When there is no attempt made to hide the model nature of the image, as in *Henry V*, it becomes impossible to have a firm sense of how to interpret the space—is it a toy, or is it London? That this level of uncertainty arises in the film's opening shot only attests to its formal uniqueness.

The opening continues to juxtapose levels of stylization. After a credits sequence that, like *Stavisky . . .* , employs stylized type design (and, in this case, antique spelling) to evoke the past, and after the opening model shot, the realistic reconstruction of the Globe begins. It is, of course, that qualified realism true of all historical fiction. Costumed extras parade about in the patterned movement typical of History Films, neither spontaneous nor chaotic, but planned to look both. After the raising of the flag, for instance, the camera begins a slow movement downward, following the lines of the architecture, from the hoister of the flag, to a group of musicians who "happen" to raise their instruments shortly after the camera reaches them. Following a newly introduced horizontal line created by the ledge of the musicians' platform, the camera pans and tracks to the theater upper galleries, where newly arrived spectators take their seats.

Having introduced this model of crowd movement, the film then cuts to the lower levels of the theater, while maintaining lateral camera movements with newly arriving spectators (see Fig. 6.23). Although the extras move in contrary directions, their options are limited, since the architecture channels them in few directions. Thus the building becomes a double excuse for architecturally motivated movement: first as the leader

Figure 6.23. *Reestablishing impersonal perspective at the Globe Theater in* Henry V.

through line of the camera to find the arriving crowd; second, after having found it, making it difficult for the extras to move in any way other than the directions prescribed by the building.

This deliberate movement of both people and camera continues as first a fruit vendor, then a gentleman move into the center of the theater. The camera travels with the gentleman until he reaches the middle of the theater, when the pan stops to rest on a centered image of the stage. The shot now takes on the impersonal "historical" perspective of the traditional wide-angle crowd shot, and the extras continue to move about in the foreground (though again, in only limited fashion, always circumscribed by the architecture).

This is the patterned, deliberate realism of the classical norm, neither too assertive nor too invisible. At the same time, this realism is deliberately undercut by shots backstage that reveal the mechanics of stage illusion. The film implicitly acknowledges that even as effort is expended to re-create the feel of Elizabethan London, the image will always differ from contemporary appearance. This is the ambiguity that the filmmakers exploit

Figure 6.24. *Realistic costumes, artificial space in* Henry V.

when they dissolve into the second section, with its painted backdrops and medieval perspectives. And yet even this conceptual preparation requires another mental flip-flop: in the Elizabethan sections, the Globe and its patrons are realistically costumed. The performers (true to period practice) are dressed *as Elizabethans,* not as characters in the fifteenth century. In the second section, on the other hand, actors are realistically *costumed* but the space is contrived and artificial (see Fig. 6.24).

Given the film's decorative experiments, it could easily have collapsed from its own ambitions. That it does not results from the film's traditional editing patterns, which are well within the norms of British classical cinema. There are, however, discreet differences between these norms and classical Hollywood practice that result from the film's theatrical adaptation and British conceptions of space.[27] Most notable among these differences is an alternative cutting rhythm built on the exchange of dialogue. In Hollywood films, dialogue is edited on the basis of (1) who is speaking (in general, the camera will be on the person talking); (2) who has a stake in what is being said (the shot of the person speaking may be interrupted by a cut to a reaction of a person with a vested interest in the line); and (3) other details of space (the reaction shot of the second character may motivate a point-of-view insert on an object, for example, even as the first character continues to speak).

As with many British films, the logic of cutting in *Henry V* is based on the completion of a block of dialogue by one character and the beginning of a new block by a second character. Speeches remain largely self-contained units uninterrupted by the editor. For example, during Henry's "Crispin's Day" speech at Agincourt, Olivier delivers the entire exhortation without reaction shots from the men in the crowd. Beginning in full shot, the speech continues and the camera tracks and pans with Olivier as he eventually crosses to and mounts a cart at the center of the image. The camera then pulls back to wide angle as Olivier completes the speech. The sound, however, remains at the same volume as in the beginning of the shot, giving the speech a primacy over the image. These techniques enable the words to register without visual competition, echoing and redounding across the landscape. They also detract, however, from the speech's emotional impact, since we are not allowed to see, until *after* the speech is concluded, the reactions of the men he is trying to persuade to fight. Or rather, the emotional impact is deflected, from the direct experience we might have by being placed in the perspectives of individual onlookers, into the more passive appreciation of the actor's delivery of great dialogue against the landscape.

The "St. Crispin's Day" delivery may be an extreme example motivated by the desire to preserve a famous speech more or less intact. It is not, however, atypical of the film's space and editing, which remain consistently actor-, voice- and dialogue-centered. It would thus be reasonable to expect the film to be heavy with close-ups. The opposite is true: unlike Hollywood's tendency to underline narrative importance through tight framings of delivery and reaction, *Henry V*'s close-ups are few and far between, and rarely tighter than medium close-up. This remains true, at least at first, even during Olivier's so-called "oblique close-up," in which he delivers a soliloquy the night before the battle. (In the shot, we see Henry's face, while hearing the soliloquy on the soundtrack as if eavesdropping on his thoughts.) The term could well be applied to all of the film's close-ups, decidedly "oblique" in their emotional impact.

As in *Stavisky* . . . , the most consistently used framings are those at the level of the set, that is, relatively full shots of actors posed against decor. Unlike *Stavisky . . .* , where these angles are cut rapidly, the framings in *Henry V* proceed with minimal editorial intrusion, allowing the actors to establish a rhythm derived from the logic of performance instead of narrative. Emphasis shifts from the unfolding of narrative through the alternation of angles and enhanced audience desire to the almost exclusive reliance on actors to communicate dialogue as crisply, dramatically, and efficiently as possible. The film becomes a record of the heroism of performance.

In Bazin's description of filmed theater, the sounds and words worm their way in and out of the spaces much as a camera would do if not linked to dialogue. This new importance of sound reverses the usual priority between sound and image. The camera changes its function from a penetrator to a recorder of space and sound. The design no longer extends from character, but from what Roland Barthes called the "grain" of the voice.[28] The story, delivered by dialogue, proceeds through the voices. The space can exist on its own, instead of furthering character identification or narrative significance. In *Henry V*, this space is self-consciously artificial, static, and pictorial and asks to be perceived as an image. We become free to notice and appreciate the charm of the setting.

For this reason, Harper's suggestion that the film offers only the self-conscious pleasures of status-mongering is a bit reductive. While *Henry V* may not provide the kind of "spontaneous" emotional sweep that Harper finds in other British costume dramas, the extraordinary stylization provides its own delights. The images so openly call attention to their artifice that they invite us to treat the film as a series of stills, to return it to the medieval images that inspired it, and to retrieve Deleuze's "privileged moment" from the forward rush of narrative. Whether such an approach works as backdrop for Shakespeare is a different issue, since the radical dissolution of our faith in the image caused by the varying levels of stylization almost certainly works in the long run to break up the play as much as the film.

Henry V is about as stylized as traditional History Films get. We should be wary, however, of carrying the deconstructive description too far precisely because of the potential pleasures the backgrounds provide. After all, the point of deconstructive cinema is to call attention to the ideological investment in Realism, to destroy faith in *any* image and by that process contribute toward the destruction of capitalism. *Henry V*, on the other hand, was meant as propaganda, and largely succeeded in that regard. If *Henry V* cannot succeed because of the contradictions its stylization throws into relief, it nonetheless presents a series of stills and acting moments that work very well indeed. The fact that the film's editing so faithfully follows the exchange of dialogue only heightens this process, since it encourages us to view each speech, and thus each shot, as a self-contained whole. It is in this sense that it qualifies as Designer History. It is a film perhaps best seen in excerpts, or on home video, where its contradictory impulses toward savoring and destruction will find a welcoming home.

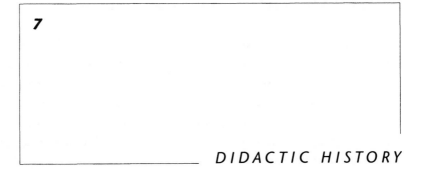

7

DIDACTIC HISTORY

The emotionally remote qualities of *Stavisky . . .* and *Henry V* may or may not derive from deliberate plan. In neither case do they result from a lack of interest *in* drama. *The Rise to Power of Louis XIV* (*La Prise de Pouvoir par Louis XIV*, Rossellini, 1966) and *Edvard Munch* (Watkins, 1976) subordinate drama to edification. The effect is remarkably similar to Designer History experientially, and the differences between *Louis XIV*, at least, and Designer History may be only a matter of degree. Both it and *Edvard Munch* are worth considering separately because of the claims made for their approaches to the cinematic re-creation of the past. As much as these claims shed light on the films, they even more powerfully reveal attitudes about how design ought to serve the reproduction of history.

The Rise to Power of Louis XIV

To judge by critical reaction, *The Rise to Power of Louis XIV* works by rules different from standard History Films. Here, political and economic history become the subject instead of the background to the narrative. While the film does not destroy the illusion of reconstructing the past, no attempt is made to make the viewer identify with the protagonist. Instead, a nonactor paces through the part, making it difficult for performance to substitute for the heroism of history. Nor does the spectacle of production assert itself through widescreen vistas of extras and commodities. Yet, despite all of this effort to serve history through neutral presentation, the film is most notable for its similarity to, not its difference from, traditional History Films.

Much of the preceding assumes that History Film is equivalent to big, if not widescreen history. John Belton has suggested some of the reasons for this association. 20th Century Fox, the studio that popularized Cinemascope, the first widely successful widescreen process, was able to naturalize the technology by associating it with History Films.[1] When designers were faced with filling this new, large frame, the art-historical precedent of the mural provided compositional conventions that could be employed on a large scale. Since the subjects of murals are also frequently historical and political, there was a double precedent for associating the political past with wide, horizontal images. As a result, not just History Film but history itself became equated with widescreen visualization.

The Rise to Power of Louis XIV was made for television, the medium against which Cinemascope was posed. We might therefore expect the shift in media to result in a rethinking of a genre so defined by the widescreen. Instead, the director chose to work within terms he already understood, which included a realization that audiences expect historical films to be spectacular: "It's very important to make the film spectacular, because above all you must entertain people. . . . They have to be spectacular and that means spending a lot of money, which you can't do for TV."[2] To the extent that *Louis XIV* transcends its budgetary limitations to give the impression of a film made for theaters, rather than for television, it displays a considerable triumph of design.

Virtually all writers on the film stress its "spectacular" nature. For example, responding to Martin Walsh's critique of the film,[3] Peter Brunette notes: "This is a forceful and cogent critique, but it is by no means clear how a film that demonstrates Louis' fostering of spectacle can itself avoid being spectacular."[4] Peter Bondanella argues:

> While retaining a scrupulous respect for historical fact and accuracy, Rossellini elevates the principle of spectacle to a philosophical level, demonstrating to his television audience that the French monarch's historical import lay precisely in his understanding of the power of spectacle and ritual over his courtiers and subjects.[5]

James Roy MacBean writes in his influential essay "Rossellini's Materialist *Mise-en-Scène* of *La Prise de Pouvoir par Louis XIV*" that the film

Figure 7.1. *The usual seventeenth-century suspects in* The Rise to Power of Louis XIV.

"admittedly has a great deal of sumptuous spectacle to divert the spectator."[6] Even Peter Burke's investigation of the spectacular "image policies" of
the historical Louis XIV makes passing reference to Rossellini's film.[7]

Having admitted to the attraction and thematic importance of the
film's surfaces (perhaps because of the uncanny appearance of the film's
seventeenth-century male attire; see Fig. 7.1), these writers proceed to demonstrate why in this case the spectacle is warranted. For example, after establishing the traditional historical film as benighted Other, Bondanella
contrasts Rossellini's "philosophical" use of visual design to the traditional
History Film, noting that "Rossellini's entire film cost approximately what
Elizabeth Taylor's jewels, wigs, and costumes cost (about $130,000) . . . [in
Mankiewicz's *Cleopatra*, 1963]."[8] As hard as he tries, Bondanella cannot
quite get past the budget and physical environment of *Louis XIV* and *Cleopatra*, if only to prove Rossellini's achievement. As a result, seeking to make
Louis XIV's spectacle special, Bondanella ends up describing it in the vulgar
material terms he insists the film transcends.

Bondanella's juxtaposition expresses the traditional, familiar, critical attitude toward spectacle. Where Rossellini, the artist attuned to the

"philosophy" of history, is able to re-create the past economically, traditional spectaculars offer only extravagant emptiness. This attitude valorizes one filmmaker's achievement, but ignores the fact that budgetary constraint is never neutral. (The comparison is also unfair. Aside from star salaries, sets are usually the largest expense on a film. *Louis XIV* could be shot in remnants from the era in which it is set. *Cleopatra* had to "build" ancient Rome and Egypt.) *The Rise to Power of Louis XIV* may have cost less than Elizabeth Taylor's jewelry, but its visual impact is not as great as *Cleopatra*'s. So limited a production as *Louis XIV* cannot impose itself on the physical environment. The design's ability to create the Totality of Space, the film's power to convince viewers that the world of Louis XIV has been presented to them, is constrained by restricted funds.

Filmmaking is an industrial procedure that, in order to produce perfect, stylized images, manipulates the physical environment. The greater the resources of the production, the more of the world it is able to marshal to its fiction. Mankiewicz's *Cleopatra* carries this process to its logical extreme by bringing together so many resources that both the story world and the production become realities unto themselves. The sequence of Cleopatra's entrance into Rome, for example, in which thousands of extras cheer Elizabeth Taylor's appearance at the head of a three-story-high sphinx drawn by dozens of slaves, has a self-enclosed totality made possible by the budget. The scene works strictly as designed. Each shot is composed for maximum visual impact, frequently in a centripetal organization. The resulting spectacle impresses for its perfection, its scope, and for being able to create precise images on a large scale.

When Rossellini shoots in real palaces for *The Rise to Power of Louis XIV*, the gain in authenticity results in a loss of precision. The stagy quality Siegfried Kracauer described in all historical re-creation, the double awareness of historicity and contemporaneity, creates a tension between spaces known to be historically true and contrived, designed images.[9] A historically true space has validity only to the extent that we recognize it exists *today*, as a survivor from the past. So, instead of the neutral background space demanded by historical re-creation, authentic spaces assert themselves as different from contemporary reality.

They also impose their own logic. For example, compare the corridor sequence in *Nicholas and Alexandra* to two similar scenes in *Louis XIV*, when the King visits the chambers of Cardinal Mazarin and his first self-consciously "spectacular" appearance. In *Nicholas and Alexandra*, a set allows the filmmakers to place spectators in ideal positions, to have a mastery over the space that reflects the production's mastery of it. If it were necessary to widen a doorway in order to move the camera down the hall for the point-of-view shots, this action was well within the production's means, reinforcing the ideal nature of the space.

When Rossellini shows Louis walking the halls, he has no such flexibility. If, for example, he had desired to move the camera through the doorways and they were too narrow, he would have had to find an alternative means of shooting the scene. The space limited the production, working against the creation of a self-referential, ideal world. Moreover, for the filmmakers to have ignored the primarily historical nature of the space by breaking down a wall to allow a camera movement would have violated the very logic of using a real location.

There is, in fact, a claustrophobic quality to *Louis XIV* that almost certainly results from the limits imposed on imagination by a real space. A real building gives Rossellini the potential to turn the camera 360 degrees to reveal a total period space, but one that is limited to the physical facticity of the location. Anything outside the ideal perspective offered in *Nicholas and Alexandra*'s corridor sequence (lights, catwalks, flats, crew members) would instantly destroy the illusion. Within these limits, each shot is organized to allow the imagination to open the space. In *Louis XIV*, authentic interiors allow the filmmakers to record as much as they like of an architectural space that does not contradict the narrative setting. It nonetheless exists independently, evoking regality and period with or without the film crew. It is both more specific and concrete (it results genuinely from the period dramatized) and more general (it does not answer the specific needs of the film story). The narrative imagination is constrained even as the real space registers with greater force.

Of course, there is a match between Rossellini's method and the restrictions imposed by a real interior. As André Bazin early on described the director's attitude:

> Rossellini is fond of saying that a love not only for his characters but for the real world just as it is lies at the heart of his conception of the way a film is to be directed, and that it is precisely this love that precludes him from putting asunder what reality has joined together, namely, the character and the setting.[10]

The film's preponderance of medium-distance framings expresses the director's desire to connect character and environment as much as the production's spatial limitations. Granting, however, the harmony between Rossellini's approach and the restrictions of low-budget shooting, the production does not so much transcend its material limitations as ignore them. They are still felt.

For example, the sequence of Fouquet's arrest, which Peter Brunette describes as "brilliantly choreographed," [11] feels undernourished, for the sequence is most notable for its lack of spectacle. Beginning with an establishing shot of the King's Council chambers, the sequence consists of only eleven shots. While three are grounded as the King's point of view of the arrest, there are no cutbacks to his face to underline reaction. Only a few extras are present; the director's relaxed framing discourages a directional gaze; the casual panning makes the frisson of a perfect composition impossible. Leger Grindon suggests that the sequence's lack of emotional delivery results from the distance Louis has established between himself and the court,[12] which is another way of saying that Rossellini translates limited resources into thematic expression. Whether the result of intention or necessity, this "climax" seems strangely anticlimactic, particularly in contrast with such large-scale scenes as the banquet.

Rossellini's use of both hidden and obvious zooms contributes to this paucity, calling attention to every use of the device.[13] The zoom does not so much reveal new space (as with a dolly shot) as redescribe the same space optically. Zooms are most frequently used by filmmakers working on a tight schedule and budget. They allow the camera to "move" in space without the added difficulties and expenses of real camera movement. This is probably the main reason why it became popular and overused in television production.

Not that Rossellini's use of the zoom merely duplicates the sloppy, repetitive use of the technique familiar from standard TV shooting (although when the film was released, the technique would almost certainly have been associated with television). When Louis walks down the hallway to Mazarin's apartments, for example, the camera simultaneously zooms rapidly with him, while panning slightly, denying the vanishing point while remaining fixed on Louis. As the King remains the central point of reference in a rush of movement, these shots embody compositional *principles* analogous to those of baroque space even as the shots miss the *surface appearance* of the squarely tectonic art of Louis XIV's period.[14]

Lest we make too much of this parallel, however, it should be pointed out that this similarity does not result from any "philosophical" use of the film medium. (The fact that Rossellini continued to use the zoom as aggressively in his other History Films should suggest there was no conscious link between the technique and the seventeenth century's worldview.) Instead, because both the art of Louis XIV's period and the cinema rely on rules of Renaissance perspective and are thus both external and materialist, both are limited to the same set of expressive options. Just as *The Leopard* accidentally embodies aspects of nineteenth-century thought by using a method as eclectic as the aesthetics of the period depicted, *The Rise to Power of Louis XIV* includes parallels with its period that would be there *regardless* of the method chosen because of the joint reliance on Renaissance perspective techniques.

This materialism of the image is a matter of technology, not, as James Roy MacBean has suggested, of intellectual inquiry. MacBean writes:

> [Rossellini's History Films] like the writings of historian Childe, evidence a very down-to-earth, commonsense materialist approach which focuses on economic conditions, the organizing of society in terms of economic functions, and the importance of technology in social change—all of which . . . are keystones of Marx's analysis of history.[15]

This effort to impute a Marxist motivation to the film's historical depiction ignores the fact that economic analysis need not equal Marxism, even when combined with the historical investigation of people and things. (Andrew Higson has shown, for example, how the British "Heritage Film" of the early 1980s, which no one would think to call Marxist, works from a similar premise.[16]) Werner Sombart's non-Marxist economic history, *Luxury and Capitalism*, provides a more apt metaphor than Marx for understanding *Louis XIV*, since it argues that luxury consumption at court stimulated capitalist development.[17]

Nor does the film provide the wide-ranging social depiction of the era that MacBean suggests. The basis of MacBean's argument seems to be the opening scene with the peasants, who are dropped once the film gets to the court and who are shown only in servile, not productive, labor. The presence of workers does not make a film Marxist, of course, even when depicted as contributing directly to economic activity. *Nicholas and Alexandra* also depicts workers, and even has them express grievances about their working conditions. That hardly makes it a "Marxist" film. On the physical evidence provided in *The Rise to Power of Louis XIV*, luxury, as in traditional History Films, comes from nowhere, produced by no one.

Leger Grindon's analysis in *Shadows on the Past: Studies in the Historical Fiction Film*[18] makes a more convincing historiographic claim for the film. Grounding his argument in a detailed formal analysis, Grindon does not find Marx, but Lucien Febvre and Fernand Braudel in Rossellini's methods. Unlike MacBean's claim for the film's Marxism, Grindon is careful only to suggest that "*The Rise to Power* displays an affinity with Annalist methods, not an allegiance."[19] That is to say that the final results bear a similarity to Braudel's histories, not that Rossellini necessarily set out to duplicate the French historian's methods.

Grindon's analogy is balanced and thoughtful. In the final analysis, however, it suffers from the same effort to make cinematic history "serious" by drawing parallels between this example of it and acceptable academic approaches. Such analogies inevitably place film at a disadvantage. Films will never have the breadth of a work like *The Mediterranean and the Mediterranean World in the Age of Philip II* for the simple reason that they are too short to embrace such scope. Moreover, such a comparison with the *Annales* school still overlooks what film *can* do, which is exactly to provide a level of sensual verisimilitude that a book can only suggest.

The similarity between Rossellini's film and the *Annales* school results from the fact that *both*, like traditional History Films, revel seriously in surface. Braudel wrote in 1950, for example, that

> just like life itself, history seems to us to be a *fleeting spectacle*, always *in movement*, made up of a web of problems meshed inextricably together and able to assume a hundred different and contradictory aspects in turn.[20]

Introducing his three-volume work *Civilization and Capitalism*, Braudel noted the

> difficult assembling of a number of *parahistoric* languages—demography, food, costume, lodging, technology, money, towns—which are usually kept separate from each other and which develop in the margin of traditional history.[21]

Louis XIV resembles Braudel's work only because the *Annales* school attempted a *cinematic* conception of history, built on surfaces. What is a work like *Civilization and Capitalism* but an epic history that uses sheer accumulated weight to trick the past into life, to achieve in a mountain of words, graphs, and statistics what the traditional History Film displays in a stream of saturated images? What does this grand conjunction of disciplines do but bring together in an academic setting the same kind of unified effort and expertise that movie productions take as a given?

What the written form of the *Annales* school's histories provides that cinema does not is an analysis of structured historical change through a macroscopic view of the past. Such a view, however, is no more accessible to Rossellini than to Joseph Mankiewicz. What is available to both directors, and what is unavailable to the scholarly historian, is the play of surfaces and objects to provide "evidence" of history beyond words. Precisely because they are bigger and more expensive, a *Cleopatra* or a *Leopard* or a *War and Peace* (Bondarchuk, 1964–1967) may actually come a little closer to Braudel's scope. In terms of spectacular girth, they, not *The Rise to Power of Louis XIV*, are the cinematic equivalents of a three-volume tome like *Civilization and Capitalism*.

Inevitably, we return to form and scope, and in this regard, Grindon's otherwise nuanced discussion reveals familiar prejudices. In order to distinguish Rossellini's film from traditional Hollywood practice, he contrasts it with Zinnemann's *A Man for All Seasons* (1966). He notes the similarities of theme and structure in the two films (*Seasons* dramatizes similar power maneuvers at the court of Henry VIII) while contrasting their formal strategies. He writes that "*A Man for All Seasons* could serve as a casebook for orthodox Hollywood editing and camera placement,"[22] where "Rossellini . . . prefers a slow camera movement, full shots, and a lingering pace."[23] He concludes that (unlike *Seasons*)

> in witnessing the practices of the seventeenth-century court, one is prompted to reflect on the power of contemporary manners. Just as people are determined by the conditions of their culture, they determine those conditions and may work to transform them. This view, Rossellini's vision, depicts the process of power and indicates the prospects for change. As such, it is emphatically political and historical.[24]

Grindon's description is largely correct. His error lies in assuming that because *A Man for All Seasons* is almost a "casebook" example of traditional Hollywood form, it serves as a useful counterexample to *Louis XIV*. *A Man for All Seasons* may be typical of Hollywood form; the historical spectacular generally is *not*. In this sense, the middle distances, carefully sculpted, recessive spaces, traditional editing strategies, and dour costuming of *Seasons* make it at least as deviant as *Louis XIV*. That Grindon, like so many others, is at pains to make this kind of contrast only attests, finally, to a discomfort with sensuous spectacle. There seems to be a desire to transform those History Films we like into something more intellectually respectable than those with which we feel uncomfortable. This is a need for the *critic*, however, not for the films, filmmakers, or most members of the audience.

Another way to approach this sense of inferiority and its effect on reception is to ask a question: If *Louis XIV* was meant to educate, what do we learn from it? Not from the interpretations offered by critics fascinated with it, but from the film itself? Some greater sense of period ritual and behavior that result from the film's unusual attention to ceremony; a greater attention to spectacle as a *subject* rather than as a by-product of a large budget. Yet while this thematic linkage between story and image is unusual, it is uncertain whether such a tie translates into the historiographic inquiry claimed for the film. Even if these claims are valid as a statement of intention, it is equally unclear whether these *images* translate into these *themes* without the intercession of a critic or teacher. For the disinterested viewer, they may simply "look nice" (if slow) the same way *Cleopatra* "looks nice."

The experiential difference between *Louis XIV* and other History Films does not lie in its surfaces, but in its doggedly undramatic presentation of a thematically justified spectacle. The use of a nonactor in the lead and the absence of traditional editing techniques virtually guarantee a lack of identification between viewer and action. Perhaps most important in this regard is the film's almost complete lack of romantic entanglements. This lack has been noted by critics, but largely overlooked in the effort to privilege the film's "philosophical" approach to history.

That "philosophy" derives from a discussion of the image grounded in narrative justification, expressed largely in two scenes. The first expression occurs when Louis summons the court tailor. As the tailor creates ever-more elaborate fripperies, the King tells Colbert how he intends to control the nobility through a conscious use of spectacular appearance. The second tie between image and subject occurs at the building site of Versailles. Here Louis notes how his new palace will become a visual symbol to the rest of Europe and to history of the glory of his reign.

These scenes justify every other sumptuous image in the film. The fact that these speeches tell us what the King is up to with these spectacles makes the *film*'s seductive surfaces acceptable. It is ultimately the film's *obvi-*

ousness that sets it apart from the rest of History Films. It is obviously *about* what we go to epics for; it obviously did not cost as much as a standard Hollywood epic, and was made by a "star" director worthy of thoughtful consideration; it is obviously serious in its avoidance of melodrama and its use of a nonprofessional lead; it obviously wants to *tell us* something about money, spectacle, and power. In short, its images can be enjoyed without guilt because they have been safely contained and defined by an academically acceptable, rationalizing narrative.

Edvard Munch

Peter Watkins's *Edvard Munch* shares several characteristics with *The Rise to Power of Louis XIV*. Like Rossellini's film, *Munch* uses a nonprofessional in the lead. It too was shot for a European television network and distributed in the United States theatrically. (The theatrical cut, edited by Watkins, is shorter than the cut prepared for Scandinavian television and was exhibited in a widescreen aspect ratio.) *Munch* expends great effort to create a realistic visual texture with limited resources. Watkins also appears to share Rossellini's goal of transcending traditional notions of cinematic history. *Louis XIV*'s design is justified by a thematic link to the King's self-conscious image policies. *Munch* motivates its distortions of cinematic realism by grounding the story and surfaces in the consciousness of an artist famous for his efforts to transcend external appearance.[25]

This motivation stems from a complete identification between filmmaker and subject of the kind described by Pasolini in the "'Cinema of Poetry.'" In a statement about the film, Watkins noted his first impressions upon seeing Munch's work:

> I remember sensing a very strong connection with Munch's experience, on the most personal level—sexual fear and inhibition, need, yearning, a remembrance of brief moments lost for ever, and half a life of aching, and longing.[26]

As a result of this recognition, Watkins notes that "I knew that I would make a film about this man, because, in that way, I knew that I would also be making a film about myself."[27] To achieve this identification, the director ignored traditional notions of history, historical representation, and narrative structure in an effort to mirror on film the intense subjectivity of the painter's work.

I have tried to deepen the subjective experience of my films . . . [and] I have tried to interweave this subjective tension within the field of historical reconstruction . . . [through] the complete breaking apart of the usual narrative structure and the use of visual and sound on a psychological and highly subjective level.[28]

It is this effort to transcend traditional cinematic history that poses the most interesting issues related to the image and design.

This desire to deepen cinematic expression through subjective identification dates at least to the Expressionist efforts of the 1920s. (To the extent that cinematic Expressionism derives from the practice of German theatrical and painterly Expressionism, Munch's work already has influenced cinema indirectly, since the Germans took directly from his experiments.[29]) Cinematic Expressionism has come to be associated with a range of particular techniques, such as low-key lighting, distorting lenses, and violent, often psychotic subject matter. This uppercase "Expressionism" established the precedent for a host of lowercase variations, including Pasolini's "'Cinema of Poetry,'" that have continued this effort to get more out of the photographed image than a material record of a place and time.

Not all of these subjective styles have used these same techniques. Neither the directors Pasolini cites nor Watkins have been associated with the kind of plastic distortions that Expressionist cinema introduced. Most of these "poetic" directors have preferred two alternative options: the expressive possibilities of camera movement (as seen in the films of Antonioni, Bertolucci, Fellini) or of editing. Godard is the chief figure of this latter tendency, although clearly Watkins also relates to this tradition.

The film's fractured editing makes *Edvard Munch* complex but not subtle or varied. Once established, the collage technique remains almost relentlessly similar in pattern, rhythm, shape, and expression. Unlike *Stavisky . . .*, which has to be examined closely to discern its constant, varying aberrations, the techniques used to achieve *Edvard Munch*'s structure are quite obvious and limited in number. Like *Stavisky . . .*, the form of *Edvard Munch* more or less *is* the film. The difference lies in the balance Resnais's "harmonics" try to achieve. *Edvard Munch* neither secures nor seeks such a balance. *Stavisky . . .*'s form is constructive, building *in time* the centripetal object the traditional History Film usually composes in space. *Munch*'s form is explosive, shattering development into a thousand pieces away from a concentrated narrative center.

Figure 7.2. *Realistic decor and costumes in "highly subjective"* Edvard Munch.

The film explores approximately eleven years in the artist's development. Although there is not a strictly linear chronology, it moves roughly forward from 1884 to 1895. In the process of exploring Munch's life and art, there are flashbacks to his childhood, intercut "interviews" with his friends, critics, relatives (all staged in period dress and decor, but addressed directly to the camera), and fragmentary repetitions of events dramatized in other parts of the film. Over most of these events, a narrator (Watkins himself) fills in gaps in the development, both about Munch's life as well as the greater social canvas of late-nineteenth-century Europe.

At one level, the design throughout remains relatively realistic. It adheres strictly to conventions of traditional period costume and decor (see Fig. 7.2). These conventions extend to the physical appearances of the actors. Geir Westby as Munch particularly reinforces this tradition, since he seems to have been selected for his marked resemblance to the painter's youthful self-portraits. With some exceptions (see below) the lighting style also largely conforms to the conventions of realistic lighting, with single light sources, such as lamps or windows, clearly motivating illumination.

Even as it is realistically dressed and lit, the film's imagery uses more deviant techniques. Most History Films employ wide spaces staged in depth as a means of showing off sets, commodities, and extras. These vistas are intercut with close-ups on exotic artifacts and shots of actors usually framed to include large amounts of the space surrounding them. Camera movement is relatively rare, and when it does occur, it is almost always executed with the extreme care, elegance, and precision that attends the careful construction of designed images. The 16-mm cinematography of *Edvard Munch* deviates significantly from these practices in its restless, frequently handheld movement. The film also relies on long-lens shots that flatten space, in direct opposition to the genre's traditional reliance on wide angles and deep space. The most obvious use of this technique occurs in the frequent shots of the daily promenades on Karl Johan Street in Christiania (Oslo).

This shaky camerawork has a counterpart in equally unconventional editing. Although traditional History Films differ from standard classical editing strategies in their efforts to impress as *image* rather than to produce patterns of *narration*, they share with most classical narrative a tendency toward impersonal forward movement. *Edvard Munch*'s editing is based on character revelation and memory. Even in *Stavisky . . .* , the closest precedent for this kind of organization that we have examined thus far, the shifting patterns of repeated imagery express the narrative's impersonal decision to repeat action. They only secondarily express character psychology. In *Edvard Munch*, the patterns are grounded as the recollections of a single person. The form results from the identification between Watkins and Munch, the filmmaker's attempt to *be* his subject and to do on film what Munch did on canvas.

This organization leads to a further deviation in that individual scenes or sequences are edited less for the creation of a coherent space or clear dramatic development than as part of the film's overall structure. There are no clearly articulated spaces in the film, and it is not unusual for scenes to be staged as a series of fractured shots with no discernible spatial relationship to each other. For example, in the opening sequence staged in a beer hall, composed of a series of medium and medium close-up shots, cut quickly, we have little sense of the spatial relationships between characters, much less any idea of an overall plan of the room. While the costumes and decor go to great lengths to establish period specificity, the editing makes it virtually impossible to distinguish one location from another. As Munch moves from

Christiania to Paris, to Berlin and back again, they could almost all be the same street and room.

Similarly, the soundtrack, which rarely serves anything other than an underlining or atmospheric function in a History Film, works to contradictory purpose in *Edvard Munch*. On the one hand, the film employs obvious distortion effects, such as the amplified sounds of Munch's paint knife scratching across the canvas, that seem to try to render some degree of subjective importance. Joseph Gomez has noted:

> Both sound and color are used in an expressionistic manner throughout the film. Background tracks run over into new scenes and often continue during the commentary only to be cut off suddenly, and the rough, hard cuts of the music tracks at unlikely moments create a surprising amount of tension.[30]

Gomez's description is certainly accurate, since the soundtrack is both assertive and occasionally irritating.

On the other hand, Gomez underplays the significance of the narration in this description. For example, discussing the sound in one sequence in the midst of Munch's affair with the pseudonymous "Mrs. Heiberg," Gomez writes, "The narrator of the film stresses that [*The Sick Child*] evolves the way it does, at least in part, as a result of Munch's relationship with 'Mrs. Heiberg.'"[31] To understand the full importance of the narration, and its relationship to the design, the passage is worth quoting in full:

> Seeking now to de-emphasize all unimportant details by blurring their images—struggling to eliminate Mrs. Heiberg from his mind—striving somehow to impart the quiver and intensity of his feelings onto the raw surface of his canvas—seeking to awaken a similar mood in the viewer—Munch works and reworks the head of his sister—detailing hair, eyes, and mouth—only to scrape the oil from the canvas and begin again. Using his knife, the back of his brush, the point of a pencil, Munch scratches and scores deep into the thick oil, as he struggles to remember, and struggles to forget.[32]

Gomez glosses over how the narration *tells us* what Munch is thinking, thus giving the image its "subjective" quality through the use of a traditionally *objective*, voice-of-God documentary technique. The film's use of narration, in fact, is virtually indistinguishable from either a traditional art-history documentary or a mainstream artistic biopic like *The Moon and Sixpence* (Lewin, 1943) or *Lust for Life* (Minnelli, 1956).

There are more similarities between *Edvard Munch* and the traditional Hollywood artist biopic than most of the film's supporters might be willing to admit. Not least among these is the concentration on the artist's emotional upheavals as the center of the story. Contrasting the film with the traditional Hollywood artist biography, Gomez, for example, notes:

> Unlike conventional film portraits of artists . . . where the artist is pictured as victim of some strangely fated madness . . . Watkins shows us Munch very much as 'one of us'—a man with fears and anxieties isolated in a repressive, hypocritical society.[33]

The fact that this description does *not* accord with experience of the film is attested to by contemporary reviews. For example, Jay Cocks's positive review is entitled "Shades of Madness,"[34] which does not suggest that the film successfully avoids Hollywood's cliché equation between artistic vision and insanity. Penelope Gilliatt's description of Munch further suggests this traditional equation: "He gazed inward, looking at fears that he knew were in danger of sending him mad."[35] John Russell's review in the *New York Times* notes that, Munch's struggles notwithstanding, it is "also true that eventually Munch could give full and glorious expression to quite other sides of life" besides anxiety and neurosis.[36] Russell would not have had this complaint if the film had not repeated Hollywood's traditional pattern of focusing on the artist's personal difficulties and isolation.

In short, it seems as if one of the consequences of an expressionist biography is an almost inevitable exploration of character psychology that, form aside, is most notable for its similarities to traditional methods. The film does not even differ that greatly in the relationship it establishes between the artist and his creations. While it is true that an unusually long amount of time is devoted in the film to the creation of the *Sick Child* canvas, most of the other artworks in the film are not examined in great detail. The level of biographical background related to their creation is also not significantly greater than what a traditional biography would provide. And in any event, length of time devoted to an artwork is no guarantee of seriousness. *The Agony and the Ecstasy* devotes two hours to one painting, and whatever its other virtues, no one would make a claim for its fidelity to Michelangelo's subjectivity.

Even the efforts to extend the expressionist logic of the director's identification with Munch into direct formal imitation have precedents in traditional Hollywood biographies. The attempt to re-create an artist's palette literally through the cinematic image, as when Watkins tries to capture the quality of the Northern light that infuses Munch's paintings, has a long cinematic pedigree. Similarly, the duplication of Munch's orange and red skies with shots of sunsets on water has plenty of precedent in traditional artist biography. *Lust for Life* is particularly adroit in its melding of painterly subjectivity and objective cinematic presentation.[37] *Rembrandt* (Korda, 1936) extends this logic further by imitating not just its subject's paintings, but those of other seventeenth-century Dutch artists.

This similarity to traditional Hollywood biography also suggests the problems in the attempt to create a "subjective" vision equal to Munch's canvases. In Chapter 1, I suggested that any attempt to create cinematic metaphor stands or falls on the willingness of the spectator to fill in the blanks with the appropriate comparison. Without such willingness, the physical fact of the Realistic image remains its first meaning. This attribute makes any effort to render space as subjective projection extremely difficult. When extended to the realm of artistic biography, it is almost impossible. A designer who wishes to show an artist at work must somehow relate the image *as created by the artist* to the space *as rendered by the camera*. The former is subjective, the latter objective.

To make the space look like the painting (*Lust for Life*'s strategy) overcomes the discrepancy, but diminishes the artist's contribution. To make the space more realistic (*Edvard Munch*'s strategy) requires some further explanation for the difference and deviance. Hollywood explains this difference through "genius." Artist biopics like *Lust for Life* appeal to the viewer's knowledge of the artist's reputation in a pseudo-objective explanation of subjective expression. We are encouraged into a mind-set something along the lines of "Van Gogh's canvases look that way because they're by Van Gogh, and why can't those dolts around him recognize the talent we all know to be true?"

Films like *Edvard Munch* try to link subjective and objective worlds through formal devices: an ultraextreme close-up on the end of a tube of red paint, for example, is juxtaposed with a brief flashback to the young, tubercular Munch coughing up blood; discussions of the distortions to physical reality provided by Munch's red skies are followed by images of sunsets; the flatness of Munch's graphic space is evoked through the use of long lenses that similarly compress perspective; and so on. These techniques may or may not work to provide the links between the film and Munch's work. Under the best circumstances, the relationships remain tenuous, dependent on the viewer catching them as the film unfolds in time. Most importantly, the

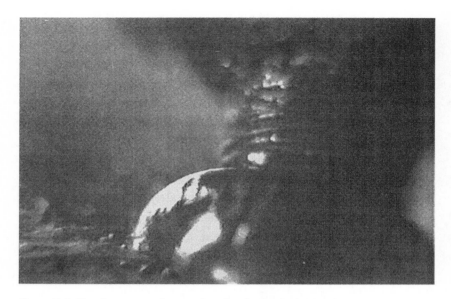

Figure 7.3. *The ultraextreme close-up of a tube of red paint in* Edvard Munch.

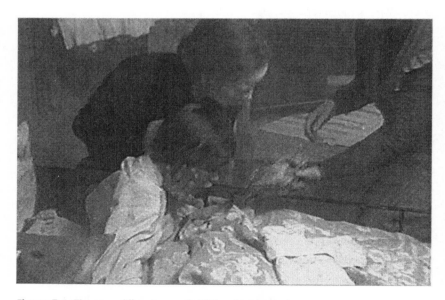

Figure 7.4. *The more diffuse image of childhood tuberculosis.*

film relies on the viewer being able to make these links as intended, rather than some other association.

For example, consider the cut from Munch's tube of red paint to his childhood bout of tuberculosis, one of the film's more successful juxtapositions. While the shot of the paint tube is so close we cannot read it as anything much more than "red" (see Fig. 7.3), the adolescent Munch is framed in medium shot (Fig. 7.4). We can barely see the blood, and even though the cut is very rapid, the shot is on-screen long enough for other details of space to register. What should be a direct *formal* linkage of color (red to red) is diffused by the differences in framing. With the help of knowing Watkins's intentions (again, an *external* reference), we can make an intellectual association between "red" and "blood," and impute a subjective moment. Without that statement, we are as likely to be confused by the cut as moved by it.

The most problematically confused associations are produced by the long-lens photography and handheld camerawork. A perceptive viewer might well establish the relationship between the film's spatial strategies and Munch's canvases, particularly since a bit of narration stresses the flat space in Munch's paintings. The shaky camerawork might also suggest the febrile state of mind of a direct participant in the action. P. Adams Sitney has made such an argument for Stan Brakhage's use of handheld "lyrical" camerawork:

> The lyrical film postulates the film-maker behind the camera as the first-person protagonist of the film. The images of the film are what he sees, filmed in such a way that we never forget his presence and we know how he is reacting to his vision. In the lyrical form there is no longer a hero; instead the screen is filled with movement, and that movement, both of the camera and the editing, reverberates with the idea of a man looking.[38]

Whether or not Watkins consciously imitated the works of avant-garde filmmakers like Brakhage, there are certainly similarities between their work, reinforced by secondary cues. Actors frequently look at the camera, for example, as if catching a viewer's glance. The framing rarely escapes the circle of feeling experienced by a body in a crowded room, establishing claustrophobically close relationships between us and the people on the screen.

Despite these efforts, we are at least equally likely to associate these techniques with the objectivity of documentary technique.[39] *Cinema verité,* not Stan Brakhage, comes to mind while watching the film. *Cinema verité* no less than Watkins attempted an immediacy between viewer and image. The problem in both cases derives from the disorientation produced by camera-work that seems always to be looking for something on which to focus. Space never settles; vision is always disrupted, and the cumulative effect is to give the soundtrack the unifying purpose the images cannot establish. (Thus, the radicalism of Brakhage's films derives precisely from their silence.) It is the soundtrack, finally, that glues these unsteady images together. As such, it becomes our locus of authority.

Just as the image cannot escape its realist tie to space and cannot create a reliable "something else" without recourse to devices beyond itself, so, too, impersonal voice-over narration cannot escape its association with authority, profundity, clarity, and stability.[40] Watkins compounds this association with impersonal references to the history of Europe in the 1880s, the state of Norwegian social welfare, the reasons why a strictly puritanical society allowed legalized prostitution, the relationship of Christiania's bohemian strata to their counterparts in France and Germany, and so on. Even if we take it on faith that this information is included in order for us to understand Munch more thoroughly, it also builds an objective structure around the painter's life. This structure works as much to distance us from Munch as to make us identify with him since the information is often interesting in itself. We may, like Watkins, share many of Munch's experiences and fixations. We do not, however, live in the same milieu the film so effectively establishes and can thus distance ourselves from his problems.

The final link between the film's design and documentary are the staged, frequently improvised interviews. Here, all the conventions of documentary interview are obeyed: subjects respond to an off-camera interlocutor; they sit in stiff, semiformal body positions; they are framed in middle distance, showing most but not all of the body, once again placing us as if we were sitting next to the subjects. Even the abandonment of handheld camera-work in these scenes works to reestablish the documentary association. Since interviews can be controlled in ways that most documentary shooting cannot, they are often photographed with more care than the rest of a documentary. So, when *Edvard Munch* apparently uses a tripod to film the interviews, the imitation is complete. Only the decor and costumes remind us of the manufactured nature of the image.

Thus, *Edvard Munch*'s undeniable difference from traditional Hollywood biopics derives not from the intensely subjective experience the director desired, but from the uncharacteristically *objective* and *social* texture the film's form allows. One may question the political and historical validity of the operatic excesses of films like *Lust for Life*. We may balk at the banality of their explanations of artistic genius. We cannot deny their success, however, in providing momentarily plausible explanations of artistic activity through a rationalizing narrative. They are able to achieve this deceptive clarity because they, much more than *Edvard Munch*, create an "intensely subjective experience" by effectively banishing social context to irrelevance.

Thus, formally and thematically, *Edvard Munch* grapples with the dual nature of the historical image, both objective and stylized at the same time. The implausibility of using a photographic medium to understand Munch's work was recognized by Munch himself. Although describing still photography, his famous aphorism "The camera cannot compete with brush and palette—as long as it cannot be used in Heaven or Hell" [41] applies equally to cinema. This comment serves as a useful close to our discussion of these attempts to make cinematic design yield more than a simple image. Design goes beyond realism, of course. Expressionism can be built into the sets; didactic narrative can point out important details. When a film like *Edvard Munch* eschews such options, it is faced with the irreducible, physical facts of the realistic image. To desire film to transcend this limitation is finally as futile as thinking of it as a substitute for a history book. Film design lives and dies by its relationship to external reality.

History Films attempting a realistic physical environment stumble over this relationship with every image. The medium demands fidelity to nature. History demands fidelity to material appearance. Historical appearance differs from contemporary reality. Thus, the "something else" that historical design delivers is less the additional meaning or subjectivity desired by its creators than the inescapable appeal of the exotic and Other. To recreate the past *requires* design and expertise. When designers are brought into this process, they bring a tendency to prettify, to translate a story's limited worldview into an aesthetically heightened space. When they are finished with history, it always *looks* more attractive than the present. Unless balanced with the greater sensual life of a *Leopard* or the self-conscious social perspective of an *Edvard Munch*, these stylish images almost inevitably result in the related phenomena of nostalgia and commodity consumption.

Part III

THE PERFECT IMAGE

8

A FEW WORDS ABOUT A HAT

Garment manufacturers were again inspired by a period picture, *Doctor Zhivago* (1965), with costumes by British designer Phyllis Dalton. . . . The Persian lamb hat worn by Omar Sharif was copied by a number of manufacturers and was widely worn.[1]

Up to this point I have restricted analysis to individual films and moments in order to understand what design brings to a film narrative, how it works with the story and characters, and some of the potential effects these interactions produce. In these concluding chapters, I would like to reconnect this discussion to the larger world. In particular, I want to examine the relationship between design and narrative, and the relation of both to commodity consumption. In the process, I would like finally to establish new terms for evaluating the relationship between film and society.

In order to achieve this synthesis, I must first resort to another textual analysis that details the interaction between design and narrative. The focus of this analysis will be less on the film's overall emotional effect than on the set of relations *Doctor Zhivago*'s design establishes with the outside world. For the purposes of analysis, we can assume that, as an example of closed, Realist History, the film's phenomenological impact is roughly equivalent to *Nicholas and Alexandra*—always allowing, of course, for the differences between the films. (Not least of these differences is the emphasis in *Zhivago* on a quasi-Lukácsian mediocre figure, as opposed to the World Historical Individuals at the center of *Nicholas and Alexandra*.)

The fashion success of the "Zhivago hat" offers a concrete instance of the influence of a film's design on the larger world. In order to understand this phenomenon, however, we must ask (1) What does the hat bring to *Doctor Zhivago* before it takes anything away? (2) What does the hat acquire from, and how does it work with, the rest of the film to achieve new associations? (3) Once understood in its new form, what about the hat would have appeared attractive enough to stimulate its purchase for the streets of 1960s America? Having answered these questions, we can then move on to the larger issue of design's place in the cycle of commodity consumption. Such a consideration, in turn, will enable us to conclude with a discussion of larger issues raised by design and "the perfect image."

The History of a Hat

We can begin to answer our first question with another question: to what extent does clothing *require* style? From a strictly utilitarian perspective, it does not. Fashion historian François Boucher expresses this difference between utilitarian garments (clothing) and more fashionable attire (costume):

> If one admits that clothing has to do with covering one's body, and costume with the choice of a particular form of garment for a particular use, is it then permissible to deduce that clothing depends primarily on such physical conditions as climate and health, and on textile manufacture, whereas costume reflects social factors such as religious beliefs, magic, aesthetics, and personal status, the wish to be distinguished from or to emulate one's fellows, and so on?[2]

Boucher concludes that style is a socially determined surplus, beyond utility.

Even a strictly utilitarian approach to fashion should expect difference once the object is related to varying social conditions. For example, a hat developed for a rainy climate might be shaped to drain water away from the head. One invented in a sunny, dry climate might develop the visor early to shield the eyes from the sun. A hat created in a cold climate might be

Figure 8.1. Omar Sharif as Doctor Zhivago. © 1966 Turner
Entertainment Co. All Rights Reserved.

heavier, and made of animal fur in order to trap as much heat as possible. Social factors determine style no less than climate, or to put it differently "utility" is a varied, not unified, concept that takes different outward forms depending on concrete conditions. A hunter/gatherer society, for example,
might plausibly use the hides and furs from their kills as means of protec-
tion; farming societies might be more inclined to develop vegetable materials, such as flax or cotton, as the basis for their clothing. All of these societies
may develop hats, but in a wide range of responses to "need."

As for the specific example of the "Zhivago hat," rounded, fur caps
in the societies of the Middle East derive from the influence of generations
of nomadic hunter/gatherer invaders. Boucher notes:

From roughly the early ninth to late eighth century BC, the civilizations of the Middle East were subject to a series of invasions from peoples of the steppes of Central Asia. . . .

For a long time all the Steppe nomads—Huns, Scythians, Alans and Sarmatians—wore the same fur and leather clothing, composed of a tunic, long trousers with or without boots, and a tall fur or felt cap.[3]

This fur cap was subsequently integrated into the attire of the Persian Empire after the death of Alexander the Great. It also influenced the clothing of the Alexandrian states of Bactria and Gandhara, from whence aspects of Central Asian style were disseminated to both India and China.

Thus, the "Zhivago hat" expresses a cosmopolitan style with deep historical roots and strong connections across cultures. Even Russia, the site of *Doctor Zhivago*'s story, and one of the cultures to receive influence from Central Asia, has historically been caught between East and West.[4] While Western societies have been subject to their own migratory patterns, these do not include successive waves of invasion by semibarbaric nomads. While the local color of British or white American culture would no doubt appear as exotic to nonnatives as non-Western societies appear to Westerners, the twentieth-century West is in the position to promote a vision of its own idiosyncrasies as "normal" while viewing other societies as deviant. The "Zhivago hat" appears exotic because its stylistic history is foreign to those making and, for the most part, viewing the film. For a citizen of one of the regions to which the hat is native, there is, of course, nothing to get excited about. It appears "natural."

Aside from the historical determinants, the hat's exotic associations also derive from such formal cues as its shape and fabric. The rounded, two-pointed shape does not conform to the twentieth-century male norm. The hat's material, fur, suggests warmth, wildness, and barbarism, the past (since fur was an exceptional fabric for the mid-1960s), and luxury. While this last association partially contradicts the wild and barbaric, it derives from several factors, many of them generated by the film. In the story, the hat is shown in luxurious settings. The "exotic" itself to some extent also implies the precious, since exotic by definition means unusual and rare. In this sense, the hat is another example of those indications of the past that work most effectively by appealing to the *present* for contrast. Moreover, hats themselves were, by the time of the film's release, something of an oddity for male attire.[5]

The association with "warmth" works negatively, much as the absence of glassware in *Barry Lyndon* suggested underdevelopment. If it is necessary to wear a "warm" hat, the climate must be cold. Therefore, the fur reinforces the story's setting, Russia, while deriving associations of Russianness by being in the setting. While the hat may in fact be made of Persian lamb's wool, with the obvious association to Persia (Iran), as set in *Doctor Zhivago*, the material becomes "Russian."

The History of an Actor

The image created by the hat relates equally to the man wearing it. The hat moves about the story on the head of "Yuri Zhivago" as embodied by Omar Sharif. The character provides the means of entry into the narrative and establishes patterns of association within the story. The actor brings the necessary connection to the contemporary world, working with it by bringing his or her history to the film. Sharif arrives at *Doctor Zhivago* with particular associations; he leaves the film with new ones. He then will add these new "*Zhivago* associations" to other films, in a continuing process until the end of his career.

Doctor Zhivago was Omar Sharif's fifteenth film.[6] Most of his earlier work had been done in his native Egypt. It is safe to assume that the majority of American, if not Western, viewers first encountered him in the supporting role of Sherif Ali in *Lawrence of Arabia* (Lean, 1962) since only five of his original fifteen appearances were in films with American or British financing. While three of his five films between *Lawrence* and *Zhivago* were either American or British productions—*The Fall of the Roman Empire* (Anthony Mann) and *Behold a Pale Horse* (Fred Zinnemann), both released in 1964, and *The Yellow Rolls Royce* (Anthony Asquith), released in early 1965—he appeared in a leading role only in the latter. Even in this case, his lead part was smaller than usual, since *The Yellow Rolls Royce* is a collection of short films centered on the car of the title, rather than a single developed narrative.

Thus, the English-speaking viewer of *Doctor Zhivago*'s first run was presented with either a completely unfamiliar lead or one perfumed heavily with an exoticism reinforced by Sharif's ethnicity. His name announces his Arab origins, and his most famous previous performance would have underlined that identification. So to viewers familiar with him from *Lawrence of Arabia* (no doubt a significant percentage of *Zhivago*'s initial audience, since both films were directed by David Lean) his casting as a Russian might have appeared bizarre. However, the remapping of his ethnicity had been prepared by his appearances as an Armenian in *Roman Empire*, a Spaniard in *Pale Horse*, and a Serb in *Rolls Royce*. Sharif qualified to play a Russian because he had been deracinated and could therefore be reshaped as a vaguely exotic object. Quite literally: in the documentary *The Making of a Russian Epic* (1995), Sharif describes the daily hours of make-up necessary to give him the Seleucid eyes and higher cheekbones of a Central Asian native.

Edward Said has discussed how the tradition of Orientalism (the study of the East by primarily Western scholars) depends on this double process of making the unfamiliar safe: "As early as Aeschylus's play *The Persians* the Orient is transformed from a very far distant and often threatening Otherness into figures that are relatively familiar."[7] Moreover, as Orientalist writers encountered the East, "something patently foreign and distant acquires, for one reason or another, a status more rather than less familiar."[8]

Sharif's deracination is one double-edged expression of this attitude toward the (Middle) East: by erasing the actor's origins, film producers enabled him to advance his career in a series of parts calculated, paradoxically, to exploit his ethnicity. The accent and dark appearance enable Sharif to use audience ignorance in a series of ethnic masquerades calculated on a variance from the western European and American norms. Sharif is Caucasian, but he is not white; he can play an Arab (*Lawrence*), a Slav (*Rolls-Royce*), or a Eurasian (*Zhivago*) because all are perceived as abnormal, exceptional, and different. As a consequence, Sharif's "ethnicity" is constructed almost entirely on the basis of his characterizations. In order for the Arab Sharif to play the Russian Zhivago, his Arabness can be remembered only to the extent that it (1) evokes a vague sense of exoticism and (2) can be reconfigured for the film's specific requirements of ethnic appearance.

He is helped in this masquerade by the equally uneasy casting of the other parts. When the British Ralph Richardson, Tom Courtenay, and Julie Christie, the American Rod Steiger, the Egyptian Omar Sharif, and the Spanish-background extras all play Russians, who can claim the most authentically "Russian" performance? The answer can only be subjective, but the success or failure of Sharif's ethnic impersonations depends on him keeping his ethnicity a shapely, enameled ewer around a wine filled and emptied for each occasion. This week a Bordeaux, next week a Green Hungarian, it does not matter. Always ethnic, he and the filmmakers who work with him must erase our knowledge of his ethnicity even while exploiting it, emphasizing some appearances when convenient (accent, almond-shaped eyes), denying or suppressing others (skin tone) that get in the way.

This ambiguous process of being/not being parallels historical design's oscillation between visibility and invisibility. Ethnic actors like Sharif provide perfect centers for History Films or period melodramas, since voice and appearance mark them as not quite of this (white, contemporary) world. Of the thirty-five films Sharif has made since leaving Egypt, at least nineteen have period settings.[9] In these films, the eras and geography remain equally vague and general. For example, in *Mayerling* (Young, 1968), a British-French coproduction, the Egyptian Sharif, the French Catherine Deneuve, the American Ava Gardner, and the British James Mason all pretend to be Austrians. That Sharif as Archduke Rudolf is meant to be the son of the Emperor Franz Josef I (Mason) and Empress Elisabeth (Gardner) merely caps the absurdity of the situation.

Mayerling may represent an extreme case of Jean-Louis Comolli's "body too much,"[10] since the dissonance between Sharif's presence and Rudolf's historical role is too great to be orchestrated successfully. However, even when the period setting is an excuse for melodrama, as in the American-set *Funny Girl* (Wyler, 1968), Sharif becomes the object of white female desire by an exploitation of his "Oriental" appearance. The publicists for *Doctor Zhivago* were equally attuned to exploiting this image. For example, among the publicity appearances scheduled by MGM for Sharif was an appearance on KNX Radio's program "Firing Line," described in the following terms: "One of the screen's handsome leading men talks to audience of housewives on differences between American and European women."[11] Sharif is asked not for his opinion of Arab women, who are merely the other half of the Other, but for his view of those women economically positioned to consume his image. Sharif was not, of course, the first male ethnic star who partially denied his background. As an Arab, however, he may be uniquely qualified to embody a general cultural fantasy. Writing about Gustave Flaubert's Oriental preoccupations, Said notes:

> Woven through all of Flaubert's Oriental experiences, exciting or disappointing, is an almost uniform association between the Orient and sex. In making this association Flaubert was neither the first nor the most exaggerated instance of a remarkably persistent motif in Western attitudes to the Orient.[12]

In all these cases, acknowledged but scrupulously undefined ethnicity becomes one more prop in the construction of the past as a collection of hothouse objects, based finally on that very Oriental image which has to be ignored even as it is acknowledged. Sharif is exotic, but denatured; sexualized, but rendered passive. Zhivago reacts to events; he rarely attempts to master them. Whether this set of impersonations is negative (Sharif is denied his "true" ethnicity) or positive (the Other acquires power by pretending to be what he is not) is a matter of opinion. For the purposes of our analysis, we need only note that as Sharif wears a "Persian wool" hat, he gives to it and takes from it multiply exotic, complexly layered associations. (He has, however, never played a Persian, unless we count his performance as an Afghan in *The Horsemen* [Frankenheimer, 1971].)

The Hat in the Text

Aside from the mutual dependence of costume and actor, the source for their new associations will be the story as it unfolds in the film. *Doctor Zhivago* dramatizes the life of a minor Russian poet caught in the throes of the Russian Revolution. Orphaned at a young age, he is brought up in the home of wealthy friends of his mother, the Gromekos. While he trains as a doctor in order to be socially useful, he writes poetry on the side. Married young to his childhood companion, Tonia Gromeko, he falls in love with Lara, the daughter of a dressmaker. When compelled to abandon his family, he spends an extended period as the physician for a group of Red partisans, from whom he escapes and returns to Lara. After a brief idyll, they are separated, and never meet again.

In both novel and film, Zhivago watches the Russian Revolution pass by. He moves neither with nor against the tides of history. He stands still as it washes over him. Although the scope of *Doctor Zhivago* is immense, it cannot, even at three hours and three minutes, replicate all the historical detail that Boris Pasternak sets in motion in the novel. (The English translation runs to 519 pages, plus another 40 pages of "Zhivago's" poetry.) Scores of minor characters are deleted. Others—such as Markel, the Gromekos' obsequious servant, who demonstrates an oily political aptitude after the Revolution—are transformed into more dramatically efficient characters, such as the house Soviet in the Gromekos' mansion. Neither can the film easily provide the insight into Yuri's reactions. What in print is a compelling portrait

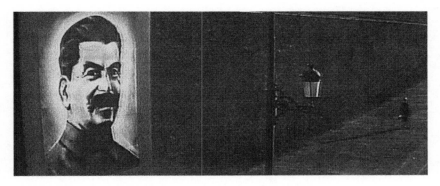

Figure 8.2. *Lara's disappearance out of history and* Doctor Zhivago.

of an artist in crisis on film becomes a large-scale spectacle with a strangely silent protagonist at the center.

Both novel and film notably lack historical figures with name recognition. In the novel this lack probably results from a deliberate strategy, to examine the consequences of the Revolution on ordinary people. True to the book, the film never mentions any of the leaders of the Revolution, even though we do see huge poster heads of Lenin[13] and Trotsky[14] as the Zhivago family waits for a train out of Moscow. More significantly, as Yevgraf, Yuri's half-brother who narrates the story, tells us about the fate of Lara—"She died, or vanished somewhere, in one of the labor camps. A nameless number on a list that was afterwards mislaid"[15]—there is a huge painted image of Stalin as Lara's tiny figure disappears into the distance (see Fig. 8.2).[16]

The interaction between this image and Yevgraf's narration produces an obvious meaning—"Lara disappeared as a result of Stalin's policies"—that depends on knowledge beyond the film. (As with the example of the Statue of Liberty in *Planet of the Apes*, this juxtaposition cannot work for a viewer who does not possess the historical knowledge necessary to make the connection between poster and dialogue.) Despite the obviousness of the intended meaning, this juxtaposition demonstrates the complex relationships possible between physical detail and historical representation. The juxtaposition also provides a good formal "clue" for deciphering how *Doctor Zhivago* works overall to create meaning. Such a clue should prove useful when moving on to the hat.

First, Lenin, Trotsky, and Stalin are never present in the film as characters or subjects of dialogue, but loom as images. At a thematic level, as expressed through action, character, and dialogue, these poster images are gratuitous. Nothing in the narrative warrants their inclusion; they are present to support the film's historical setting with physical evidence. The poster images ground the story in temporal specifics, and allow it to draw on the material world and the viewer's *a priori* historical knowledge. They exemplify the classical strategy of redundancy, since they are no more visually necessary than they are for the story. The film's physical production is elaborate enough to convince realistically that the past has been re-created. Nonetheless, by resorting to images that immediately conjure up the period through the appearance of well-known personalities, the posters further anchor the film's physical world to the era.

At the same time, this reliance is contradictory, since all three poster images, despite separation in projection time by over an hour and narrative time by several years, are executed in the same style: red, black, and white murals. This uniform style seems to be employed to reinforce the same general meaning: Soviet life was so mundane that even political posters did not change over the years. Yet this general meaning is achieved by contradictory historical precedent. The limited palette, for example, clearly harkens to Constructivist experimentation in the 1920s. The large scale, Realistic mural painting was, however, a product of Socialist Realism, which was posed *against* Constructivism. This association with "dull Soviet life" is helped by other cues, such as the drab gray and brown walls on which the images are hung or painted, and the very nature of large-scale political imagery, with its implied intrusion of politics into daily life. These dominant associations may overpower the contradiction of evoking period through antagonistic movements like Socialist Realism and Constructivism. The contradiction is nonetheless an inevitable by-product of underlining period through pastiche evocations.

The image of Lara walking along the wall also literally depicts what the dialogue describes. "She disappeared" (in a labor camp) is juxtaposed with an image of her disappearance, out of the frame. Lara's step out of the frame is a step out of existence (narrative), out of history. That frame is depicted *as* history by the representation of Stalin that dominates it. Lara's figure, on the other hand, is almost invisible from the beginning. And she disappears along insistent perspective lines rushing to the vanishing point. She not only disappears *out* of the frame and history, but *into* the transcendent infinity of baroque composition.

Baroque transcendence ties the shot to its overall importance in the film's story. For this shot is Yevgraf's *remembered* image. It is explicitly grounded as his point of view, a perspective reinforced by his voice-over. It is thus a subjective, not an objective, image, which means that the dominant associations of history revealed through physical detail above are expressed through an individual, rather than a social, consciousness. Thus, Lara's retreat to infinity makes some sense as Yevgraf's wish fulfillment for Lara (if not an ascendance to Heaven, at least a vanishing toward something greater), as a *fond* image. That sentiment, however, makes no sense against the historical, social nature of the image.

The fact that the shot takes place on a street reinforces its contradictory functions: the point at which the production engages the greater *social* life is here rendered as the memory of an individual, looking *at* an individual. And yet, *not* an individual, since the mural forcibly imposes history onto a subjective image. These contradictions are made greater by the social world depicted by the story. The simplicity of the image is made possible partly by the absence of refuse and distracting details that the film has previously associated with the immediate postrevolutionary period. (The novel identifies this period as that of the New Economic Policy,[17] but the film never makes this connection. Emphasizing Stalin's importance in relation to the NEP would produce yet another contradiction, since Lenin and Bukharin, not Stalin, were associated with the policy. Such historical "smudging" is typical of the film, which never quite makes sense as chronology.)

This cleanliness, coming after the disorder and violence with which these streets have been associated, is a positive, internal association generated by the story. Most of the social actions that occur in the film take place on the Moscow street set, and most (such as the massacre of the protesting workers, Lara's seduction by Komarovsky, and the Christmas drunkenness of the proletariat prior to Lara's attempted shooting of Komarovsky) are negative. Thus, the clean postrevolutionary streets can be read against the dirty, violent prerevolutionary streets. At the same time, it is also the space in which we see Tonia and Yuri kiss for the first time; it is the space in which Lara and Zhivago first meet (although they do not realize it), and so on. The street is not just the space in which the contradictory aims of the physical representation battle for supremacy, but also where thematics compete for attention.

I do not want to deny the obvious, or to suggest that any of these complexities call attention to themselves as we view the scene. In the forward rush of narrative, the viewer is most likely to interpret this as a simple, uncomplicated message, a character's farewell from the story, and nothing more. That is the point: if an obvious, relatively foregrounded moment of design like Lara's disappearance works in such complexly contradictory fashion to achieve what *feels* like a simple, uncomplicated image, such "background" design as costuming should be examined for similar contradictions. Or, to put it differently, simplicity is an effect achieved by complex techniques. And while the story may successfully hide that complexity, the multifaceted nature of the design opens the story to new associations beyond the narrative.

At least one potential opened up by this suppressed complexity is a pattern of similarity and difference within the film. We therefore have to examine not only Zhivago's hat, but all the hats in the film since an object acquires at least part of its naturalness and invisibility by being grounded in a context in which it is not exceptional, but one of many of the same type. This type of grounding is parallel to the familiar redundancy principle, but with slightly different purpose. Whereas narrative information is usually repeated in order to assure that the audience will get important story information, redundant design works at least as much to guarantee that we do *not* get the message. To isolate objects in self-consciously emptied, rarefied frames calls attention to the limited contents. To embed them in a texture of similar objects distracts from individual artifacts while contributing toward the overall objectification of the image itself through enhanced appearance. If Zhivago were the only man to wear a hat in the film, it would have much more obvious presence. Instead, it is merely one of many bits of headgear in a tapestry of hat association woven across the surface of the film.

The hat's social function, its utilitarian purpose, is the warp in this tapestry to the woof of Zhivago's personality, which determines individual expression. Hats as objects work to evoke a general social image of turn-of-the-century Russia. The similarities between types of hats in the film work to construct a background social texture through visual devices. The differences between individual hats are meant to express individual character traits. This situation provides the potential conflict noted in Chapter 2, when story and character demands may work at cross-purposes. The most obvious potential for contradiction arises over the extent to which the "individual" hat worn by Zhivago also must look like other hats in order to achieve the background purpose of design.

Figure 8.3. *Villains can also wear hats: Komarovsky in* Doctor Zhivago.

For example, Zhivago is not the only one to wear a rounded woolen hat (see Fig. 8.3). Komarovsky also wears a very similar one the night he seduces/rapes Lara. This link between the two characters is reinforced when Yuri, wearing his fur hat, kisses Tonia as they ride down the same street on which Komarovsky raped Lara, in the same mode of transport, a sleigh. The obvious rhyming of these two scenes is justified by an exchange of dialogue between Zhivago and Komarovsky, who has just been shot by Lara. As Zhivago dresses Komarovsky's wounds, he asks:

> ZHIVAGO: What happens to a girl like that when a man like you is finished with her?
>
> KOMAROVSKY: Interested? I give her to you.[18]

Zhivago's disgust at Komarovsky's attitude proves ironic, of course, when he has his extended affair with Lara.

Thematic linkage and physical similarities between their hats establish a degree of complicity and equivalence between Yuri and Komarovsky, the villain. At the same time, Yuri has other characteristics, such as his status as a student and poet, and his career as a physician, that can be linked to other characters and situations. For example, in early scenes, Yuri is shown wearing a student's cap that matches a similar cap worn by Pasha, Lara's first husband (see Fig. 8.4). It is also reminiscent in style with a soldier's cap (worn most prominently in the film by Yevgraf) and with workers' caps. All of these caps work together, playing to and off each other, to develop associations and new meanings within the story.

Figure 8.4. *Students also used to wear hats: Pasha in* Doctor Zhivago.

The similarities between Yevgraf's, Pasha's, and Zhivago's student caps link them visually, at least for a time. When Zhivago abandons that cap for the woolen hat, he marks his entry into the bourgeoisie. He also indicates his development as a character, since the new woolen hat physically marks his changed status. Pasha, on the other hand, abandons his student's cap for a very similar soldier's cap, marking his failure to develop emotionally. Read in contrast to Zhivago, Pasha's failure to develop becomes negative confirmation of Zhivago's greater emotional maturity and sensitivity, and thus his greater appropriateness as a partner for Lara.

While the new woolen hat indicates Zhivago's emotional development, it also marks Zhivago's similarities to Komarovsky. As such, the historical associations of barbarity that contradict its image as a solid bourgeois artifact rise to the surface, since Komarovsky's behavior is hardly ideal. While these historical associations do not have to be known specifically by the viewer, it certainly is necessary for the hat to read generally as exotic for it to convey a sense of "Russianness." The associations that produce this sense exceed narrative requirements. Combined with Sharif's ambiguous ethnicity, the hat's exoticism and contradictory associations do more, finally, than characterize Zhivago. The hat marks itself as worthy of attention, something slightly *apart* from the general narrative background, a *stylish*, different object capable of being overvalued.

The Edge of the Frame

I have sketched this description of the "Zhivago hat" in order to demonstrate how the most insignificant portion of a design works, both in service to a narrative and beyond it. The importance of the "Zhivago hat," however, lies not so much in its function within the story, or even the new meanings it acquired by being part of the film, but in the social fact of its acceptance as a mass consumer item. The coffee pot in *The Leopard* and the glassware in *Barry Lyndon* did not appear in department stores after those films' releases. Saint Laurent's gowns for Anny Duperey in *Stavisky* . . . did not lead to a revival of 1930s women's wear, even in the midst of a general revival of the period.

Doctor Zhivago apparently did lead to a fashion craze. The commercial success of Zhivago fashions moves them out of Idealist meaning into economics, thus politics. The relevance of the hat's meaning lies in the degree to which it helps us to understand the motives of people who purchased replicas of it. In particular, the complexities involved in film design help us to realize that a simple formula to describe audience reception cannot adequately account for *any* reaction, much less one as indirect as the purchase of knock-off commodities from a film. On the other hand, design does *not* "work in mysterious ways." Nothing would be served by using the complexities we have uncovered to produce a new obfuscation of the process. Instead, we should think of design as offering a multifaceted appeal to an audience, opening up several potential avenues for dialogue, interaction, and pleasure. Any one of these facets may succeed or fail in engaging the viewer. The cumulative effect is to overwhelm through variety. We have seen how that variety is produced; it remains to be seen how it is used.

9

THE POLITICS OF CONSUMPTION

Like most film decor, *Doctor Zhivago*'s opulent visual stylization is divorced from production and labor. The richly decorated and furnished home of the Gromekos, for example, just *is*, apart from any obvious means of support. As such, it merely fulfills its purpose, to remain in the background to character emotions. To ask how these characters pay for the world around them distracts from the action. The film is hardly exceptional in this separation of rich surroundings from material means. *Doctor Zhivago* compounds the general phenomenon by its closed organization around a period setting. The compositions always point inward, drawing the gaze into frames cluttered with exotica, shutting out all intrusion.

While Conservative Stylization may successfully keep design in check, below consciousness, the cumulative force of these artfully planned environments cannot be underestimated. This is one reason why it was necessary to foreground single pieces of design. If we are to understand an object's appeal, we have first to comprehend what it does in the narrative context, even as it "hides" from visibility. Having brought some of the complexities involved in the "Zhivago hat" into the light, I would now like to move on to a description of the wider environment in which the hat was received and the relationship between film design and commodity consumption.

That *Doctor Zhivago* was promoted on the basis of its spectacle and design is not controversial. Page 11 of a fact booklet distributed to exhibitors, for example, gives statistics about the Moscow street set ("170,000 linear feet of pine, 46,200 square feet of hard board, 95,000 square feet of plywood, 42,000 feet of laths, 44,500 square feet of cane screening, 32,800 square feet of asbestos sheets"),[1] which filtered into several reviews. In the booklet, production designer John Box is interviewed about creating "reality from illusion," a process detailed enough to extend to re-creating newspapers in Russian that are never shown in close-up. Even the published screenplay has pictures of the street set in its front and back covers and title page.

Nor should there be any debate that the film was a part of a campaign to sell hats. In a publicity packet that followed the Academy Awards, there are interviews with costume designer Phyllis Dalton, who won an Oscar® for her designs. There is also a sidebar in the packet, "Accent on Furs in 'Doctor Zhivago'" that details the influence of the women's furs worn in the film on the upcoming fashion season. "The 'Zhivago' look has influenced and been incorporated in fashions from the leading couture houses of the world and is featured in the collections of St. Laurent, Dior [etc.]" (This piece also includes side comments about the men's costumes, although nothing about Zhivago's hat.)

Publicity for the film did not stop with clothes and sets. One of the more intriguing suggestions from MGM's publicity department is worth quoting in detail:

> Vodka Gift to Movie Critics: In tune with the Russian background of *Doctor Zhivago*, you might send a bottle of vodka to the local paper's amusement page staffers (or a jar of caviar to those whom you have reason to believe are non-drinkers). Daily columnists might be included as well. An accompanying note with the vodka could read as follows [in Russian, followed by the English translation] Here is a bottle of vodka with our compliments, and we hope you enjoy *Doctor Zhivago*.[2]

This suggestion merely takes the commodity consumption encouraged by the movies to a logical conclusion: literal consumption into our bodies. The idea must have met with some success. According to a contemporary article in *Esquire*, "This is the year when vodka may outsell gin."[3]

This kind of evidence can be used to construct a familiar, top-down theory of commodity consumption. Under such a scenario, *Doctor Zhivago* hits with an audience. Other businesspeople, alert to the possibilities offered by the film's physical depiction, exploit the film's popularity by offering facsimiles of its design. The producers, in turn, reexploit that dissemination of the film's image by using it as further publicity for the film. More spectators are brought into the theater on the basis of the "look," the successful "look" of the film confirms its importance, and so forth.

Nonetheless, there is equal evidence to suggest that the MGM publicity department created the "Zhivago" look in only a limited sense. Much of the fashion craze that the film supposedly set in motion was already moving. For example, in an advertisement of early 1964, a woman dressed in a fur suit, with a fur hat very similar to those worn by the women in *Doctor Zhivago*, is used to sell VO Whiskey.[4] This ad predates release of the film (December 22, 1965) by nearly two years. If newspaper advertisements are any indication, fur hats for women were already highly popular at the time of the film's release. Virtually every ad for women's clothing in the fall 1965 issues of both the *New York Times* and *Los Angeles Times*, for example, prominently feature hats with passing similarities to those worn by the women in the film.

As for men's hats, in an inserted catalog for B. Altman's in the Sunday *New York Times* of November 14, 1965, there is an ad for an "Embassy" hat that is virtually identical to the one worn by Sharif in the film. This example is admittedly ambiguous, since in the next issue of the *Times*, November 15, 1965, there is the first advertisement for advanced booking of the premiere of *Zhivago*. So, the hat's promotion in the Altman's catalog might have been part of a saturation campaign before release of the film. If so, however, there is remarkably little evidence elsewhere to confirm such intentions, since this is the only advertising appearance of the hat in the entire fall and winter months of 1965–1966 in the *New York Times*.

It seems more likely that the appearance in the Altman's catalog is coincidental, part of a broader context than the film's promotion. Thus, the fact that the "Zhivago hat" was a commercial success relates as much to existing fashion and taste as to the film's popularity. While explanations of that context must remain tentative and partial, the evidence provided by *Doctor Zhivago* suggests one possible explanation centered on male Eastern exoticism. Since both Sharif and the hat appeared complexly, if obviously, foreign to American and British audiences, images of similarly foreign men from the mid-1960s may have provided the unconscious contemporary texture around the exotic artifact.

In 1965, there would have been several precedents for the Sharif/ Zhivago image. Among these would have been Jawaharlal Nehru of India (who died in 1964, and whose image was still probably familiar to audiences),

Kwame Nkrumah of Ghana, and Ayub Khan of Pakistan.[5] The most direct precedent, however, was probably President Sukarno of Indonesia, who was stripped of power late in the year. His appearance would thus have been fresh in people's minds at the film's release. A familiar component of Sukarno's style was his two-pointed cap. While not made of fur, the hat's overall shape is very close to Zhivago's. Sukarno offers an ambiguous, potentially dangerous image to a Western viewer, triply Other—Third World, socialist, Muslim. This danger in fact could have reinforced the hat's association with "wildness," and could have thus worked to underline the hat's story function.

Of course, even granting this possibility does little to explain why the mid-1960s consumer would want to look like Sukarno, or any other similarly exotic Eastern male. However, there are hints that the middle-class American male's self-image underwent a change in the mid-1960s. This shift might temporarily have expressed itself through a sympathy with vaguely Eastern design. The June 1966 issue of *Esquire*, for example, noted:

> Something . . . has persuaded the American man to spend $400,000,000 a year to smell good and look pretty. . . . Depending upon how the [male cosmetics] market is defined, estimates of its total potential for 1966 range from $355,000,000 to $435,000,000. Many of the manufacturers and distributors in the business have experienced sales increases during the past two years of 300 to 400 percent.[6]

Doreen Yarwood writes about postwar male fashion:

> Though less subject to the rapid changes in fashion seen in feminine dress, men's clothes since 1950 have altered dramatically. The trend has been towards more variety of wear for different temperatures and occasions, less formality and greater casualness.[7]

Whether considered a feminization of men, a new dandyism, exoticism, or casualness, this phenomenon of a "new" concern with grooming, vanity, and appearance suggests a movement away from a squarely Establishment image, or at least a change *of* that image. For it has to be recognized that whatever may register as "Establishment" itself changes with shifting fashion until yesterday's deviation becomes today's norm.

It is for this reason—the ability of dominant images of correct dress to change with the times—that questions of whether or not *Doctor Zhivago* created a fashion craze for woolen hats, or merely exploited an existing context, become secondary. More important is the way in which Zhivago fashions participated in the self-confirming cycle of commodity consumption. The film exists, with hats. People see the film, buy the hats. The hats enter the street as "Zhivago hats" and become popular. Popular commodities breed desire in those who do not have them to the extent these people wish to conform to an "in" group. Meanwhile, as more hats appear on the streets, the film acquires new viewers, at least partially on the basis of its fashions. For those viewers now familiar with the hat, it ceases being a foreign object, but continues to create value. Except that the terms of value have shifted to being an item worthy of contemporary emulation, rather than imitation of a specific character's dress.

This cycle is not endless. Certainly one film's success is not enough to perpetuate an object's popularity. A commodity must intersect with a general fantasy greater than a single film's popularity to insure its continued marketability. The brief appearance, for example, of a similar hat in *Nicholas and Alexandra*—which is set during the same period, in the same country, designed by the same person (John Box), and produced only a few years after *Zhivago*—suggests that the hat had insufficient staying power to become anything more than a recurring period detail. This failure may result from its very exoticism, the fact that it is different enough to call attention to itself. Because of this deviance from the norm, the hat remained unsuitable for a society structured on visual conformity. The hat does not move to the forefront as a normalized object; instead, it retreats into the background as an exotic one.

Thése shreds of evidence help to construct the mental image the 1965–1966 consumer may have had at the moment of purchase. It is important to build such a construction since luxury commodities like the "Zhivago hat" move beyond simple utility. Its purchase can only be understood as a question of desire, not need. Wolfgang Haug has suggested that utility enters into this equation only to the extent that we justify our desire for commodities by the utility they offer.[8] I tell myself I am paying so much for a hat, for example, not because I have desire for it built by *Doctor Zhivago* and advertising, but because it will help to keep my head warm. Such a justification ignores the particular aesthetic form that exists apart from the hat's utility, but which is, of course, the reason I choose one hat over another.[9] Aesthetic illusion thus enters as an independent force. As a result, "Whoever controls the product's appearance can control the fascinated public by appealing to them sensually."[10]

Most feature films are not explicitly meant to sell a product other than themselves.[11] They nonetheless do something more important toward the creation of the commodity fetish. By creating an "invisible" background both more attractive than everyday life and seemingly accessible without work, designed features help to create an idealized world that identifies commodities with this beauty and ease. The thirty-second ad is explicitly presentational, and thus invites rejection. The feature film nests products in a much more seductive, because cumulative and silent, world that is no less designed than an advertisement, but that does not *seem to* rely on style for its message. Commodities can be strewn with calculated casualness across the frame, appearing somehow just there, attainable without effort, no more important than a shrug, immediately, unproblematically available. The narrativized commodity is thus the ultimate alienated object, for not only is the labor necessary for its production excluded; that needed to *purchase* the object is suppressed.

Stuart Ewen has described this tendency to view the past apart from material realities:

> As style becomes a rendition of social history, it silently and ineluctably transforms that history from a process of human conflicts and motivations, an engagement between social interests and forces, into a market mechanism, a *fashion show*.[12]

Ewen is interested in the raiding of past styles to create fashion, but his description is as apt for the general tendency of period re-creation in film. While the museum metaphor may work more precisely to describe History Film's attitude toward the past than Ewen's fashion show, both descriptions suggest the evacuation of meaning from objects, extraction from physical and material contexts to be reset in a privileged frame.

Unfortunately, neither Haug's nor Ewen's theories can explain much about single acts of consumption. As a description of general phenomena, Haug offers a convincing model of supraindividual socioeconomic structures that at most suggests the external, social causes that may motivate a person to buy an individual commodity. Even more problematic is Haug's commitment to the utilitarian fallacy. Much of his discussion tries to show how socialist societies (particularly East Germany) more "rationally" distribute goods on the basis of use and need, rather than manufactured desires. Yet not every person who saw *Doctor Zhivago* bought a hat;

not every person who saw the film liked it; there were probably some people who did not care for the film but who bought the hat because they *did* like *it*. Individual acts of consumption, however determined they may be by external factors, must ultimately be evaluated on the problematic notion of taste.

Pierre Bourdieu has suggested in *Distinction: A Social Critique of the Judgement of Taste* that taste itself is sociologically determined. For Bourdieu, any decision to purchase will be based on economic and cultural capital. Economic capital is the simple means to purchase; cultural capital is the education necessary to understand the object's style. In Haug's terms, style adds value, and thus is part of fetishization. For Bourdieu, cultural capital is thus itself grounded in economics. The ability to savor culture and make distinctions between artifacts presupposes sufficient leisure time to indulge such interests. Those engaged in a daily struggle to survive lack this luxury and will therefore always work at a disadvantage.

> The denial of lower, coarse, vulgar, venal, servile—in a word, natural—enjoyment, which constitutes the sacred sphere of culture, implies an affirmation of the superiority of those who can be satisfied with the sublimated, refined, disinterested, gratuitous, distinguished pleasures forever closed to the profane. That is why art and cultural consumption are predisposed, consciously and deliberately or not, to fulfil a social function of legitimating social differences.[13]

As a result of these ever-greater distinctions, the excluded internalize the image the dominant class has of them as their *self*-image, and view themselves as inferior because of their lack of education.

Bourdieu's theory suggests that an individual who purchased the "Zhivago hat" first considered whether or not he could afford it. After that calculation, he measured the hat's appearance against an internalized self-image based on education and economic class. ("Is it me?") Such an approach refines models like Haug's, but it still reduces all nonutilitarian purchase to economics, since cultural capital, the currency of subjective evaluation, has an economic base. Yet Ewen, investigating the historical origins of the American aesthetic, suggests that patterns of consumption *themselves* create a class image.[14] After describing the emerging middle class of the late nineteenth and early twentieth centuries, he goes on to note that "'Middle class' status [in the nineteenth century] was becoming something founded purely on one's ability to purchase, construct, and present a viable social self."[15]

If Ewen is correct, "cultural capital" at best serves the secondary function of recognizing what is "in" at any given moment.

Ewen's description allows a degree of personal empowerment, while at the same time acknowledging the power relationships that this process hides. The objects with which we clutter our lives are part of a self-conscious theatricalization in which appearances are part of a role played at a given point in time. Under this model, I buy the hat to perpetuate a fantasy set in motion by the film. My hat, and the way I wear it, then enter the dance of appearances made possible by consumer society. When seen on the street, my hat becomes "evidence" of my sophistication to the extent that I see other people on the street with similar images also wearing the hat. I purchase the hat to "say something" about myself, but the "something" I express is the desire to be like other people with similar tastes.

At first glance, this model seems both more likely and more attractive than Bourdieu's description. It allows elbow-room for individual personality, while not denying the social determinants in the construction of individuality. The Bourdieu model, on the other hand, depends on an essentialist notion of both utility and class taste. This essentialism can easily lead to the vulgarization that the uneducated will *always* dress "badly" while middle- and upper-class consumers will *always* have an advantage, since they control the processes of classification that define taste. It further assumes that those who live at a subsistence level have no desire for adornment beyond the utilitarian style they are forced to adopt out of poverty.

However, Ewen's model is ultimately just as flawed as Bourdieu's, not least because of the play that is enacted under it. The "Zhivago hat" is purchased almost as if the selection is arbitrary, as if the play of appearances successfully suppresses *Doctor Zhivago* and the historical threads attached to it. This suppression is just as problematic, for if an individual act of consumption cannot be explained entirely in terms of supratextual machines of oppression, neither can those social structures be dismissed as random. To choose a particular image is to choose all the associations with it. And even if, as Ewen suggests, credit makes that image more generally available than Bourdieu's strictly economically based model, there remains a bottom line: credit is not arbitrarily extended; it arises from the wages the worker receives, which in turn derives from levels of skill and education. In short, the class component remains.

To avoid despairing of any explanation, however, thinking of the film, hat, and audiences with these theories in mind may help to explain the complex set of reasons motivating an individual purchase. For it is the fissures of complexity and contradiction opened by the texts (hat, film, character, etc.) that capitalism exploits. It is the very multiplicity and diversity of meaning provided by the hat's grounding in a narrative setting that makes the hat (or any other commodity) appeal to consumers. To sell, it is necessary only to find in each person the point or complex of associations that will motivate purchase. I want to look Russian, I want to look like Omar Sharif, I want to possess Julie Christie, I want to be a poet, I want to pretend I'm participating in the Russian Revolution, I want it because everyone else has it—the combinations are, if not endless, certainly various enough to insure a wide range of possible motivations to purchase.

In light of this situation, it could be argued that Bourdieu, not Ewen, offers the more optimistic scenario. The unified self produced by an internalized class-image may produce a sense of inferiority, but it also allows the possibility of genuine *resistance* to coercive consumption. By recognizing "that which I am not," the unified self can establish a set of personal values apart from desire. The atomized, diverse consumer, on the other hand, presents too many opportunities to exploit. Lacking a self-image, this consumer has the virtue of play, but cannot resist coercion. The fragmented self has no values beyond the very variety exploited by capitalism.

Of course, to the extent variety allows a bit of subversive meaning to sneak into otherwise repressive contexts, consumption can lead to personal satisfaction and empowerment. If I work in a staid bank, for example, my "Zhivago hat" may add a dash of exoticism to my office. This is the progressive, internal aspect of consumption, the personal satisfaction that may derive from an alienated object, the revolt of style against conformity. If my boss demands I get rid of the hat, however, it would be gone immediately, unless I have sufficient means to exist without a job. Moments of subversive form quickly evaporate in the heat of economic and power realities. At most, style subverts style—"Zhivago hat," not button-down Oxford. Subjected to social demands and expressed in an impersonal object, such revolts are at best momentary and usually lead to further commodity consumption.

The "Society of the Spectacle"

In a polemic against consumer society yet to be equaled in force, Guy DeBord described a "Society of the Spectacle," in which "all of life presents itself as an immense accumulation of *spectacles*" predicated on alienation and objectified vision.[16] Jean Baudrillard, in only somewhat less polemical terms, has also argued that it may no longer even be possible to speak of use value in our society.[17] Very few contemporary commodities have a purely utilitarian purpose, and even those that clearly empower the user (such as a personal computer) do so largely within the rarefied realm of the super-superstructure. (Computers are only powerful because society depends on them, not out of any inherent power.) Is, then, such a thing as "progressive consumption" possible?

Jane Gaines, Charlotte Herzog, and the other authors in *Fabrications: Costume and the Female Body* would like to suggest it is. Although self-consciously restricting their discussion to female appearance, these writers provide several alternative readings of the relationship between capitalist production and commodity (specifically clothing) consumption. Gaines immediately confronts the implicit moralism of traditional feminist (and by extension, socialist) fear of fashion.

> For feminist scholars, confronting our own moralism and replacing it with acceptance has meant an extention [sic] of the horizon of our research. . . . Wearing high culture blinders, we are unable to appreciate the strength of the allure, the richness of the fantasy, and the quality of the compensation, especially if our analysis consists only of finding new ways to describe the predictable mechanisms of patriarchial [sic] culture.[18]

This emphasis on the potential pleasures of consumption offers a different approach to the topic. Gaines also suggests that the notion of resistance as formulated by the British cultural studies tradition and Antonio Gramsci can give consumption a directly political, progressive flavor. The resistance scenario suggests that people do not simply buy objects in order to reproduce the dominant meaning contained in them, but to subvert or reshape that meaning.[19]

Elizabeth Wilson also takes a significant forward step by pointing out the limitations of a strictly utilitarian approach to consumption. In particular, she focuses on the double standard that applies to fashion, as opposed to other forms of consumption:

> Fashions in clothing are, of course, open to the objection that although we "need" clothes, we don't "need" fashion. Yet we never hear the argument that although we need food, we don't "need" pizzas, Peking Duck, or *nouvelle cuisine*.[20]

After making this useful comparison, Wilson continues with the equally important task of revealing the contradictions of leftists' attitudes toward dress, and their frequently moralistic fear of pleasure.

All of these arguments offer significant advances. By restoring pleasure as a valid criterion of commodity evaluation, we foreground one of the most obvious aspects of consumption, namely that it is something we enjoy doing. By establishing resistance as a possibility, we are prevented from slipping into the essentialism of Bourdieu's position, with its fundamental equivalence between utilitarianism and working-class taste. Resistance also helps to check Haug's implication that such pleasure, derived from an aesthetic form over which the consumer has no control, is a form of false consciousness. If the consumer genuinely engages in a form of *conscious* resistance, and derives pleasure from that political act, rather than the commodity itself, it is difficult to insist that he or she somehow has been duped by the system. Resistance also works against Ewen's insistence that the image we choose to wear merely duplicates the systems of power that victimize us in the first place.

The "Zhivago hat" at one level lends credence to this scenario. A vulgar interpretation of the "top-down" model might lead one to the conclusion that a consumer would seek to reproduce the *Doctor Zhivago* environment in toto, or at least try to dress overall in a manner that did not conflict with the hat. The 1960s obviously did not witness a general return to the buttoned-up blacks, browns, and grays of early Soviet-era fashion. The fur cap, in fact, was probably most popular in the youth counterculture, and was quickly incorporated into the creation of a new image of 1960s rebelliousness based on colorful, "psychedelic" patterns, loosely fitting fabrics, and a general rejection of social responsibility. Fashion historian Madge Garland lends further support to this possibility in her description of fashion trends in the 1960s. After mentioning the new importance of the middle and working classes in the creation of fashion taste, she notes:

> The phenomenon of the Sixties was principally that fashion was no longer a question of dictate, but of individual taste and invention—even though this came to be well marketed and exploited by clever young designers working in London.[21]

Zhivago's rejection of traditional bourgeois norms *and* Soviet-style repression might have accorded well with this audience's self-image. They did not literally re-create the film's milieu in their new image; they merely "capped" their self-expression with his hat. (See, for example, the cover picture of the LP *The Byrds' Greatest Hits.*)

The problem with this approach can be neatly summarized by a passage that Gaines apparently means to be taken positively:

> The suggestion that there is a symmetry between production and consumption is not new, but the use of "production" taken over from industrial manufacture as a metaphor for signification has eroded the Leftist prohibition against stating outright that commodity consumption is the course of the worker's alienation. . . . In this shading, then, production and consumption become almost indistinguishable.[22]

This semantic merger of production and consumption achieved by the *metaphorical* operation of linking the former with *signification*, is postmodernism's equivalent to the utilitarian fallacy. Accepting this metaphor makes it easy to conclude that because each of us *produces* meaning by our choice of commodities, we thereby can *resist* because it is impossible for capitalism entirely to control our purchases. If, for example, I purchase an expensive suit and wear it with high-top sneakers, this partially "subverts" the dominant image of power and display contained in the suit and substitutes for it my own sense of humor. With this new use and meaning, I neatly become a "producer."

This conflation and attendant subversion are only possible, however, because of the flattening of distinction between the idealist process of signification and the materialist production of goods. If it is obvious that power suits and high-tops do not "go together," it should be equally obvious that not all forms of production are created equal. Each of us also *produces* offal as a result of consumption, for example, but we should (I hope) be loath to construct a cultural theory on the basis of the results. Furthermore, if I believe that the meaning produced by personal style is secondary to the primary fact that the clothes I wear are produced by people over whom I have no control (Garland's "clever young designers" marketing and exploiting new trends, such as wearing high-top sneakers with business suits), I am likely to find "resistance" little better than nose-thumbing.

Moreover, even if we accept the potentially progressive aspects of consumption, such an emphasis still privileges the intellect over the body, a privilege at least as "productive" of contemporary alienation as the commodity fetish. The mental pleasures of subversion are at best no greater than the physical pleasures of the body. To return to Wilson's analogy, clearly it is true that to submit fashion to a set of standards that we do not apply to other consumables, such as food, is unfair. Let us extend that analogy to its implicit conclusion, however. Eating does not make us chefs, wearing clothes does not make us couturiers, and watching films does not make us filmmakers. If we cook, the rewards we derive from the process are that much greater—at the level of bodily pleasures (the food tastes better because we have spiced it *literally* to our "tastes") and *also* at the level of mental pleasures (the satisfaction of a job well done). Presumably if we sew our clothes, design our environments, shoot our own videos, even greater satisfaction could be expected.

Does the choice made by a consumer express self? Yes, but it is a limited definition of self, filtered through someone else's definition, a willingness to have others determine what is our correct image. Whatever the emotional satisfactions such consumption may create, we must assume that they would pale next to a *self*-defined self. In this regard, "resistance" as a form of political statement in many ways is a confession of bankruptcy. Having lost faith in the ability of the working class to create a revolution, we now emphasize its (undeniable) ability to revolutionize style.

The unanswered question remains: if the unemployed working-class youths of Britain, or the inner-city underclass in the United States, had the money to buy Armani, would they choose to wear worn-out jeans? Or would they rather participate in the cycle of conspicuous consumption, discard their "resistance," and revel in the material pleasures their newly found wealth would make possible? This is another way of saying that a theory of "progressive consumption" ultimately remains too negative. It focuses on what people do *in spite of* the system, not *instead of* it.

To slip back into a puritanical Marxism that denies pleasure in favor of utility is not the answer. Neither is a giddy acceptance of everything. Embracing everything respects nothing, least of all oneself. The decision to purchase must be governed by a personal morality based on a knowledge of self in relation to the greater social fabric. Only in this double sense of "self" can any hope of real empowerment occur. My "need" to buy an exotic commodity like the "Zhivago hat" will inevitably return so long as I am frustrated by my personal life. And that frustration has no chance of ending until I recognize that the hat, as the expression of an egotistical desire to establish individuality through conformity, is as much a *cause* of the frustration as a relief from it. My personal rejection at the level of style, is a purely tactical response to capitalism's long-term strategy to sell.

This, then, is the central paradox of the "Society of the Spectacle." The very devices we use to make our lives more pleasant contribute only to our long-term frustration. The very pleasures we indulge guarantee nothing except a later desire to repeat, augment, and surpass them. In this cycle, we can at best carve out a small space of personal resistance where we "give the finger" to forces beyond our control. The designed image works as an important part of this process, generating desire, stimulating imagination, fostering an image of potential that can never be realized. It might seem that there is no way out, that we are doomed to this endless round of victimization. This bankrupt surrender at least has the beauty of nihilism. It nonetheless is unnecessary, for we do not have to be victims, we do not have to be passive observers, we do not have to accept other people's images. We can, in fact, use those images as the first step in a new form of *production* that serves no needs but our own.

10

PRODUCTIONISM

Our discussion in the previous chapter might just as easily have been called "The Politics of Signification." Any overview of the relationship between films and consumption assumes that at some level the film "means something" to the person who buys an artifact from it. I have suggested, however, that to concentrate exclusively on what a commodity "means" leads to a politically untenable position that, while it empowers consumers at one level, victimizes us at another. We can agree with at least one aspect of the traditional Marxist scenario. Part of the designed image's power lies in the environmental unconscious it creates, in which objects seem to sit naturally, just *there*. Because they have been aesthetically heightened, they also work as a standard against which we measure our daily lives. As such, they are guaranteed to raise the frustration that is the first step to commodity consumption.

Is there any way out of this cycle of surrender to the "Society of the Spectacle"? In this chapter, I want to sketch a new way of thinking about the relationship between image and consumer and thereby to provide a provisional, positive answer to that question. Attention to consumption extends film and design beyond the narrow confines of aesthetics and meaning. It does nothing to offer an active politics of resistance, except in the negative fashion of "subverting" dominant meaning. I wish to offer a more interventionist model, one that acknowledges the problems of artistic activity, but because of that realization offers a new social position for both artist and consumer. In effect, I wish to erase that distinction completely in favor of a politics of *personal* production.

Production: Against

But first, the negatives. While I have no hard evidence to support my claim, I would be willing to bet that few people who allow a film crew to use their property agree a second time. Those who do so almost certainly ask for more money. The reasons for this reluctance derive from the same reason they were willing to permit a film crew into their lives in the first place: the designed image. Someone who has never witnessed a film shoot and who has never had his or her life disrupted by one is most likely to think that by agreeing to this intrusion, his or her life (or at least personal space) will be transformed into the magically perfect images of the cinema. Once acquainted with the realities of movie production, however, people realize that this glamorous hyperrealism is achieved through the complete disruption, if not destruction, of existing space. The ideal comes at a high price.

To understand why this should be so, we should return briefly to Léon Barsacq's description of the film designer's profession. According to Barsacq, first there was the realistic image achieved by using the camera as a recorder. Second, there was the stylized image that grafted theatrical practice onto cinematic space. Because each story has individual requirements from the physical environment, it became necessary to dress images in terms specific to narratives. Finally, there came the development of architectural space that transcended the limitations of the fixed spectator position in favor of the roving camera eye. Where stylization makes the realistic record inadequate, architectural space introduces the possibility of multiple ideal perspectives. What had in the Méliès tradition been a matter of a single, ideal camera position became with the development of editing devices a matter of dozens, even hundreds of ideal angles.

The production of multiple, ideal images to record the same dramatic content is an expensive, complex process justified in terms of emotional impact. Once multiple camera positions became an integral part of cinematic expression, more efficient and cost-effective production methods as well as greater control over lighting and decor became necessary. These latter considerations eventually led to the development of the closed studio and assembly-line methods of production. In this limited sense, production design *is* a form of industrial design, since it dresses a serially produced commodity in an attractive package. And so long as the production of narrative features was largely confined to studio backlots—that is, to enclosed, assembly-line methods—the disruptive impact on the environment was minimal. In this sense, film has always been a relatively "clean" industry.

However, once studio production gave way to location shooting as the norm, the power relationship between feature film production and external reality shifted considerably, sullying film production's "clean" image. Few filmmakers venture outside studio walls with the intention of giving up the expressive advantages they enjoy in the studios. Locations are chosen for their "authenticity," but that validity is *not* defined in terms of the space's existence in reality. A factory floor would not serve simply to reveal the machinery of capitalist production, for example, but as the *realistic background* to a traditional narrative, such as in *Norma Rae* (Ritt, 1979). Or, a city like Prague can be used to stand in for Dresden, in *Slaughterhouse Five* (Hill, 1972), or for Vienna, in *Amadeus* (Forman, 1984), rendering its charms as *someone else's* in order to serve the script.

Consider a simple example. Assume I agree to allow a film crew to shoot in my apartment. It was selected because it "reads" as the space inhabited by a university professor. When the designer and crew arrive, they begin to filter out those details that do not accord with their story. So, for example, assume that the story's professor teaches English and hates movies. All my movie posters, videotapes, and discs would have to disappear, probably to be replaced by books. The facts of my life give way to narrative demands. The designer then realizes that in order to achieve a particular shot, the mirror in my bathroom will have to be removed because it inconveniently reflects the camera crew. He has it taken down, and in the process, it breaks. I am paid to replace it, but no one pays me for the time I will waste going to the store to select it, load it, put it back up, and so on.

It is at just this grubby level of physical detail and trivial inconvenience that the *least* disruptive location shooting works. Combined with the Romantic rhetoric of auteurism, this kind of physical displacement takes on a far more pervasive, dangerous, and questionable aspect. The filmmaker convinced of his or her artistry (and what one isn't?) abandons all moral scruples in favor of a greater "vision"—itself no doubt inspired by the designed image. This "vision" justifies everything, from pollution, to astronomical budgets, to even the death of actors. At its worst, the designed image makes filmmakers forget that they operate in the real world, or rather, the *production* takes on a reality of its own that transcends all other considerations.

For example, consider these comments from production designer Bruno Rubeo about the production of *Platoon* (Stone, 1986). Asked about the use of Philippine locations to re-create the jungles of Vietnam, Rubeo noted:

> There was no road there. We had to build roads and dams over two bridges and a river to get to the location. . . .
>
> We made a village and real rice fields. We found a river which was quite far away and had a system of pumps to water the valley down. . . . We ended up planting thousands of trees. . . . The dry season came, and things started turning brown. Suddenly, there was no jungle there. One day I was in the middle of the valley talking to a construction guy when all of a sudden I hear, whoosh. It was spontaneous combustion. It was so hot; the valley just caught on fire. . . . We had to keep on pumping water into the valley.[1]

It is difficult to decide which is more disturbing about these anecdotes, the ecological destruction in the service of a film narrative, or the blasé attitude of the man responsible for it, as if this is "of course" something that had to be done to insure the "right look." Not that Rubeo should be singled out for this incident; his comments merely encapsulate a general attitude. Steven Bach's *Final Cut: Dreams and Disaster in the Making of Heaven's Gate*, for example, documents the consequences when a director single-mindedly focuses on a film's appearance at the expense of every other consideration. The tragedy of *The Twilight Zone Movie*, when two child extras and the film's lead, Vic Morrow, were killed because of a special effect that went out of control, merely extends this logic to its ultimate conclusion. Unfortunately, this logic is also as integral to industrial filmmaking as clear-cutting is to logging, smokestacks to steel mills, and despoliation to mining.

When accidents like that on the set of *The Twilight Zone Movie* occur, the laws of physics wreak their revenge on the designed image. Physical space does not lend itself easily to narrative demands. It must be shaped into the spectacular surfaces that yield so much pleasure. The process of achieving these surfaces need not result in death, but it almost always involves at least inconvenience to those around the production and can frequently pose active dangers. Designer Richard Sylbert described the filmmaker's attitude succinctly to journalist Julie Salamon:

To me a movie is a war. And if you don't know it's a war you're missing something. . . . The war is between the problems, the people with the ideas, and the people with the money. The crazies versus the bean counters.[2]

This statement, of course, merely repeats the self-flattering ideology of Romanticism, as applied to cinema. Its terms are nonetheless disarmingly similar to an argument made by the syndicalist philosopher Georges Sorel:

Whenever we consider questions relative to industrial progress, we are led to consider art as an *anticipation* of the highest and technically most perfect forms of production . . . This analogy is justified by the fact that the artist dislikes reproducing accepted types; . . . the inventor is an artist who wears himself out in pursuing the realisation of ends which practical people generally declare absurd; and who, if he has made any important discovery is often supposed to be mad. . . . This state of mind is, moreover, exactly that which was found in the first armies which carried on the wars of Liberty.[3]

Sorel characterizes the soldiers of the "wars of Liberty" (those of the French Revolution and Napoleonic eras) as a collective of heroes:

In the wars of Liberty each soldier considered himself as an *individual* having something of importance to do in the battle . . . Battles under these conditions . . . became collections of heroic exploits accomplished by individuals under the influence of an extraordinary enthusiasm.[4]

Sorel's linking of this "heroic individualism" economically to the American nineteenth-century entrepreneur merely completes the parallel to the contemporary film worker. Film technicians and artists no longer serve on payroll at a corporation with a fixed physical plant. They are independent contractors who sell their skills to the highest bidder for projects in which they presumably have a vested emotional interest.

There is, then, an antagonistic relationship between mainstream filmmakers and the environments they seek to control. Once they succeed in doing so, the results circulate in the wider world of meaning. In Chapter 2, we briefly touched on some of the consequences of appropriating landscapes to narrative ends. In a political consideration of this problem, the relative power of the local population and of a film crew will inevitably affect the finished images. When, for example, the film crew and local population are on relatively equal footing, there is some insurance that the result will not too actively distort the image presented to the rest of the world. The benefit may even accrue to the location's favor if, for example, the pure images presented in the film help to create a relatively clean industry like tourism for an otherwise impoverished area.

However, when the production intrudes into less developed spaces, the situation is more complex. For example, *Burn!* (Pontecorvo, 1970) tries to offer a sympathetic view of a Third World struggle. Its production process, however, inevitably reproduces the structures it criticizes because of the industrial nature of big-budget filmmaking. Of course, no single film can be held responsible for the realities of capitalist production. Good political intentions, however, do not mitigate the appropriation of landscapes in Africa, Colombia, and Caribbean islands to create the fictional island of Quemada. Nor can they erase the fact that real fields are burned to produce the film's ravishing swirls of fire and smoke, that flesh-and-blood people give the director the baroquely dynamic crowd scenes he seems to desire, that real buildings have become stage sets for a plot part operetta, part white-man's fantasy.

Luis Pico Estrada has described this process of First World productions set in Latin America. While Estrada acknowledges the value of attention to the region's history, he also points out the problems of such depiction from the outside:

> It must be added that, for the Latin American market, every one of these films suffered from the natural remoteness of a work designed for international markets and not for specific ones. So in the "liberal" international filming of Latin American themes we find a lack of verisimilitude in the details (scenes, equipment, costumes and even gestures and attitudes), the absence of a certain complicity "from within" and finally the barrier of a different language, especially in the treatment of historical subjects.[5]

Estrada sees the alienation of space and decor in these films as a political failure. The "appropriation" of Latin American history to the thematic concerns of European and American filmmakers reconfigures local issues as the exotic—exotic to those spectators in developed countries positioned to patronize the films, and equally, if differently, exotic to the populations depicted, since they have been distorted and alienated out of recognition from their own concerns and experience. Moreover, *any* space outside the parochial perspective of filmmakers gets warped by their partial vision of the world. (As someone originally from New England, for example, I have been struck by Hollywood's inability to convey any sense of what it is like to live there. I assume that people everywhere, confronted with similar images of themselves, feel equally baffled or amused.)

Production: For

I have not, however, come to bury production, but to praise it. The reasons are simple: consumption is not enough to supply the emotional satisfactions that artistic production provides. In the previous chapter, we examined some of the attitudes around consumption, particularly in light of Marxist theory. These attitudes largely condemn consumption as a theft of our psychic lives. Such a position is untenable because it refuses to acknowledge the potential emotional satisfactions consumption may provide, *even if* we consume as victims of the "Society of the Spectacle." Instead, I suggest that we view consumption as a necessary first step toward a new, personalized production.

At one level, there is nothing new in this position. If Marxism became a matter of distributing poverty more equally, it did not start out that way. Engels, for example, recognized the problem offered by capitalism not as a matter of money, but of production:

> The old [capitalist] mode of production must therefore be revolutionized from top to bottom, and in particular the former division of labour must disappear. Its place must be taken by an organization of production in which, on the one hand, no individual can throw on the shoulders of others his share in productive labour . . . and . . . on the other hand, productive labour, instead of being a means of subjugating men, will become a means of their emancipation, by offering each individual the opportunity to develop all his faculties, physical and mental, in all directions and exercise them to the full—in which, therefore, productive labour will become a pleasure instead of being a burden.[6]

Marx located this burden in the alienation of labor produced by capitalist production methods.

> Owing to the extensive use of machinery and to division of labour, the work of the proletarians has lost all individual character, and consequently, all charm for the workman. He becomes an appendage of the machine, and it is only the most simple, most monotonous, and most easily acquired knack, that is required of him.[7]

A primary tenet of Marxist theory is that because the worker has no personal investment in his or her work, labor becomes displeasurable. Restore the personal stake to the worker, and his or her effort will cease being unpleasant and become instead an active extension of psychic life. We must be wary at this juncture, however, to avoid falling into the utilitarian fallacy. Recognizing the personal expression provided by consumption provides one means to avoid this pitfall. To recognize the potential emotional, irrational values that an impersonal commodity may provide is to point out that just because an object is *useful* in productive terms does not make it *valuable* in emotional ones. To insist further, as does traditional Marxism, that this "value" is false and produced by the commodity fetish does not get us very far, since such a position insists that the transcendent, socially determined value of utility should override all personal values.

In this sense, Sorel's analogy between art and larger human activity is helpful. It points out the extremes to which a person with a vested interest in his or her work will go in order to achieve quality production. It reintegrates the *emotional stake* of production and suggests the possibility of a social organization based not on a leveling to the lowest common denominator, but on the greatest human achievements made possible by group struggle. This group, moreover, remains a collection of individuals, each of whom brings specialized talents, and who reach greatest satisfaction by exercising those skills in a common effort.

Thus, contemporary film production does offer a helpful model of industrial organization, since it brings together a collection of talents working toward a common goal. Unfortunately, as an industrial activity, large-scale film and television production is essentially coercive, manipulative, and frequently destructive. Furthermore, the classical narrative model is a closed system that allows spectators no participation beyond attending or staying away, the pseudodemocracy of the marketplace. Industrialized narrative filmmaking thus offers a potentially progressive mode of *organization* in the service of a reactionary *process*.

There are at least two possible responses to this situation. First, at the level of consumption, we can exercise what little control we have over the process by occasionally rejecting commercial production. The terms for this rejection will have to be determined by each person. The point is to recognize media consumption as a political act and to participate in those politics in an informed manner. This position does not require a Luddite rejection of technology, merely a degree of thought about what we consume. In short, I advocate a politics of *taste* that runs directly counter to Pierre Bourdieu's insistence that all distinction serves the interest of the ruling class. Clearly it does not, since one aspect of a consumer society is the need for producers to sell. If we have the political courage to say no on occasion, we can recognize distinction as a potentially *progressive* action when directed against the proper targets.

There are obvious precedents for such a politics of taste. The efforts in the 1970s and 1980s to boycott companies doing business in South Africa is one example. So too are the efforts of ecological groups to encourage consumers to avoid producers with particularly bad environmental records. However, although these models are useful, they are also isolated, dependent on individual, clearly definable goals, and do not help to create an overall aesthetic morality that can be applied in other instances. Moreover, these examples are purely negative. The consumer is asked to give up a direct, sensual pleasure in favor of the debatable rewards of virtue. Such boycotts run the danger of reintroducing the antipleasure strain of the most puritanical, utilitarian Marxism.

Instead, we need a politics of taste based *first* on pleasure. Without it, we have no chance of withstanding the appeals of the worst of capitalism, which has always succeeded in appealing to people's "tastes." At the same time, we have to maintain a large enough perspective to recognize when our pleasures may interfere with others. Just as a movie crew searching for the "perfect image" runs the risk of intruding in the lives of innocent bystanders, so too the consumer thinking only of pleasure risks slipping into the grossest egotism.

The Greek philosopher Epicurus offers one of the most enduring and reasonable compromises between selfish pleasure and social responsibility. Defining pleasure largely on the basis of the absence of pain, he divides it into three general types.[8] The first of these are natural and necessary pleasures. These include the satisfaction of hunger, thirst, and other basic, bodily needs. At one level, this category does not involve film at all, since cinema clearly does not fulfill a bodily need. Nonetheless, incorporating such thinking into film theory would be a blessing, since it begins with the *body*, so frequently overlooked in the privileging of meaning. If film cannot *satisfy* hunger, for example, it can certainly *stimulate* it.

The second category of Epicurean pleasures are those that are natural, but unnecessary. Since such pleasures do not depend on the removal of pain, they are gratuitous. Herein lies one of the major flaws of Epicurean pleasure theory, namely that it is purely negative. Since the removal of pain provides the maximum pleasure, these types of pleasure cannot provide increase, only variety. For example, rich food may change the object of our pleasure, but not increase its quantity since the basic pleasure of satisfying hunger can be achieved equally by simple food.

At the same time, Epicurus warns that such pleasures may also be accompanied by painful effects that outweigh their pleasure. As such, this category is useful in a contemporary theory of commodity consumption and production since it recognizes that excess can be more trouble than it is worth. For example, while there is little need to worry about compulsive filmgoing, such a balanced view of television viewing might prove useful, since it acknowledges the *pleasure* of watching television while still suggesting that too much of it may be harmful in the long run.

The third Epicurean category of pleasures consists of those that are neither natural nor necessary. Epicurus views these as the fulfillment of desires that have been prompted by "empty imagination." As such, they are to be avoided. They also create a problem for anyone attempting an Epicurean approach to media, or indeed, to contemporary commodity consumption in general since few of the articles of late capitalist production are either natural or necessary. This problem again results from the purely negative definition Epicurus gives to pleasure as the absence of pain. This negative definition leads him logically to call for a withdrawal from society into the pleasures of "The Garden," the name he gave his school, where he and like-minded sages and students would debate and refine the master's philosophy.

However, Epicurus allowed for a "way out" of this withdrawal. He acknowledged that although the only way to achieve *eudaemonia* (happiness) was through *ataraxia* (peaceful contentment), the means of achieving either would vary from one person to the next. He also recognized that the fulfilling of secondary and tertiary pleasures could, in moderation, help a person toward the greater goal of happiness and that furthermore the self-conscious *denial* of pleasure was as harmful as overindulgence. He thus opened a relativist door that allows us to evaluate the pleasures of media under the guiding principle of *phronesia*—balanced, prudent evaluation.

It remains, however, to overcome the basic negativism of the Epicurean definition of pleasure. Nietzsche characterized Epicurus unflatteringly as "a typical decadent," since his theory of pleasure was based on a "development of hedonism on a thoroughly morbid basis." [9] While Nietzsche's *Thus Spake Zarathustra* might well seem to describe the Epicurean sage par excellence, with his withdrawal from society to achieve a greater truth, the German philosopher's attention to style might be more helpful in overcoming the negative aspects of Epicureanism. He also provides a useful link back to Sorel in his description of the heroism of artistic production:

> It is the weak characters without power over themselves who *hate* the constraint of style. . . . Such spirits—and they may be of the first rank—are always out to interpret themselves and their environment as *free* nature.[10]

From Sorel, we take a restatement of the Marxist position of both utilitarian and emotional rewards of production; from Epicurus, we can add an awareness of the importance of the body and the consequences of overindulgence; from Nietzsche, an attention to artifice and self-control. Together, we can forge a definition of everyday heroism: the style of personal production.

Why the importance of style? Because the success of the designed image in creating desires or in directing them toward commodity consumption suggests that "reality" does not satisfy our emotional needs. To resort, as extreme Marxists have done, to the assertion that these needs are themselves produced only by the displeasure of capitalism is to pin an idealist definition of human desire on the hope of a future deliverance. Instead of viewing style as an evil to be gotten past in order to discover the truth, it should be *valorized* as the purest expression of individuality.

Why the importance of production? Because Marxists are right to point out that productive labor, tied to individual interest, can be immensely rewarding emotionally, far more so than the mere acquisition of goods. The varieties of late capitalist commodity production insure consumers a wide range of products with which to "express themselves." Yet the satisfaction of having found, say, the perfect suit can never last so long as the contentment produced by my knowing that I have written this book. Whatever its flaws, it is nonetheless something *I* did. This is the egotism of artistry, of course, but it is also the personal happiness produced by the satisfaction of inner needs, a happiness only I can fulfill for myself because only I can know it fully.

To balance this egotism, Epicurus offers a hedonism based on a selfish calculus. In it, desires like the "Will to Style" can be understood as an individual form of need. This desire must nonetheless be measured against the potential harm its untrammeled satisfaction might entail. Outside the legal complications unfettered will might introduce, the social isolation Nietzsche himself experienced in life might be seen as one of the inevitable consequences of "too much style." Presumably, too, the death of actors even if accidental is too much to ask for to achieve "the perfect image." The potential pleasure such an image might provide to viewers has to be balanced against the cost of achieving it.

A Way Out; the Way Ahead

Thirty-odd years of deconstruction have left us with little faith. That was, of course, the purpose of the exercise: to expose people to the contradictions of modern ideology and thereby liberate them from it. Even people who have never heard the term must grapple daily with some of its effects, such as extremes of moral relativism. Yet, the liberation has not quite happened. Instead, reactionary politics combined with libertarian economics (an unsteady mixture if ever there were one) have replaced Marxism as the driving ideological force of the Western world. In the arts, there has been no switch to the "writerly text" Roland Barthes envisioned.[11] Instead, traditional narrative has been enthroned not just as the dominant discourse for conservative industries like the cinema, but also as the object of study in academic departments dedicated to deconstruction. Rather than overthrowing the classical novel, these departments have become its last defense.

Not all poststructuralists espouse Marx's doctrines, but most would probably agree with the attitude expressed in the title of a letter written to Arnold Ruge in 1843: "For a Ruthless Criticism of Everything Existing."[12] If it is the one thing picked up by middle-class deconstructionists from Marxism, it may also be the most unfortunate. For Marx also wrote at roughly the same time (1845) that

> the chief defect of all hitherto existing materialism . . . is that the thing, reality, sensuousness, is conceived only in the form of the object or of *contemplation*, but not as *human sensuous activity, practice*, not subjectively.[13]

Instead of concentrating on "human sensuous activity" and "practice," deconstruction has become a sterile exercise in academic contemplation, so far removed from the pleasures created by the objects it studies as to qualify as nothing better than pure displeasure. That may be its purpose, but that does not mean we have to applaud. And it has proved incapable of presenting any alternative to traditional ideology beyond its own negativism. It is a purely *defensive* philosophy.

Marx's comments nonetheless point to a way out: sensuous activity and practice, or better, practice *as* sensuous activity. It is time for critics to cease *contemplation* and become producers in their field of study. There was a time when media scholars were relieved of this obligation because of the expense of the medium they studied. However, with the popularization, dispersion, and general drop in cost of home video and graphically oriented computers, it is no longer possible to insist that knowing *how* to produce meaning visually is less important than discussing *what* meaning is produced. It is time to redefine "visual literacy" with the same double meaning that verbal literacy has always involved: not just the ability to "read" images, but the ability to "write" with them as well.

I do not mean to suggest that this obligation holds only for those studying the image. It should no longer be possible to discuss the use of music, for example, without a working knowledge of composition and musical notation, the ability to *produce* music as well as discuss it. An architect who does not know the basics of 3-D computer imaging no longer knows his or her field. Can the architectural critic proceed without similar knowledge?

Unfortunately, these examples also run the risk of instilling the fear in critics that they should know these tools in order to survive, instead of inspiring them to recognize the *pleasures* and the personal *rewards* possible through the exploitation of new technologies like video and personal computers. The architecture critic discussing another's work can now provide active alternatives at no greater cost than he or she would invest in the time necessary to write a book. The film critic discussing design can design the discussion in ways that augment the words. The music critic discussing Mozart does not have to resort to graphic representations of his music, but can simply play it.

Will these new media replace the book and written essay? My having written this one should testify that I do not believe in the book's demise. CD-ROMs and videos cannot offer the depth or density of a book, and for now, they cannot replicate its convenience. That is just another way of saying, however, that a CD-ROM is not as good as a book because it is not a book. Print cannot offer the breadth of hypertextual organization or multimedia's range of expressive potential either. The *political* task we face is to recognize these differences and to fight any attempt either to suppress these new potentials or to evaluate them in terms by which they are guaranteed to fail. Instead, we must work for an environment that does not *fear* the image (or music, or the senses) but *uses* it as one tool among many.

Our new production should be governed by three main principles:

(1) A primary emphasis on pleasure. The product must be pleasurable, *first* to the producer and only secondarily to the audience. There may be no audience. Guilty adherence to standards (aesthetic, moral, political) destroys pleasure and must be resisted. The path to a genuine altruism is through a personally satisfied ego that can impose limits on itself in the recognition that not *all* pleasure leads to happiness.

(2) An ethically, theoretically, politically informed approach to the image. The producer must recognize as much as possible the contradictions of his or her position. This recognition does *not* imply a particular approach to the image. For those whose personal needs are best met by professional standards, so be it. For those for whom lack of talent or equipment result in a rough image, fine. The *value* attached to *either* approach must be removed. To the Right, this means a willingness not to denigrate a production for its lack of "production values." To the Left, this means a recognition that no form of signification is more "correct" than any other. (The Left's sentimental attraction to rough edges, for example, should have died with the success of MTV: the absence of style does not guarantee the presence of virtue.) People must be free to develop personal style, which is another way of saying that people must be free to express their feelings. Style is thus the highest moral principle.

(3) Personal, not industrial, production. Hollywood cannot be saved from within. The progressive producer who sells his or her abilities to Hollywood always is compromised by the system much more than he or she can change it. Liberal reformism may have validity in a parliamentary democracy; it has none in a setting as hierarchical as the entertainment industry. If a producer succeeds in sneaking a subversive moment into an otherwise standard product, that means only that "subversion" has entered the vocabulary of techniques available to industrial filmmaking. The most progressive political act a producer can do is to *reject* industrial practice.

The problems of the designed image can be overcome if we take the pleasures created in its production back from professionals, if we reacquire a direct stake in our work. It is not enough to resist; we must produce. We have been taking things apart for thirty years. It is time to begin putting them back together.

Notes

Introduction

1. Stephen Heath, *Questions of Cinema*, 19–75.

1. What Is Production Design?

1. For example: " 'Most directors are hyphenates,' explains [*Blade Runner* art director David] Snyder. 'They can be actor-directors or editor-directors. Because Ridley [Scott] was an art director–director, he spent the majority of his time with the art department.' In fact, when Snyder was first introduced as the film's art director, Scott, in a hint of things to come, shot a look at the man and said simply, 'Too bad for you, chap.' " Kenneth Turran, "Blade Runner," *Los Angeles Times Magazine*, September 13, 1992, 20.

2. Charles Affron and Mirella Jona Affron, *Sets in Motion: Art Direction and Film Narrative*, 4. See also Beverly Heisner, *Hollywood Art: Art Direction in the Days of the Great Studios,* for a description of studio art departments.

3. Léon Barsacq, *Caligari's Cabinet and Other Grand Illusions: A History of Film Design*, 7.

4. David O. Selznick, memo dated September 1, 1937, quoted in *Memo from David O. Selznick*, selected and edited by Rudy Behlmer (New York: Viking Press, 1972), 152.

5. Affron and Affron, 83.

6. Affron and Affron, 40.

7. At least in France. For a "how-to" primer from the British perspective, see *Film Design*, compiled by Terence St. John Marner in collaboration with Michael Stringer. See also Vincent LoBrutto, *By Design: Interviews with Film Production Designers,* and Heisner for a discussion of Hollywood practice. Together, the books suggest no significant divergence in approach between the design professions in these three major film industries.

8. Barsacq, 6–7.

9. Barsacq, 4.

10. Barsacq, 123.

11. LoBrutto, 32.

12. LoBrutto, 38.

13. LoBrutto, 94.

14. LoBrutto, 99.

15. LoBrutto, 168.

16. LoBrutto, 174.

17. Heisner argues (see in particular Chapter 1, 7–23) that Hollywood design makes most sense as an expression of studio style, thus a means of product differentiation. For a thorough discussion of the relationship between design and exchange value, see Wolfgang Fritz Haug, *Critique of Commodity of Aesthetics: Appearance, Sexuality, and Advertising in Capitalist Society*, trans. Robert Bock. We will explore this issue in detail in Chapter 9.

18. For example, see Donald Albrecht's *Designing Dreams: Modern Architecture in the Movies* for a detailed discussion of the transformation of general associations of Modernist architecture, from democratic mass potential to elitist exclusivity.

19. Pier Paolo Pasolini, "'The Cinema of Poetry,'" in *Heretical Empiricism*, 171.

20. Pasolini, 171.

21. For just such an adamantly literal approach to the image, see Nicola Chiaromonte, "On Image and Word," *Movies as Medium*.

22. For an elaborated discussion of the overwhelming of the dominant by the minor, see my "'Reading' Design in *The Go-Between*."

23. Michel Ciment, *Conversations with Losey*, 341–342.

24. On the *punctum*, see Roland Barthes, *Camera Lucida*; for the musical metaphor, see Barthes's *S/Z*.

25. For a discussion of *phronesia* in Epicurean philosophy, see Richard W. Hibler, *Happiness through Tranquility: The School of Epicurus* (Lanham, Md.: University Press of America, 1984), 62–64.

2. Circles of Feeling

1. Christian Norberg-Schulz, *Existence, Space, and Architecture*. Gaston Bachelard, in *The Poetics of Space*, offers a similar, body-centered description of space.

2. Jane Gaines, "Costume and Narrative: How Dress Tells the Woman's Story," in Jane Gaines and Charlotte Herzog, eds., *Fabrications: Costume and the Female Body*, 180–211.

3. Barsacq, 128.

4. George F. Custen, *Bio/Pics: How Hollywood Constructed Public History*.

5. Barsacq, 128. It is in this light that we should examine Jean-Louis Comolli's discussions of the actor's body in historical representation; see "Historical Fiction: A Body Too Much." For a discussion of the evolution of mid-nineteenth-century Western male fashion and capitalist development, see Walter Benjamin, *Charles Baudelaire: A Lyric Poet in the Era of High Capitalism*, 76–77. For a discussion of the representation of early-nineteenth-century male fashion, see my "The Bourgeois Gentleman and the Hussar."

6. Norberg-Schulz, 20.

7. Barsacq, 7.

8. See, in particular, Alain Robbe-Grillet, "Nature, Humanism, Tragedy," in *For a New Novel: Essays on Fiction*, 49–76.

9. See John Berger, *Ways of Seeing*, for a discussion of the relationship between advertising and traditional arts.

10. Norman Bryson, *Looking at the Overlooked: Four Essays on Still Life Painting*, 64.

11. "The existence of the things *quâ* commodities, and the value-relation between the products of labour which stamps them as commodities, have absolutely no connexion with their physical properties and with the material relations arising therefrom. There it is a definite social relation between men, that assumes, in their eyes, the fantastic form of a relation between things. In order, therefore, to find an analogy, we must have recourse to the mist-enveloped regions of the religious world. In that world the productions of the human brain appear as independent beings endowed with life, and entering into relation both with one another and the human race." Karl Marx, *Capital: A Critique of Political Economy* 1:77.

12. Barsacq, 122.

13. Barsacq, 124–125.

14. LoBrutto, 76.

15. Affron and Affron, 83.

16. Affron and Affron, 39.

17. Norberg-Schulz, 27; emphases in original.

18. Barsacq, 180.

19. Siegfried Kracauer, *Theory of Film: The Redemption of Physical Reality*, 62.

20. Norberg-Schulz, 27; emphases in original.

21. Norberg-Schulz, 20.

22. Rudolf Arnheim, *Art and Visual Perception: A Psychology of the Creative Eye, the New Version*, 294.

23. Edmund Burke, *A Philosophical Enquiry into the Origin of Our Ideas of the Sublime and Beautiful*, 107–108.

24. Robert Rosenblum, *Modern Painting and the Northern Romantic Tradition: Friedrich to Rothko*. For another discussion of the relationship between the Northern painting tradition, religious affect, and cinema, see Anne Hollander, *Moving Pictures*, particularly Chapter 11.

25. Heinrich Wölfflin, *Principles of Art History: The Problem of the Development of Style in Later Art*, 9–10.

3. Imaging

1. Charles F. Altman, "Psychoanalysis and Cinema: The Imaginary Discourse," in *Movies and Methods* 2:517–531.

2. Arnheim, *Art and Visual Perception*, 239.

3. Rudolf Arnheim, *Film as Art*, 17.

4. Arnheim, *Film as Art*, 73–74.

5. André Bazin, *What Is Cinema?* 1:105.

6. Leo Braudy, *The World in a Frame: What We See in Films*, 65–66.

7. Braudy, 37.

8. Braudy, 15.

9. Braudy, 77.

10. Heinrich Wölfflin, *Principles of Art History: The Problem of the Development of Style in Later Art*, 124.

11. Wölfflin, 126; emphasis in original.

12. Wölfflin, 27.

13. Altman, 521.

14. See also Noël Burch, *Theory of Film Practice*, 29–30, for a discussion of camera movement and its relation to spatial illusion.

15. For the importance of part/whole relationships in baroque form, see Paul Frankl, *Principles of Architectural History: The Four Phases of Architectural Style, 1420–1900*.

16. See John Belton and Lyle Tector, "The Bionic Eye: The Aesthetics of the Zoom," for an overview of uses of the zoom.

17. Gilles Deleuze, *Cinema 1: The Movement-Image*, 12.

18. Deleuze, 12.

19. Deleuze, 13.

20. Deleuze, 14.

21. Deleuze, 12.

22. Joseph Losey, "The Individual Eye," 14.

23. Robbe-Grillet, "On Several Obsolete Notions," in *For a New Novel*, 27. See also David Bordwell, Janet Staiger, and Kristin Thompson, *The Classical Hollywood Cinema: Film Style and Mode of Production to 1960*, 13, for the relationship between character and filmic space.

24. Deleuze, 16.

25. Deleuze, 12.

26. Charles Barr, "Cinemascope: Before and After," in *Film Theory and Criticism: Introductory Readings*, 3d ed., 139–163.

27. John Belton, *Widescreen Cinema*, 196.

28. Belton, 194–195.

29. "The greater density of the sound-Scope-color image requires a more precise control than the simple 'unit' image does." Barr, 144.

30. Leon Shamroy, "Filming the Big Dimension," 232.

31. Lyle Wheeler, quoted in "CinemaScope—What It Is; How It Works," 133.

32. Barr, 146.

33. Pasolini, 149.

34. See, for example, *"Les images d'Antonioni": Livre de photos—catalogue de l'Exposition "Cher Antonioni . . ." (les films d'Antonioni en deux cent images en noir et blanc et en couleur)*, ed. Carlo di Carlo (Rome: Cinecittà International, 1988).

35. My basis for evaluation of the film is the video version broadcast on American Movie Classics in late 1990. I do not know if all prints have been similarly censored.

4. Historical Design

1. Sue Harper, *Picturing the Past: The Rise and Fall of the British Costume Film*; Leger Grindon, *Shadows on the Past: Studies in the Historical Fiction Film*. In addition to these works, *Hollywood and History: Costume Design in Film*, a compilation of essays organized by Edward Maeder to accompany a costume exhibition at the Los Angeles County Museum of Art, provides an excellent overview of issues related to costume and makeup design from the production perspective, particularly in relation to historical fidelity.

2. Pierre Sorlin, *The Film in History: Restaging the Past*, 61.

3. Harper, *Picturing the Past*, 2.

4. Custen, 2.

5. See, for example, Saul Friedländer, *Reflections of Nazism: An Essay on Kitsch and Death*.

6. Ellen Draper, " 'Untrammeled by Historical "Fact" ': *That Hamilton Woman* and Melodrama's Aversion to History," 58.

7. Grindon, 223.

8. György Lukács, *The Historical Novel*, trans. Hannah Mitchell and Stanley Mitchell.

9. Lukács, 92.

10. Lukács, 188–189.

11. Lukács, 189.

12. For discussions of the relation between painting and historical re-creation, particularly the artist biopic, see my "When History Films (Try to) Become Paintings," *Cinema Journal*; Griselda Pollock's "Artists Mythologies and Media Genius, Madness, and Art History," *Screen*; John Walker's *Art and Artists on Screen*; and Norman King's *Abel Gance: A Politics of Spectacle*. See also Chapter 7 here.

13. Walter Benjamin, "The Work of Art in the Age of Mechanical Reproduction," in *Illuminations*, 232–233.

14. Thomas Elsaesser, "Tales of Sound and Fury: Observations on the Family Melodrama." In addition to Elsaesser, see Peter Brooks, *The Melodramatic Imagination*; Christine Gledhill, ed., *Home Is Where the Heart Is*; Geoffrey Nowell-Smith, "Minnelli and Melodrama"; et al.

15. Foster Hirsch, *The Hollywood Epic*, 29.

16. For discussions of French academicism, see Donald Drew Egbert, *The Beaux-Arts Tradition in French Architecture, Illustrated by the Grands Prix de Rome*; Philippe Grunchec, *The Grand Prix de Rome: Paintings from the Ecole des Beaux-Arts, 1797–1863*; and Hugh Honour, *Neo-Classicism*.

17. For a discussion of the nineteenth-century attitude toward history painting as a degenerated form, see Linda Nochlin, *Realism*, 23–25.

18. Honour, 82.

19. For a discussion of this style in relation to the Warner biopics of the 1930s, see Thomas Elsaesser, "Film History as Social History: The Dieterle/Warner Bros. Biopic," 28.

20. Michael Marrinan, *Painting Politics for Louis-Philippe: Art and Ideology in Orléanist France, 1830–1848*, 91.

21. Marrinan, 24–25.

22. Marrinan, 20.

23. Marrinan, 39.

24. Marrinan, 56.

25. Marrinan, 25.

26. Marrinan, 53.

5. Realist History

1. Robert K. Massie, *Nicholas and Alexandra*, vii.

2. Massie, viii.

3. Massie, 16–17.

4. Leon Trotsky, *The History of the Russian Revolution*, trans. Max Eastman, 1:53–55.

5. Peter Kurth, *Tsar: The Lost World of Nicholas and Alexandra*, 32.

6. Massie, 125.

7. *Variety*, January 24, 1968; *Film Daily*, January 25, 1968.

8. According to *Variety*, August 5, 1970.

9. Massie, 103–104.

10. Press kit, Horizon Films and Columbia Pictures.

11. Giuseppe di Lampedusa, *The Leopard*, 50.

12. This analysis is based on a videotape copy of the 1983 rerelease of the Italian-language version of the film. The rerelease replaced most of the footage edited out by 20th Century Fox for the initial American release in 1963. Presumably the scene described in Lampedusa's novel was never filmed.

13. Chris Chase, "At the Movies," *New York Times*, September 2, 1983, sec. C, 6.

14. Walter F. Korte, "Marxism and Formalism in the Films of Luchino Visconti," 10.

15. Korte, 10.

16. Karl Marx, "Economic and Philosophic Manuscripts of 1844," *The Marx-Engels Reader*, 93.

17. Albert Boime, *The Art of the Macchia and the Risorgimento*, 57.

18. Boime, 70.

19. Boime, 133.

20. Victor Cousin, *Lectures on the True, the Beautiful, and the Good*, 178. For a brief genealogy of Cousin's relationship to the philosophy of nineteenth-century art and architecture, see Christopher Curtis Mead, *Charles Garnier's Paris Opéra*, 204–206.

21. On the relationship between cinema and static arts, see Gilles Deleuze, *Cinema 1: The Movement-Image*, 4–5. For readers interested in Fattori's painting, see the reproduction on page 158 of Boime.

22. Boime, 159.

6. Designer History

1. See Josef Von Sternberg, *Fun in a Chinese Laundry* (New York: Macmillan, 1965).

2. Alain Resnais, interview with Richard Seaver, in Jorge Semprun and Resnais, *Stavisky . . .* , 153.

3. For a brief description of the historical Stavisky and the controversy surrounding him, see Richard Seaver's introduction to the published *Stavisky . . .* screenplay.

4. Resnais, 162.

5. Pauline Kael, *Reeling*, 420.

6. Jonathan Rosenbaum, "Paris," 2.

7. Jan Dawson, "Film Festival Preview," 38.

8. Michael Wilmington, "'Stavisky': Resnais' 'Almost' Masterpiece," *Los Angeles Times*, September 19, 1991, sec. F, 3.

9. "Stavisky," 6.

10. Semprun and Resnais, 122. All quotations of dialogue are taken from the published English screenplay, rather than from subtitles.

11. For a discussion of similar moments in 1930s films, see Charlotte Herzog, "'Powder Puff' Promotion: The Fashion Show-in-the-Film," in Gaines and Herzog, 134–159. Jane Gaines also notes a similar "rhythm of costuming" at work in many Women's Films in "Costume and Narrative," 180–211.

12. Resnais, 158.

13. Semprun and Resnais, 12.

14. I do not know if an equivalent subtitle is superimposed on French original prints. There is no on-screen graphic to give the information, and it may be that it was assumed French audiences could recognize the hotel and its location.

15. Semprun and Resnais, 20.

16. For a thorough overview of the various combinations of point of view, see Edward Branigan, *Point of View in the Cinema: A Theory of Narration and Subjectivity in Classical Film.*

17. Semprun and Resnais, 31.

18. Kael, 416.

19. See David Bevington and David Scott Kastan, "*Henry V* in Performance," in William Shakespeare, *Henry V*, xxvii–xxxiii.

20. Laurence Olivier, *On Acting* (New York: Simon and Schuster, 1986), 271, quoted in Affron and Affron, 136.

21. Bazin, "Theater and Cinema—Part Two," *What Is Cinema?* 1 : 102.

22. Bazin, 1 : 106.

23. Affron and Affron, 5.

24. Harper, *Picturing the Past*, 87.

25. Raymond Durgnat, *A Mirror for England: British Movies from Austerity to Affluence*, 107.

26. Affron and Affron, 5.

27. For the relationship between British theater and cinema, see Geoff Brown's "'Sister of the Stage': British Film and British Theater," in *All Our Yesterdays*, 143–167. For a discussion of the differences between American and British spatial sensibilities, and their effect on historical representation, see my "Fear and Loathing of British Cinema," *Spectator*, 22–37.

28. Roland Barthes, "The Grain of the Voice," *Image, Music, Text*, 188.

7. Didactic History

1. Fox's contribution to the development of the History Film is a subject unto itself, and outside the scope of this look at the genre. See, however, both Belton and Heisner, Chapter 7.

2. Roberto Rossellini, "A Panorama of History," interview with Rossellini by Francisco Llinas and Miguel Marias, 86.

3. Martin Walsh, "*Rome, Open City, The Rise to Power of Louis XIV*: Re-Evaluating Rossellini," *Jump Cut*, 13–15. Walsh burdens Rossellini with the usual list of "materialist" critical opprobrium: idealism, humanism, illusionism.

4. Peter Brunette, *Roberto Rossellini*, 286.

5. Peter Bondanella, *The Films of Roberto Rossellini*, 131.

6. James Roy MacBean, "Rossellini's Materialist *Mise-en-Scène* of *La Prise de Pouvoir par Louis XIV*," 29.

7. Peter Burke, *The Fabrication of Louis XIV*, 199.

8. Bondanella, 130–131.

9. "Unlike the immediate past, the historical past must be staged in terms of costumes and settings completely estranged from present-day life. Consequently, it is inevitable that any movie goer susceptible to the medium should feel uneasy about their irrevocable staginess. . . . he does not naïvely succumb to the magic of the allegedly recaptured past but remains conscious of the efforts going into its construction." Kracauer, 77.

10. Bazin, 2:97–98.

11. Brunette, 285.

12. Grindon, 148–149.

13. Both Bondanella and Brunette discuss the director's use of the Pancinoor zoom lens in some detail, but do so largely from the standpoint of the degree of freedom and control the lens offered the director.

14. For a discussion of the work of the famous court painter Charles Lebrun, for example, and his debt to the conventions of High Renaissance painters like Raphael, see P. Burke, 191.

15. MacBean, 20.

16. Andrew Higson, "Re-presenting the National Past: Nostalgia and Pastiche in the Heritage Film," in *Fires Were Started: British Cinema and Thatcherism*, 118.

17. Werner Sombart, *Luxury and Capitalism*, trans. W. R. Dittmar.

18. Grindon, 123–178.

19. Grindon, 156.

20. Fernand Braudel, "The Situation of History in 1950," in *On History*, 10; emphases added.

21. Fernand Braudel, *Civilization and Capitalism: 15th–18th Century* 1:27; emphasis in original.

22. Grindon, 164.

23. Grindon, 165.

24. Grindon, 165–166.

25. Ragna Stang, who is thanked for her assistance in the film's credits, has written perhaps the most authoritative study of the artist's work, *Edvard Munch: The Man and His Art*. More directly relevant to some of the issues raised in this discussion is Arne Eggum's *Munch and Photography*.

26. Peter Watkins, "*Edvard Munch*: A Director's Statement," 17.

27. Watkins, 17.

28. Watkins, 19.

29. For a discussion of the relationship between Munch and German Expressionism, see Stang, 277–283. See Lotte Eisner's *The Haunted Screen: Expressionism in the German Cinema and the Influence of Max Reinhardt* for a description of the development of Expressionist narrative cinema.

30. Joseph A. Gomez, "Peter Watkins's *Edvard Munch*," 45.

31. Gomez, 41.

32. Watkins, quoted in Gomez, 41–42. The passage occurs at 1:02:15–1:03:03 on the VHS video release from New Yorker films.

33. Gomez, 45.

34. Jay Cocks, "Shades of Madness," 97.

35. Penelope Gilliatt, "The Current Cinema," 114.

36. John Russell, "*Edvard Munch*—a Film Truer to Life than to Art," 33.

37. For a discussion of *Lust for Life*'s uneasy relationship between art and life, see Griselda Pollock's "Artists Mythologies and Media Genius, Madness and Art History," and my "When History Films (Try to) Become Paintings." Angela Dalle Vacche's *Cinema and Painting: How Art Is Used in Film* does not discuss either *Edvard Munch* or *Lust for Life* particularly, but does provide a unique take on the use of art-historical reference in film.

38. P. Adams Sitney, *Visionary Film: The American Avant-Garde*, 142.

39. For a discussion of the evolution of direct cinema and cinema verité, see Erik Barnouw, *Documentary: A History of the Non-Fiction Film*, 83–182.

40. See Barnouw, 229–262.

41. Quoted in Eggum, 6.

8. A Few Words about a Hat

1. Satch LaValley, "Hollywood and Seventh Avenue: The Impact of Period Films on Fashion," in *Hollywood and History*, 94.

2. François Boucher, *20,000 Years of Fashion: The History of Costume and Personal Adornment*, 9.

3. Boucher, 68.

4. See Trotsky's *History of the Russian Revolution* 1:3 for a brief description of Russia's medieval past.

5. "Hats are now [1950 onward] only rarely part of the masculine wardrobe." Doreen Yarwood, *Fashion in the Western World, 1500–1990*, 155.

6. The discussion of Sharif's career is based on information culled from *Film Actors Guide*, compiled and edited by Steven A. LuKanic.

7. Edward W. Said, *Orientalism*, 21.

8. Said, 58.

9. This estimation is based only on those Sharif films that I have seen or read about, or whose titles clearly announce a period setting.

10. Jean-Louis Comolli, "Historical Fiction: A Body Too Much."

11. Quoted in MGM publicity packet available in the University of Southern California Cinema-Television library. Unfortunately, it is unclear whether this packet contains one or several publicity packets. My references, therefore, must remain imprecise.

12. Said, 188.

13. References in this discussion will give preference to the 1988 Turner Entertainment laserdisc, which will be referred to as "MGM," followed by the side number, minute, and second. For example, this reference, "MGM S2:48.31." References to the published screenplay will be made as "Bolt" followed by the page number; references to the original novel will be made as "Pasternak" followed by the page number.

14. MGM S2:49.15.

15. MGM S4:39.19.

16. In the published screenplay, the painted images of Lenin and Trotsky were meant to be followed by a similar image of Stalin (Bolt, 126). At some point, the decision must have been made to remove it. The mural of Stalin at the end, however, is described as showing him surrounded by admiring children (Bolt, 220). Note too that the screenplay calls for Lara to disappear into a crowd.

17. Pasternak, 473.

18. MGM S2:14.11.

9. The Politics of Consumption

1. MGM publicity packet.

2. MGM publicity packet.

3. *Esquire* 66, no. 4 (October 1966): 96.

4. As seen in *Esquire* 44, no. 2 (February 1964): 48.

5. Nkrumah is pictured in the February 25, 1966 issue of the *New York Times*; Khan is pictured with Lyndon Johnson in the December 19, 1965 issue of the *Los Angeles Times*.

6. *Esquire* 45, no. 6 (June 1966): 111. The October 1965 issue (129) also featured an article on Sukarno, pictured in his ubiquitous hat.

7. Yarwood, 154.

8. Haug, *Critique of Commodity Aesthetics*, 144.

9. Haug, 16.

10. Haug, 17.

11. Charles Eckert, in "The Carole Lombard in Macy's Window," suggests otherwise. Investigating the relationship between several 1930s releases and product placements and tie-ins, he demonstrates the usefulness Hollywood served in disseminating positive images for products. However, Eckert's discussion has limited relevance to this discussion, since he wants to demonstrate the generation of desire for contemporary (1930s) commodities, rather than the exotic period objects we are considering here. For a more general discussion of the integration of "modern" commodities into public consciousness, see Donald Albrecht, *Designing Dreams: Modern Architecture in the Movies*.

12. Stuart Ewen, *All Consuming Images: The Politics of Style in Contemporary Culture*, 248; emphasis in original.

13. Pierre Bourdieu, *Distinction: A Social Critique of the Judgement of Taste*, 7.

14. Ewen, 61; emphasis in original.

15. Ewen, 68.

16. Guy Debord, *Society of the Spectacle*.

17. Jean Baudrillard, "The Political Economy of the Sign," in *Selected Writings*.

18. Jane Gaines, "Introduction: Fabricating the Female Body," in Gaines and Herzog, 6.

19. Gaines, "Introduction," 7.

20. Elizabeth Wilson, "All the Rage," in Gaines and Herzog, 28.

21. J. Anderson Black and Madge Garland, *A History of Fashion*, 263. Note the decidedly "Russian" look of the fashions in the bottom photograph on the same page.

22. Gaines, "Introduction," 13.

10. Productionism

1. LoBrutto, 257–258.

2. Julie Salamon, *The Devil's Candy: "The Bonfire of the Vanities" Goes to Hollywood*, 77. For an extended examination of the relationship between war and filmmaking, see Paul Virilio, *War and Cinema: The Logistics of Perception* (London: Verso, 1989).

3. Georges Sorel, *Reflections on Violence*, 287; emphasis in original.

4. Sorel, 282–283; emphasis in original.

5. Pico Estrada, "Latin American Historical Films: The Epic of the Underdogs," in *Flashback: Films and History*, 178–179.

6. Friedrich Engels, "On the Division of Labour in Production," *The Marx-Engels Reader*, ed. Robert C. Tucker, 323.

7. Karl Marx and Friedrich Engels, "The Communist Manifesto," *Marx-Engels Reader*, 341.

8. There are several works that discuss Epicurean philosophy. Among them, Cyril Bailey's *Epicurus: The Extant Remains* provides translations of all surviving Epicurean texts as well as critical commentary. *The Essential Epicurus* (Buffalo, N.Y.: Prometheus Books, 1993), translated by Eugene O'Connor, includes all of the philosopher's major works in a compact form. Howard Jones's *Epicurean Tradition* (London: Routledge, 1989) provides a concise summary of Epicurean thought including an overview of the history of the philosophy in the West, through the seventeenth century. Jones emphasizes the philosopher's physical, atomistic theory, rather than his ethics or aesthetics. Readers interested in the latter aspects of Epicureanism can consult Phillip Mitsis's *Epicurus' Ethical Theory: The Pleasures of Invulnerability*, which provides a critical examination of Epicureanism in the light of both classical Greek philosophy and modern hedonism.

9. Friedrich Nietzsche, "The Antichrist," in *The Portable Nietzsche*, 602.

10. Nietzsche, "The Gay Science," *Portable Nietzsche*, 99.

11. Barthes, *S/Z*.

12. Karl Marx, "For a Ruthless Criticism of Everything Existing," *Marx-Engels Reader*, 7.

13. Karl Marx, "Theses on Feuerbach," *Marx-Engels Reader*, 107; emphases in original.

Film List

Many of the films in this filmography have been discussed in some detail in this book. Additional titles are presented for those interested in continuing to explore issues raised here. Readers interested in film design generally can refer to the filmographies in Affron and Affron, Barsacq, Heisner, and LoBrutto. For those interested in historical film representation, the filmographies in Hirsch, Custen, and *Hollywood and History* provide excellent starting points.

This is an admittedly eclectic variety of films. Given the thrust of the discussion, there is an understandable bias toward History Films, costume melodramas, and to a lesser extent, science fiction and fantasy. I have also included titles outside these genres that pose interesting questions about design. Chief among these are films from directors known for pronounced visual styles or works from filmmakers frequently overlooked in other considerations of design. On the other hand, I have *not* included works from filmmakers (such as Sirk) already recognized for their *mise-en-scène*, except in those instances where they have contributed to the History Film or science fiction.

Animated titles are conspicuous by their absence. At the risk of a pun, one has to draw the line somewhere. Although animation might seem to carry design to its logical extreme, I found little benefit, finally, in conflating the two professions. Production design ultimately is about making a fictional world look real; animation makes everything look designed.

Non-English titles have been listed under their American release titles for the sake of convenience, except in those instances where the original language title is more familiar (e.g., *L'avventurra*, not *The Adventure*). Years are based on American release dates.

The Abominable Dr. Phibes (Fuest, 1971)

Accident (Losey, 1967)

The Adventures of Robin Hood (Keighley/Curtiz, 1938)

Age of Innocence (Scorsese, 1993)

The Agony and the Ecstasy (Reed, 1965)

Alexander Nevsky (Eisenstein, 1938)

Alexander the Great (Rossen, 1956)

Alien (R. Scott, 1979)

Amadeus (Forman, 1984)

American Gigolo (Schrader, 1980)

An American in Paris (Minnelli, 1951)

Andrei Rublev (Tarkovsky, 1966)

The Andromeda Strain (Wise, 1971)

Anne of the Thousand Days (Jarrott, 1970)

Antonio das Mortes (Glauber Rocha, 1969)

Apocalypse Now (Coppola, 1979)

Arabesque (Donen, 1966)

The Assassination of Trotsky (Losey, 1972)

L'avventurra (Antonioni, 1960)

Barry Lyndon (Kubrick, 1975)

Batman (Burton, 1989)

The Battle of Algiers (Pontecorvo, 1967)

Battleship Potemkin (Eisenstein, 1925)

Becket (Glenville, 1964)

Ben Hur (Wyler, 1959)

The Betsy (Petrie, 1978)

The Birth of a Nation (Griffith, 1915)

Black Narcissus (Powell, 1947)

Blade Runner (R. Scott, 1982)

Blow-Up (Antonioni, 1966)

The Blue Max (Guillermin, 1966)

The Bonfire of the Vanities (DePalma, 1990)

Bram Stoker's Dracula (Coppola, 1992)

Braveheart (Gibson, 1995)

Brazil (Gilliam, 1985)

The Buccaneer (DeMille, 1958)

Burn! (Pontecorvo, 1970)

Cabaret (Fosse, 1972)

The Cabinet of Dr. Caligari (Wiene, 1919)

Cabiria (Pastrone, 1914)

Caligula (Brass, 1979)

Camelot (Logan, 1967)

Caravaggio (Jarman, 1986)

Carnal Knowledge (Nichols, 1971)

Casablanca (Curtiz, 1942)

Cat People (Lewton, 1942)

Cat People (Schrader, 1982)

Chapaiev (Vasiliev and Vasiliev, 1934)

The Charge of the Light Brigade (Richardson, 1968)

Charlie Chan at the Olympics (Humberstone, 1937)

Charlie Chan at the Race Track (Humberstone, 1936)

Chinatown (Polanski, 1974)

El Cid (Mann, 1961)

Citizen Kane (Welles, 1941)

Cleopatra (Mankiewicz, 1963)

A Clockwork Orange (Kubrick, 1971)

The Collector (Wyler, 1965)

Colonel Redl (Szabó, 1985)

Conan the Barbarian (Milius, 1982)

The Conformist (Bertolucci, 1971)

Conquest (Brown, 1937)

Contempt (Godard, 1964)

The Cotton Club (Coppola, 1984)

Cries and Whispers (Bergman, 1972)

Cromwell (Hughes, 1970)

Cyrano de Bergerac (Rappeneau, 1990)

The Damned (Visconti, 1969)

Danton (Wajda, 1982)

The Day of the Locust (Schlesinger, 1975)

Days of Heaven (Malick, 1978)

Death in Venice (Visconti, 1971)

The Decameron (Pasolini, 1971)

Desirée (Koster, 1954)

Despair (Fassbinder, 1978)

Desperately Seeking Susan (Seidelman, 1985)

The Devils (Russell, 1971)

Dick Tracy (Beatty, 1990)

Die Hard (McTiernan, 1988)

Diva (Beneix, 1981)

Doctor Zhivago (Lean, 1965)

Don Giovanni (Losey, 1979)

Don't Look Now (Roeg, 1973)

Douce (Autant-Lara, 1943)

Dracula (Browning, 1931)

Dracula (Fisher, 1958)

Dracula (Badham, 1979)

The Draughtsman's Contract (Greenaway, 1982)

The Duellists (R. Scott, 1977)

Edvard Munch (Watkins, 1976)

The Egyptian (Curtiz, 1954)

1860 (Blassetti, 1933)

Elvira Madigan (Widerberg, 1967)

The Empire Strikes Back (Kershner, 1980)

Excalibur (Boorman, 1981)

Fahrenheit 451 (Truffaut, 1966)

The Fall of the Roman Empire (Mann, 1964)

Faust (Murnau, 1926)

Fellini Satyricon (1969)

Fiddler on the Roof (Jewison, 1971)

55 Days at Peking (Ray, 1962)

Fire Over England (Howard, 1937)

Fitzcarraldo (Herzog, 1982)

Floating Weeds (Ozu, 1959)

Forbidden Planet (Wilcox, 1956)

The Fortune (Nichols, 1975)

1492: The Conquest of Paradise (R. Scott, 1992)

The French Lieutenant's Woman (Reisz, 1981)

Funny Girl (Wyler, 1968)

Galileo (Losey, 1974)

Gandhi (Attenborough, 1982)

The Garden of the Finzi-Continis (DeSica, 1970)

Glengarry Glen Ross (Foley, 1993)

The Go-Between (Losey, 1971)

The Godfather (Coppola, 1972)

The Godfather, Part II (Coppola, 1974)

The Golem (Wegener, 1920)

Gone with the Wind (Fleming, 1939)

The Good, the Bad, and the Ugly (Leone, 1966)

The Gospel According to St. Matthew (Pasolini, 1964)

The Great Gatsby (Clayton, 1974)

The Great Train Robbery (Crichton, 1979)

Hammett (Wenders, 1982)

Heaven's Gate (Cimino, 1980)

Henry V (Olivier, 1944)

The Hindenburg (Wise, 1975)

History Lessons (Straub/Huillet, 1972)

History of the World, Part 1 (Brooks, 1981)

The Horsemen (Frankenheimer, 1971)

The Hunchback of Notre Dame (Dieterle, 1939)

The Hunger (T. Scott, 1983)

The Immortal Beloved (Rose, 1994)

The Incredible Shrinking Man (Arnold, 1957)

The Innocent (Visconti, 1979)

Intolerance (Griffith, 1916)

Investigation of a Citizen above Suspicion (Petri, 1970)

Ivan the Terrible (Eisenstein, 1944, 1949)

Jason and the Argonauts (Chaffey, 1963)

Jesus Christ Superstar (Jewison, 1973)

JFK (Stone, 1991)

Journey to the Center of the Earth (Levin, 1959)

Juarez (Dieterle, 1939)

Kafka (Soderbergh, 1991)

Kagemusha (Kurosawa, 1980)

The Kennel Murder Case (Curtiz, 1933)

Khartoum (Dearden, 1966)

Kind Hearts and Coronets (Hamer, 1949)

The King and I (Lang, 1956)

King David (Beresford, 1985)

King of Kings (Ray, 1961)

The King's Whore (Corti, 1990)

The Lady from Shanghai (Welles, 1948)

The Lady Vanishes (Hitchcock, 1938)

Ladyhawke (Donner, 1985)

The Last Emperor (Bertolucci, 1987)

Last Tango in Paris (Bertolucci, 1973)

Last Year at Marienbad (Resnais, 1961)

Lawrence of Arabia (Lean, 1962)

The Leopard (Visconti, 1963)

Letter from an Unknown Woman (Ophuls, 1948)

The Life and Death of Colonel Blimp (Powell, 1943)

Lifeboat (Hitchcock, 1944)

Lili Marleen (Fassbinder, 1981)

The Lion in Winter (Harvey, 1968)

Lola Montes (Ophuls, 1955)

Ludwig: The Mad King of Bavaria (Visconti, 1973)

Lust for Life (Minnelli, 1956)

McCabe and Mrs. Miller (Altman, 1971)

The Madness of King George (Hytner, 1994)

The Magnificent Ambersons (Welles, 1942)

Mahler (Russell, 1974)

The Maltese Falcon (Huston, 1941)

A Man for All Seasons (Zinnemann, 1966)

The Manchurian Candidate (Frankenheimer, 1962)

Manhattan (Allen, 1979)

Marie Antoinette (Van Dyke, 1938)

The Marquise of O . . . (Rohmer, 1976)

The Masque of the Red Death (Corman, 1964)

Mélo (Resnais, 1986)

Mishima: A Life in Four Chapters (Schrader, 1985)

Mission: Impossible (DePalma, 1996)

The Moderns (Rudolph, 1988)

Modesty Blaise (Losey, 1966)

Monty Python's Life of Brian (T. Jones, 1979)

The Moon and Sixpence (Lewin, 1943)

Morocco (von Sternberg, 1930)

Moulin Rouge (Huston, 1953)

Mr. Klein (Losey, 1976)

Murder on the Orient Express (Lumet, 1974)

Muriel (Resnais, 1963)

The Music Lovers (Russell, 1971)

My Darling Clementine (Ford, 1946)

Mystery of the Wax Museum (Curtiz, 1933)

The Name of the Rose (Annaud, 1986)

Napoleon (Gance, 1927)

New York, New York (Scorsese, 1977)

Nicholas and Alexandra (Schaffner, 1971)

The Night Porter (Cavani, 1974)

Nijinsky (Ross, 1980)

1984 (Radford, 1984)

1900 (Bertolucci, 1977)

Nosferatu (Murnau, 1922)

Nosferatu the Vampyre (Herzog, 1979)

Notorious (Hitchcock, 1946)

October (Eisenstein, 1928)

Odd Man Out (Reed, 1947)

Oliver! (Reed, 1968)

Once Upon a Time in the West (Leone, 1968)

One from the Heart (Coppola, 1982)

Orphée (Cocteau, 1949)

The Other Francisco (Giral, 1974)

Out of Africa (Pollack, 1985)

Outland (Hyams, 1981)

Pandora and the Flying Dutchman (Lewin, 1951)

Parsifal (Syberberg, 1982)

A Passage to India (Lean, 1984)

The Passenger (Antonioni, 1975)

Passion (Godard, 1982)

Patton (Schaffner, 1970)

Persona (Bergman, 1966)

Picnic at Hanging Rock (Weir, 1979)

The Picture of Dorian Gray (Lewin, 1945)

Pierrot le Fou (Godard, 1965)

Planet of the Apes (Schaffner, 1968)

The Private Life of Henry VIII (Korda, 1933)

The Private Lives of Elizabeth and Essex (Curtiz, 1939)

Prospero's Books (Greenaway, 1991)

Providence (Resnais, 1977)

Quai des Brumes (Carné, 1938)

Queen Margot (Leconte, 1994)

Quintet (Altman, 1979)

Quo Vadis (Le Roy, 1951)

Raiders of the Lost Ark (Spielberg, 1981)

Ran (Kurosawa, 1985)

The Red and the White (Jansco, 1969)

Red Desert (Antonioni, 1964)

The Red Shoes (Powell, 1948)

Rembrandt (Korda, 1936)

The Return of Martin Guerre (Vigne, 1982)

Return of the Jedi (Marquand, 1983)

Reversal of Fortune (Schroeder, 1990)

Richard III (Loncraine, 1995)

The Rise to Power of Louis XIV (Rossellini, 1966)

The Robe (Koster, 1953)

Robin and Marian (Lester, 1976)

Robinson Crusoe on Mars (Haskin, 1964)

The Romantic Englishwoman (Losey, 1975)

Rome: Open City (Rossellini, 1945)

Romeo and Juliet (Zeffirelli, 1968)

Rosa Luxemburg (von Trotta, 1986)

Rosencrantz and Guildenstern Are Dead (Stoppard, 1990)

Royal Flash (Lester, 1975)

The Rules of the Game (Renoir, 1939)

The Sand Pebbles (Wise, 1966)

Sansho the Bailiff (Mizoguchi, 1954)

Savage Messiah (Russell, 1972)

The Scarlet Empress (von Sternberg, 1934)

The Sea Hawk (Curtiz, 1940)

The Seven-Per-Cent Solution (Ross, 1976)

The Seventh Seal (Bergman, 1956)

Shanghai Express (von Sternberg, 1932)

The Shining (Kubrick, 1980)

Slaughterhouse Five (Hill, 1972)

Sodom and Gomorrah (Aldrich, 1962)

Solaris (Tarkovsky, 1972)

Solomon and Sheba (Vidor, 1959)

Soylent Green (Fleischer, 1973)

Spartacus (Kubrick, 1960)

Special Section (Costa-Gavras, 1975)

Stalker (Tarkovsky, 1979)

Star Trek: The Motion Picture (Wise, 1979)

Star Wars (Lucas, 1977)

Stavisky (Resnais, 1974)

The Story of Adèle H (Truffaut, 1975)

A Tale of Two Cities (Conway, 1935)

Tales of Hoffman (Powell, 1951)

The Taming of the Shrew (Zeffirelli, 1967)

The Ten Commandments (DeMille, 1956)

The Thomas Crown Affair (Jewison, 1968)

The Three Musketeers (Lester, 1973)

Time Bandits (Gilliam, 1981)

Tom Jones (Richardson, 1963)

Tomb of Ligeia (Corman, 1965)

Tombstone (Cosmatos, 1993)

Triumph of the Will (Riefenstahl, 1935)

20,000 Leagues under the Sea (Fleischer, 1954)

Two or Three Things I Know about Her (Godard, 1970)

2001: A Space Odyssey (Kubrick, 1968)

Ugetsu (Mizoguchi, 1953)

The Untouchables (DePalma, 1987)

Valentino (Russell, 1977)

Vera Cruz (Aldrich, 1954)

Vertigo (Hitchcock, 1958)

Victor/Victoria (Edwards, 1982)

Les Visiteurs du Soir (Carné, 1942)

The Wannsee Conference (Schirk, 1984)

War and Peace (Bondarchuk, 1964–1967)

The War Lord (Schaffner, 1965)

War of the Worlds (Haskin, 1953)

Weekend (Godard, 1967)

West Side Story (Robbins/Wise, 1961)

Who Framed Roger Rabbit (Zemeckis, 1988)

The Wild Bunch (Peckinpah, 1969)

Wilson (King, 1944)

Wind from the East (Godard, 1970)

The Wizard of Oz (Fleming, 1939)

You Only Live Twice (Gilbert, 1967)

Young Winston (Attenborough, 1972)

Zabriskie Point (Antonioni, 1970)

Zardoz (Boorman, 1974)

Zelig (Allen, 1983)

Bibliography

Design, Art History, Architecture

Ackerman, Gerald M. *The Life and Work of Jean-Léon Gérôme*. London; New York: Sotheby's Publications, 1986.

Affron, Charles, and Mirella Jona Affron. *Sets in Motion: Art Direction and Film Narrative*. New Brunswick, N.J.: Rutgers University Press, 1995.

Albrecht, Donald. *Designing Dreams: Modern Architecture in the Movies*. New York: Harper & Row and the Museum of Modern Art, 1986.

Allen, Richard. "Representation, Illusion, and the Cinema." *Cinema Journal* 32, no. 2 (Winter 1993): 21–48.

Arnheim, Rudolf. *Art and Visual Perception: A Psychology of the Creative Eye, the New Version*. Berkeley: University of California Press, 1974.

———. *The Dynamics of Architectural Form*. Berkeley: University of California Press, 1977.

Banham, Reyner. *Theory and Design in the First Machine Age*. 2d ed. New York: Praeger Publishers, 1960.

Barsacq, Léon. *Caligari's Cabinet and Other Grand Illusions: A History of Film Design*. Revised and edited by Elliott Stein. New York: New American Library, Times Mirror, 1976.

Berger, John. *Ways of Seeing*. London: British Broadcasting Corporation, 1972.

Black, J. Anderson, and Madge Garland. *A History of Fashion*. London: Macmillan, 1990.

Boucher, François. *20,000 Years of Fashion: The History of Costume and Personal Adornment*. New York: Harry N. Abrams, n.d.

Boullée, Etienne-Louis. "Essais sur l'architecture." In *Boullée and Visionary Architecture*, ed. Helen Rosenau. New York: Harmony Books, 1976.

Bryson, Norman. *Looking at the Overlooked: Four Essays on Still Life Painting*. Cambridge: Harvard University Press, 1990.

Buscombe, Edward. "Painting the Legend: Frederic Remington and the Western." *Cinema Journal* 23, no. 4 (Summer 1984): 12–27.

Carrick, Edward, comp. *Art and Design in the British Film: A Pictorial Directory of British Art Directors and Their Work*. London: Dennis Dobson Ltd., 1948.

Chiaromonte, Nicola. "On Image and Word." In *The Movies as Medium*. Selected, arranged, and introduced by Lewis Jacobs. New York: Farrar, Straus & Giroux, 1970.

Ciment, Michel. *Conversations with Losey*. London: Methuen & Co., 1985.

Le Corbusier. *Towards a New Architecture*. Translated by Frederick Etchells. New York: Dover Publications, 1986.

Dalle Vacche, Angela. *Cinema and Painting: How Art Is Used in Film*. Austin: University of Texas Press, 1996.

De Marly, Diana. *Fashion for Men: An Illustrated History*. New York: Holmes & Meier Publishers, 1985.

Dillon, Carmen. "The Art Director." *Films and Filming* 3, no. 8 (May 1957): 12–13.

Dondis, Donis A. *A Primer of Visual Literacy*. Cambridge: MIT Press, 1973.

Dreyer, Carl. "Color and Color Films." In *The Movies as Medium*. Selected, arranged, and introduced by Lewis Jacobs. New York: Farrar, Straus & Giroux, 1970.

Egbert, Donald Drew. *The Beaux-Arts Tradition in French Architecture, Illustrated by the Grands Prix de Rome*. Princeton: Princeton University Press, 1980.

Eisner, Lotte H. *The Haunted Screen: Expressionism in the German Cinema and the Influence of Max Reinhardt*. Berkeley: University of California Press, 1969.

Frankl, Paul. *Principles of Architectural History: The Four Phases of Architectural Style, 1420–1900*. Cambridge: MIT Press, 1968.

Giedion, Sigfried. *Space, Time, and Architecture: The Growth of a New Tradition*. 5th ed., rev. and enl. Cambridge, Mass.: Harvard University Press, 1967.

Golomstock, Igor. *Totalitarian Art in the Soviet Union, the Third Reich, Fascist Italy, and the People's Republic of China*. Translated by Robert Chandler. New York: Icon Editions, 1990.

Gombrich, E. H. *The Sense of Order: A Study in the Psychology of Decorative Art*. Ithaca, N.Y.: Cornell University Press, 1979.

Gray, Martin. "Design for Living," *Film and Filming* 3, no. 4 (January 1957): 8–9.

Gropius, Walter. *Scope of Total Architecture*. New York: Collier Books, 1955.

Grunchec, Philippe. *The Grand Prix de Rome: Paintings from the Ecole des Beaux-Arts, 1797–1863*. Washington, D.C.: International Exhibitions Foundation, 1984.

Head, Edith, and Jane Kesner Ardmore. *The Dress Doctor*. Boston: Little, Brown & Co., 1959.

Heisner, Beverly. *Hollywood Art: Art Direction in the Days of the Great Studios*. Jefferson, N.C.: McFarland & Company, 1990.

Henderson, Brian. "Notes on Set Design and Cinema." *Film Quarterly* 42 (Fall 1988): 17–28.

Higson, Andrew. "Space, Place, Spectacle: Landscape and Townscape in the 'Kitchen Sink' Film." *Screen* 25, no. 4–5 (July–October 1984): 2–21.

Hinz, Berthold. *Art in the Third Reich*. Translated from the German by Robert Kimber and Rita Kimber. New York: Pantheon Books, 1979.

Hollander, Anne. *Moving Pictures*. Cambridge: Harvard University Press, 1991.

Hollywood and History: Costume Design in Film. Organized by Edward Maeder. Los Angeles: Los Angeles County Museum of Art; London: Thames and Hudson, 1987.

Honour, Hugh. *Neo-Classicism.* Harmondsworth, England: Penguin Books, 1968.

Hudson, Roger. "Three Designers." *Sight and Sound* 34, no. 1 (Winter 1964–1965): 26–31.

Jencks, Charles. "Late Modernism and Post-Modernism." In *Architectural Design, 1978, in Late-Modern Architecture and Other Essays.* New York: Rizzoli, 1980.

Kybalová, Ludmila, Olga Herbenová, and Milena Lamarová. *The Pictorial Encyclopedia of Fashion.* Translated by Claudia Rosoux. New York: Crown Publishers, 1968.

Laugier, Marc-Antoine. *An Essay on Architecture.* Los Angeles: Hennessey & Ingalls, 1977.

Lindsay, Vachel. *The Art of the Moving Picture.* New York: Liveright, 1970.

LoBrutto, Vincent. *By Design: Interviews with Film Production Designers.* Westport, Conn.: Praeger, 1992.

Losey, Joseph. "The Individual Eye." *Encore* (London) (March–April 1961): 5–15.

Marner, Terence St. John, and Michael Stringer, comps. *Film Design.* London: Tantivy Press; New York: A. S. Barnes, 1974.

Mead, Christopher Curtis. *Charles Garnier's Paris Opéra: Architectural Empathy and the Renaissance of French Classicism.* New York: The Architectural History Foundation; Cambridge: MIT Press, 1991.

Mitchell, William J. *The Reconfigured Eye: Visual Truth in the Post-Photographic Era.* Cambridge: MIT Press, 1992.

Nochlin, Linda. *Realism.* New York: Penguin Books, 1971.

Norberg-Schulz, Christian. *Existence, Space, and Architecture.* New York: Praeger Publishers, 1971.

———. *Intentions in Architecture.* Cambridge: MIT Press, 1965.

Peterson, Steven. "Space and Anti-Space." *Harvard Architecture Review* 1 (Spring 1980): 89–113.

Polt, Harriet R. "Notes on the New Stylization." *Film Quarterly* 19, no. 3 (Spring 1966): 25–29.

Porphyrios, Demetri. *Sources of Modern Eclecticism: Studies on Alvar Aalto.* London: Academy Editions; New York: St. Martin's Press, 1982.

Rasmussen, Sten Eiler. *Experiencing Architecture.* Cambridge: Technology Press of Massachusetts Institute of Technology, 1959.

Rosenblum, Robert. *Modern Painting and the Northern Romantic Tradition: Friedrich to Rothko.* New York: Harper & Row, 1975.

Schwartz, Allen K. "The Impressionism of *Elvira Madigan.*" *Cinema Journal*, 8 (Spring 1969): 25–31.

The Second Empire, 1852–1870: Art in France under Napoleon III. Philadelphia: Philadelphia Museum of Art, 1978.

Silver, Alain J. "The Fragments of the Mirror: The Use of Landscape in Hitchcock." *Wide Angle* 1, no. 3 (1976): 53–61.

Sontag, Susan. *On Photography*. New York: Farrar, Straus & Giroux, 1977.

Sparke, Penny. *An Introduction to Design and Culture in the Twentieth Century*. London: Allen & Unwin, 1986.

Tashiro, Charles Shiro. "'Reading' Design in *The Go-Between*." *Cinema Journal* 33, no. 1 (Fall 1993): 17–34.

Turim, Maureen. "Symmetry/Asymmetry and Visual Fascination." *Wide Angle* 4, no. 3 (1980): 38–47.

Venturi, Robert. *Complexity and Contradiction in Architecture*. New York: Museum of Modern Art, 1966.

Vitruvius. *Ten Books of Architecture*. Translated by Morris Hicky Morgan. New York: Dover Publications, 1960.

Whittock, Trevor. *Metaphor and Film*. Cambridge: Cambridge University Press, 1990.

Wittkower, Rudolf. *Architectural Principles in the Age of Humanism*. New York: W. W. Norton, 1971.

Wölfflin, Heinrich. *Principles of Art History: The Problem of the Development of Style in Later Art*. New York: Dover Publications, 1950.

Yarwood, Doreen. *Fashion in the Western World, 1500–1990*. New York: Drama Book Publishers, 1992.

General Film History and Theory

Apra, Adriano, and Patrizia Pistagnesi, coordinators. *The Fabulous Thirties: Italian Cinema, 1929–1944*. Milan: Electa International Pub. Group, 1979.

Armes, Roy. *A Critical History of the British Cinema*. New York: Oxford University Press, 1978.

Arnheim, Rudolf. *Film as Art*. Berkeley: University of California Press, 1957.

Barnouw, Erik. *Documentary: A History of the Non-Fiction Film*. 2d rev. ed. New York: Oxford University Press, 1993.

Bazin, André. *What Is Cinema?* Translated by Hugh Gray. 2 vols. Berkeley: University of California Press, 1967–1971.

Bordwell, David, and Kristin Thompson. *Film Art: An Introduction*. 4th ed. New York: McGraw-Hill, 1993.

Branigan, Edward. *Point of View in the Cinema: A Theory of Narration and Subjectivity in Classical Film*. Berlin; New York: Mouton Publishers, 1984.

Braudy, Leo. *The World in a Frame: What We See in Films*. Garden City, N.J.: Anchor Books, 1977.

Brown, Geoff. "'Sister of the Stage': British Film and British Theater." In *All Our Yesterdays*, 143–167. London: BFI Publishing, 1986.

Burch, Noël. *Theory of Film Practice*. New York: Praeger Publishers, 1973.

Casebier, Allan. *Film and Phenomenology: Toward a Realist Theory of Cinematic Representation*. Cambridge: Cambridge University Press, 1991.

Coursodon, Jean-Pierre. *American Directors*. 2 vols. New York: McGraw-Hill, 1983.

Dayan, Daniel. "The Tutor-Code of Classical Cinema." *Film Quarterly* 28, no. 1 (Fall 1974): 22–31.

Eisenstein, Sergei. *Film Form: Essays in Film Theory*. Edited and translated by Jay Leyda. New York: Harcourt, Brace & World, Inc., 1949.

———. *Film Sense: Essays in Film Theory*. Edited and translated by Jay Leyda. New York: Harcourt, Brace & World, Inc., 1947.

Ellis, John. *Visible Fictions: Cinema, Television, Video*. Rev. ed. London: Routledge, 1992.

Elsaesser, Thomas. "Tales of Sound and Fury: Observations on the Family Melodrama." In *Movies and Methods*, ed. Bill Nichols, 2: 165–189.

Heath, Stephen. *Questions of Cinema*. Bloomington: Indiana University Press, 1981.

Kracauer, Siegfried. *Theory of Film: The Redemption of Physical Reality*. New York: Oxford University Press, 1960.

LuKanic, Steven A., comp. and ed. *Film Actors Guide*. Los Angeles: Lone Eagle Publications, 1991.

McConnell, Frank. *Storytelling and Mythmaking: Images from Film and Literature*. New York: Oxford University Press, 1979.

Metz, Christian. *The Imaginary Signifier: Psychoanalysis and the Cinema*. Translated by Celia Britton, Annweyl Williams, Ben Brewster, and Alfred Guzetti. Bloomington: Indiana University Press, 1982.

Nichols, Bill, ed. *Movies and Methods*. 2 vols. Berkeley: University of California Press, 1976–1985.

Nowell-Smith, Geoffrey. "Minnelli and Melodrama." In *Movies and Methods*, ed. Bill Nichols, 2: 190–195.

Pasolini, Pier Paolo. "The 'Cinema of Poetry.'" In *Heretical Empiricism*, 167–186. Bloomington: Indiana University Press, 1988.

Pudovkin, V. I. *Film Technique and Film Acting*. Translated by Ivor Montagu. New York: Grove Press, 1958.

Renov, Michael. "Topos Noir: The Spacialization and Recuperation of Disorder." *Afterimage* 15, no. 3 (October 1987): 12–16.

Sitney, P. Adams. *Visionary Film: The American Avant-Garde*. 2d ed. New York: Oxford University Press, 1979.

Sobchack, Vivian Carol. *The Address of the Eye: A Phenomenology of Film Experience*. Princeton: Princeton University Press, 1992.

Tashiro, Charles Shiro. "Fear and Loathing of British Cinema." *Spectator* 14, no. 2 (Spring 1994): 22–37.

Film Technology and Production

Bach, Steven. *Final Cut: Dreams and Disaster in the Making of Heaven's Gate*. New York: William Morrow and Co., 1985.

Barr, Charles. "Cinemascope: Before and After." In *Film Theory and Criticism: Introductory Readings*, 139–163. New York: Oxford University Press, 1985.

Belton, John. *Widescreen Cinema*. Cambridge: Harvard University Press, 1992.

Belton, John, and Lyle Tector. "The Bionic Eye: The Aesthetics of the Zoom." *Film Comment* 16, no. 5 (September–October 1980): 11–17.

Bordwell, David, Janet Staiger, and Kristin Thompson. *The Classical Hollywood Cinema: Film Style and Mode of Production to 1960*. New York: Columbia University Press, 1985.

Carr, Robert E., and R. M. Hayes. *Wide Screen Movies: A History and Filmography of Wide Gauge Filmmaking*. Jefferson, N.C.: McFarland & Co., 1988.

"CinemaScope—What It Is; How It Works." *American Cinematographer* 34 (March 1953): 112+.

Clarke, Charles G., comp. and ed. *American Cinematographer Manual*. 5th ed. Hollywood: American Society of Cinematographers, 1980.

Reisz, Karel, and Gavin Millar. *The Technique of Film Editing*. 2d enl. ed. New York: Hastings House, 1968.

Salamon, Julie. *The Devil's Candy: "The Bonfire of the Vanities" Goes to Hollywood*. New York: Dell Publishing, 1991.

Shamroy, Leon. "Filming the Big Dimension." *American Cinematographer* 34 (May 1953): 216+.

General Philosophy

Aristotle. *The Poetics of Aristotle*. Translated by Stephen Halliwell. Chapel Hill: University of North Carolina Press, 1987.

Bachelard, Gaston. *The Poetics of Space*. Translated from the French by Maria Jolas. Boston: Beacon Press, 1964.

Barthes, Roland. *Camera Lucida*. Translated by Richard Howard. New York: Hill and Wang, 1981.

——. *Image, Music, Text*. New York: Noonday Press, 1977.

——. *S/Z*. Translated by Richard Miller. New York: Hill and Wang, 1974.

Benjamin, Walter. *Charles Baudelaire: A Lyric Poet in the Era of High Capitalism*. New York: Verso, 1983.

——. *Illuminations*. New York: Schocken Books, 1968.

Brooks, Peter. *The Melodramatic Imagination: Balzac, Henry James, Melodrama, and the Mode of Excess*. New Haven: Yale University Press, 1976.

Burke, Edmund. *A Philosophical Enquiry into the Origin of Our Ideas of the Sublime and Beautiful*. 2d ed. Menston, England: The Scolar Press, 1970.

Cousin, Victor. *Lectures on the True, the Beautiful, and the Good*. Translated by O. W. Wight. New York: D. Appleton & Co., 1857.

Deleuze, Gilles. *Cinema 1: The Movement-Image*. Minneapolis: University of Minnesota Press, 1986.

———. *Cinema 2: The Time-Image*. Minneapolis: University of Minnesota Press, 1989.

Epicurus, the Extant Remains; with Short Critical Apparatus. Translated by Cyril Bailey. Oxford: Clarendon Press, 1926.

Foucault, Michel. *Discipline and Punish: The Birth of the Prison*. Translated by Alan Sheridan. New York: Vintage Books, 1977.

———. *Power/Knowledge: Selected Interviews and Other Writings, 1972–1977*, ed. Colin Gordon; trans. Colin Gordon, Leo Marshall, John Mepham, and Kate Soper. New York: Pantheon Books, 1980.

Freud, Sigmund. *The Interpretation of Dreams*. Translated by James Strachey. New York: Avon Books, n.d.

Jameson, Fredric. "Postmodernism; or The Cultural Logic of Late Capitalism." *New Left Review*, no. 146 (July 1984): 53–92.

Kubler, George. *The Shape of Time: Remarks on the History of Things*. New Haven: Yale University Press, 1962.

Marx, Karl. *Capital: A Critique of Political Economy*, vol. 1. Edited by Frederick Engels; translated by Samuel Moore and Edward Aveling. New York: International Publishers, 1967.

Marx, Karl, and Friedrich Engels. *The Marx-Engels Reader*. Edited by Robert C. Tucker. New York: W. W. Norton, 1972.

Mitsis, Phillip. *Epicurus' Ethical Theory: The Pleasures of Invulnerability*. Ithaca, N.Y.: Cornell University Press, 1988.

Nietzsche, Friedrich. *The Birth of Tragedy and The Case of Wagner*. Translated by Walter Kaufmann. New York: Vintage Books, 1967.

———. *The Portable Nietzsche*. Translated by Walter Kaufmann. New York: Viking Press, 1954, 1968.

Robbe-Grillet, Alain. *For a New Novel: Essays on Fiction*. Translated by Richard Howard. Evanston, Ill.: Northwestern University Press, 1965.

Said, Edward W. *Orientalism*. New York: Vintage Books, 1978.

Sorel, Georges. *Reflections on Violence*. Authorized translation by T. E. Hulme. New York: Peter Smith, 1941.

Film-Specific Information

Nicholas and Alexandra

Kim, Erwin. *Franklin J. Schaffner*. Metuchen, N.J.: Scarecrow Press, 1985.

Kurth, Peter. *Tsar: The Lost World of Nicholas and Alexandra*. Boston: Little, Brown & Co., 1995.

Massie, Robert K. *Nicholas and Alexandra*. New York: Dell Publishing, 1967.

Trotsky, Leon. *The History of the Russian Revolution*. 3 vols. Translated by Max Eastman. Ann Arbor: University of Michigan Press, 1932, 1957.

The Leopard

Boime, Albert. *The Art of the Macchia and the Risorgimento: Representing Culture and Nationalism in Nineteenth-Century Italy*. Chicago: University of Chicago Press, 1993.

Dalle Vacche, Angela. *The Body in the Mirror: Shapes of History in Italian Cinema*. Princeton: Princeton University Press, 1992.

Holt, Edgar. *The Making of Italy, 1815–1870*. New York: Atheneum, 1971.

Korte, Walter F. "Marxism and Formalism in the Films of Luchino Visconti." *Cinema Journal* 11, no. 1 (Fall 1971): 2–12.

Lampedusa, Giuseppe di. *The Leopard*. Translated by Archibald Colquhoun. London: Pantheon Books, 1960.

Leprohon, Pierre. *The Italian Cinema*. Translated by Roger Greaves and Oliver Stallybrass. New York: Praeger Publishers, 1966.

Lovett, Clara M. *The Democratic Movement in Italy, 1830–1876*. Cambridge: Harvard University Press, 1982.

Mack Smith, Denis. *Victor Emanuel, Cavour, and the Risorgimento*. London: Oxford University Press, 1971.

Marrinan, Michael. *Painting Politics for Louis-Philippe: Art and Ideology in Orléanist France, 1830–1848*. New Haven: Yale University Press, 1988.

Nowell-Smith, Geoffrey. "Lampedusa Revisited." *Sight and Sound* 52, no. 4 (Autumn 1983): 285.

———. *Luchino Visconti*. New York: Viking Press, 1973.

Stirling, Monica. *A Screen of Time: A Study of Luchino Visconti*. New York: Harcourt Brace Jovanovich, 1979.

Stavisky . . .

Armes, Roy. *The Cinema of Alain Resnais*. New York: A. S. Barnes & Co., 1968.

Dawson, Jan. "Film Festival Preview." *Film Comment* 10, no. 5 (September/October 1974): 38.

Kael, Pauline. "Pure Chrome." In *Reeling*. Boston: Little, Brown & Co., 1976.

Kreidl, John Francis. *Alain Resnais*. Boston: Twayne Publishers, 1977.

Monaco, James. *Alain Resnais*. New York: Oxford University Press, 1979.

Rosenbaum, Jonathan. "Paris." *Film Comment* 10, no. 2 (March–April 1974): 2–6.

Semprun, Jorge, and Alain Resnais. *Stavisky . . . .* Translated from the French by Sabine Destrée. New York: Viking Press, 1975.

"Stavisky." *Independent Film Journal* 74, no. 10 (October 16, 1974).

Sweet, Freddy. *The Film Narratives of Alain Resnais*. Ann Arbor, Mich.: UMI Research Press, 1981.

Ward, John. *Alain Resnais; or The Theme of Time*. Garden City, N.Y.: Doubleday & Company, 1968.

Wilmington, Michael. "'Stavisky': Resnais' 'Almost' Masterpiece." *Los Angeles Times*, September 19, 1991, sec. F, 3.

Henry V

Allmand, Christopher. *Henry V*. Berkeley: University of California Press, 1992.

Durgnat, Raymond. *A Mirror for England: British Movies from Austerity to Affluence*. New York: Praeger Publishers, 1971.

Earle, Peter. *The Life and Times of Henry V*. London: Weidenfeld and Nicolson, 1972.

Labarge, Margaret Wade. *Henry V: The Cautious Conqueror*. New York: Stein and Day, 1975.

Landy, Marcia. *British Genres: Cinema and Society, 1930-1960*. Princeton: Princeton University Press, 1991.

Shakespeare, William. *Henry V*. New York: Bantam Books, 1988.

The Rise to Power of Louis XIV

Bondanella, Peter. *The Films of Roberto Rossellini*. Cambridge; New York: Cambridge University Press, 1993.

Brunette, Peter. *Roberto Rossellini*. New York: Oxford University Press, 1987.

Burke, Peter. *The Fabrication of Louis XIV*. New Haven: Yale University Press, 1992.

Erlanger, Philippe. *Louis XIV*. Translated by Stephen Cox. New York: Praeger Publishers, 1970.

Gareau, Michel. *Charles LeBrun: First Painter to King Louis XIV*. New York: Harry N. Abrams, 1992.

Goubert, Pierre. *Louis XIV and Twenty Million Frenchmen*. Translated by Anne Carter. New York: Random House, 1966.

Kauffmann, Stanley. *Living Images: Film Comment and Criticism*. New York: Harper & Row, 1975.

Lublinskaya, A. D. *French Absolutism: The Crucial Phase, 1620-1629*. Translated by Brian Pearce. London: Cambridge University Press, 1968.

MacBean, James Roy. "Rossellini's Materialist *Mise-en-Scène* of *La Prise de Pouvoir par Louis XIV*." *Film Quarterly* 25, no. 2 (Winter 1971-1972): 20-29.

Rossellini, Roberto. "A Panorama of History." Interview with Rossellini by Francisco Llinas and Miguel Marias. *Screen* 79 (Winter 1973-1974): 83-109.

Sarris, Andrew. "Rossellini Rediscovered." *Film Culture*, no. 32 (Spring 1964): 60-63.

Tapié, Victor-L. *France in the Age of Louis XIII and Richelieu*. Translated by D. McN. Lockie. London: Macmillan, 1974.

Walsh, Martin. "*Rome, Open City, The Rise to Power of Louis XIV*: Re-Evaluating Rossellini." *Jump Cut* 5, no. 15 (1977): 13–15.

Edvard Munch

Cocks, Jay. "Shades of Madness." *Time* 108 (October 18, 1976): 97.

Eggum, Arne. *Munch and Photography*. Translated by Birgit Holm. New Haven: Yale University Press, 1989.

Gilliatt, Penelope. "The Current Cinema." *New Yorker* 52 (September 20, 1976): 114–118.

Gomez, Joseph A. "Peter Watkins's *Edvard Munch*." *Film Quarterly* 30, no. 2 (Winter 1976–1977): 38–46.

Russell, John. "*Edvard Munch*—a Film Truer to Life than to Art." *New York Times*, September 12, 1976, sec. 2, 33.

Stang, Ragna. *Edvard Munch: The Man and His Art*. Translated from the Norwegian by Geoffrey Culverwell. New York: Abbeville Press, Inc., 1979.

Watkins, Peter. "*Edvard Munch*: A Director's Statement." *Literature/Film Quarterly* 5, no. 1 (Winter, 1977): 17–22.

Doctor Zhivago

Bolt, Robert. *Doctor Zhivago: The Screenplay*. New York: Random House, 1965.

Pasternak, Boris. *Doctor Zhivago*. New York: Pantheon Books, 1958.

Silverman, Stephen M. *David Lean*. New York: Harry N. Abrams, 1989.

History and Historical Representation

Braudel, Fernand. *On History*. Translated by Sarah Matthews. Chicago: University of Chicago Press, 1980.

———. *Civilization and Capitalism, 15th–18th Century*. Vol. 1. *The Structures of Everyday Life: The Limits of the Possible*. New York: Harper & Row, 1981.

———. *Civilization and Capitalism, 15th–18th Century*. Vol. 2. *The Wheels of Commerce*. New York: Harper & Row, 1982.

———. *Civilization and Capitalism, 15th–18th Century*. Vol. 3. *The Perspective of the World*. New York: Harper & Row, 1984.

Carnes, Mark C., ed. *Past Imperfect: History According to the Movies*. New York: Henry Holt and Co., 1995.

Comolli, Jean-Louis. "Historical Fiction: A Body Too Much." *Screen* 19, no. 2 (Summer 1978): 41–53.

Custen, George F. *Bio/Pics: How Hollywood Constructed Public History*. New Brunswick, N.J.: Rutgers University Press, 1992.

Draper, Ellen. "'Untrammeled by Historical Fact': *That Hamilton Woman* and Melodrama's Aversion to History." *Wide Angle* 14, no. 1 (January 1992): 56–63.

Edelson, Edward. *Great Movie Spectaculars*. Garden City, N.Y.: Doubleday & Company, 1976.

Elley, Derek. *The Epic Film: Myth and History*. London; Boston: Routledge & Kegan Paul, 1984.

Elsaesser, Thomas. "Film History as Social History: The Dieterle/Warner Bros. Bio-pic." *Wide Angle* 8, no. 2 (1986): 16–31.

Farber, Stephen. "The Spectacle Film: 1967." *Film Quarterly* 20, no. 4 (Summer 1967): 11–22.

Flashback: Films and History. S.l.: The Unesco Press and la Baconnière, 1974.

Foucault, Michel. *The Order of Things: An Archaeology of the Human Sciences*. New York: Vintage Books, 1970.

Friedländer, Saul. *Reflections of Nazism: An Essay on Kitsch and Death*. Translated by Thomas Weyr. New York: Harper & Row, 1984.

Greenblatt, Stephen. *Marvelous Possessions: The Wonder of the New World*. Chicago: University of Chicago Press, 1991.

Grindon, Leger. *Shadows on the Past: Studies in the Historical Fiction Film*. Philadelphia: Temple University Press, 1994.

Harper, Sue. "Historical Pleasures: Gainsborough Costume Melodrama." In *Home Is Where the Heart Is*, ed. Christine Gledhill, 167–196. London: BFI Publishing, 1987.

———. *Picturing the Past: The Rise and Fall of the British Costume Film*. London: BFI Publishing, 1994.

———. "Studying Popular Taste: British Historical Films in the 1930s." In *Popular European Cinema*, ed. Richard Dyer and Ginette Vincendeau, 101–111. London: Routledge, 1992.

Higson, Andrew. "Re-presenting the National Past: Nostalgia and Pastiche in the Heritage Film." In *Fires Were Started: British Cinema and Thatcherism*, 109–129. Minneapolis: University of Minnesota Press, 1993.

Hirsch, Foster. *The Hollywood Epic*. South Brunswick, N.J.: Barnes, 1978.

King, Norman. *Abel Gance: A Politics of Spectacle*. London: British Film Institute, 1984.

LaCapra, Dominick. *History and Criticism*. Ithaca, N.Y.: Cornell University Press, 1985.

Landy, Marcia. *Cinematic Uses of the Past*. Minneapolis: University of Minnesota Press, 1996.

Lukács, György. *The Historical Novel*. Translated from the German by Hannah Mitchell and Stanley Mitchell. London: Merlin Press, 1962.

──────. *History and Class Consciousness: Studies in Marxist Dialectics*. Translated by Rodney Livingstone. Cambridge: MIT Press, 1971.

Lunn, Eugene. *Marxism and Modernism: An Historical Study of Lukács, Brecht, Benjamin, and Adorno*. Berkeley: University of California Press, 1982.

Neale, Steve. "*Triumph of the Will*: Notes on Documentary and Spectacle." *Screen* 20, no. 1 (Spring 1979): 63–86.

Nietzsche, Friedrich. *The Use and Abuse of History*. Translated by Adrian Collins. Indianapolis: Bobbs-Merrill, 1949.

Pollock, Griselda. "Artists Mythologies and Media Genius, Madness, and Art History." *Screen* 21, no. 3 (1980): 57–96.

Rosen, Philip. "History of Image, Image of History: Subject and Ontology in Bazin." *Wide Angle* 9, no. 4 (1987): 7–34.

Rosenstone, Robert A. *Visions of the Past: The Challenge of Film to Our Idea of History*. Cambridge, Mass.: Harvard University Press, 1995.

──────, ed. *Revisioning History: Film and the Construction of a New Past*. Princeton: Princeton University Press, 1995.

Searles, Baird. *Epic!: History on the Big Screen*. New York: Harry N. Abrams, 1990.

Sorlin, Pierre. *The Film in History: Restaging the Past*. Totowa, N.J.: Barnes & Noble Books, 1980.

Tashiro, Charles Shiro. "The Bourgeois Gentleman and the Hussar." *Spectator* 13, no. 2 (Spring 1993): 32–45.

──────. "When History Films (Try to) Become Paintings." *Cinema Journal* 35, no. 3 (Spring 1996): 19–33.

Toplin, Robert Brent. *History by Hollywood: The Use and Abuse of the American Past*. Urbana: University of Illinois Press, 1996.

Walker, John A. *Art and Artists on Screen*. Manchester; New York: Manchester University Press, 1993.

Wind, Edgar. "The Revolution of History Painting." *Journal of the Warburg and Courtauld Institutes* 10 (1947): 159–162.

Consumption

Baudrillard, Jean. *Selected Writings*. Stanford, Calif.: Stanford University Press, 1988.

Bourdieu, Pierre. *Distinction: A Social Critique of the Judgement of Taste*. Translated by Richard Nice. Cambridge: Harvard University Press, 1984.

Debord, Guy. *Society of the Spectacle*. Detroit: Black & Red, 1983.

Eckert, Charles. "The Carole Lombard in Macy's Window." *Quarterly Review of Film Studies* 3, no. 1 (Winter 1978): 1–21.

Ewen, Stuart. *All Consuming Images: The Politics of Style in Contemporary Culture*. New York: Basic Books, 1988.

Gaines, Jane, and Charlotte Herzog, eds. *Fabrications: Costume and the Female Body*. New York: Routledge, 1990.

Hanson, Philip. *Advertising and Socialism: The Nature and Extent of Consumer Advertising in the Soviet Union, Poland, Hungary, and Yugoslavia*. White Plains, N.Y.: International Arts and Sciences Press, Inc., 1974.

Haug, Wolfgang Fritz. *Critique of Commodity Aesthetics: Appearance, Sexuality, and Advertising in Capitalist Society*. Translated by Robert Bock. Minneapolis: University of Minnesota Press, 1971.

Sombart, Werner. *Luxury and Capitalism*. Translated by W. R. Dittmar. Ann Arbor: University of Michigan Press, 1967.

Index

Lightning Source UK Ltd.
Milton Keynes UK
24 February 2011

168124UK00001B/41/P